Health and Health Care Policy

Health and Health Care Policy

A Social Work Perspective

Cynthia Moniz
Plymouth State College

Stephen Gorin
Plymouth State College

Boston   New York   San Francisco
Mexico City   Montreal   Toronto   London   Madrid   Munich   Paris
Hong Kong   Singapore   Tokyo   Cape Town   Sydney

Series Editor: *Patricia Quinlin*
Editorial Assistant: *Annemarie Kennedy*
Marketing Manager: *Taryn Wahlquist*
Editorial-Production Service: *Omegatype Typography, Inc.*
Composition and Prepress Buyer: *Linda Cox*
Manufacturing Buyer: *JoAnne Sweeney*
Cover Administrator: *Kristina Mose-Libon*
Electronic Composition: *Omegatype Typography, Inc.*

For related titles and support materials, visit our online catalog at www.ablongman.com.

Between the time Website information is gathered and published, some sites may have closed. Also, the transcriptions of URLs can result in typographical errors. The publisher would appreciate notification where these errors occur so that they may be corrected in subsequent editions.

Library of Congress Cataloging-in-Publication Data

Moniz, Cynthia.
    Health and health care policy : a social work perspective / Cynthia Moniz, Stephen Gorin.
        p.   cm.
    Includes bibliographical references and index.
    ISBN 0-205-30672-1
        1. Medical policy—United States.   2. Health policy—United States.   3. Social workers.   I.
    Gorin, Steven H.   II. Title.
    RA394 .M665   2003
    362.1'042'0973—dc21

                                                                        2002018676

Printed in the United States of America

10 9 8 7 6 5 4 3 2   07 06 05 04

For our parents, Mary and Tony, and
Ros and Jerry

CONTENTS

LIST OF FIGURES

Chapter 3

Chapter 4

Chapter 5

Chapter 6

PREFACE

The profession of social work has been inextricably linked with health care since its beginning. At the turn of the twentieth century, social work leaders such as Jane Addams and Lillian Wald advocated public health reforms to prevent the spread of communicable diseases in poor urban and rural neighborhoods. They raised concern about high infant mortality rates and participated in early efforts to establish maternal and child health programs through the U.S. Children's Bureau. Others took the lead in mental health reform efforts to change the inhumane treatment of patients in public asylums.

During the New Deal, settlement house worker Frances Perkins became secretary of labor and fought for compulsory universal health insurance as part of the Social Security Act. Later, social workers played an active role in the enactment of Medicare and Medicaid, which established reimbursement mechanisms for social workers in a variety of health settings, including hospitals, mental health clinics and centers, and nursing care facilities. During the 1990s, the National Association of Social Workers developed its own legislative proposal for national health care reform, which was introduced by Senator Inouye (D-HI) in 1992. Today, at the turn of the twenty-first century, the growth of managed care in health and behavioral health has dramatically altered social work practice while concerns about the lack of universal coverage are beginning to surface again.

This book is an effort to fill a void that currently exists in the social work literature on health and health care policy. It was written for students at both the undergraduate and graduate level in social work education but should be of interest to practitioners and policy advocates in the public health and health policy arena, as well. Social work students and practitioners are often interested in clinical practice, but they must also be informed about the changing environment in which they practice.

In this book, we provide an overview of the development of health policy in the United States, with a particular focus on the role of social workers and the nation's failure to achieve universal coverage. A balanced view of the Clinton administration's Health Security Act and the battle for health care reform in the 1990s is included. We discuss the role of private and public insurance, including Medicare and Medicaid, in health care and examine the uninsured population. The critical role of managed care in health and mental health, including the growth of mental health carve-out plans, is part of this review. The book provides an integrated view of health and mental health and the impact of managed care on social work and health/mental health policy.

The book also introduces the study of epidemiology, which is central to public health efforts to improve the nation's health and reduce health disparities among different segments of the population. We provide a comprehensive overview of the health status of at-risk groups, specifically people of color, women, children, and elderly adults, and discuss the need to improve health outcomes in infant mortality, cardiovascular disease, HIV/AIDS, cancer, diabetes, and infectious diseases. We examine risk factors particular to each of these groups, such as violence against women, and analyze the role of federal health and welfare policies, such as S-CHIP or child welfare legislation, in prevention or health promotion or access to care. We have developed charts and graphs to highlight disparities in health and access to health care, and have included website addresses in the text to help readers update this information.

Finally, writing this book has given us the opportunity to introduce readers who might be unfamiliar with the social determinants of health literature to a perspective for understanding health and improving health policy that is truly compatible with social work's biopsychosocial perspective. There is no social work and health policy book that explores the implications for social work and health care policy of this important framework. The social determinants of health perspective clearly demonstrate the impact of the social environment on individual and population health, and provide insight into potential directions for the future of health policy.

Acknowledgments

Although we did all our own research, we would like to acknowledge several people who helped along the way. Specifically, we would like to thank the following: Jennifer Quigley-Harris for suggesting we write the book in the first place; Sam Flint, a friend for more than twenty years and almost a coauthor of this book; Kevin Corcoran, another long-time friend, who generously shared his insights into research, writing, and publishing; Sharon Keigher, editor of *Health and Social Work,* who encouraged us in the work; Madeline Golde, Cathy Hurwitt, and the people at Families USA, who taught us much about the health care systems; Don Wharton and Virginia Barry, the president and vice president at Plymouth State College, who understood the importance of our work; Steve Gleason, Rick Boxer, Irwin Redlener, Pat Ford-Roegner, and Chris Jennings, friends and colleagues from the president's health care task force, a brilliant, though unfortunately unappreciated effort to do the right thing; Ann Crowley, who started as a student and became a friend; Michael Rachlis and Debby Copes, who gave us insight into the Canadian health care system, introduced us to the social determinants of health, and provided warm hospitality in Toronto; and Bruce Kennedy and Ichiro Kawachi, who appeared on Steve's radio program and deepened our understanding of the impact of inequality on health. We would also like to acknowledge the generous support of the Whiting Foundation. We owe a special debt to Richard Wilkinson for his pathbreaking research, friendship, and support. We have fond memories of walking with him through a sheep pasture overlooking Brighton, England. We also thank the reviewers of this edition for their helpful suggestions: Jeanne A. Barrett, Lorain County Community College; Joan Dworkin, California State University, Sacramento; Sophia Dziegielewski, University of Central Florida; Howard Karger, University of Houston; and Carol Shutt, Morehead State University.

1 Efforts to Establish National Health Insurance: 1865–1946

In the first two chapters of this book, we provide an overview of the history of health care policy in the United States. The first chapter examines the period dating from the end of the Civil War to World War II (1865–1946). This is a crucial period in the development of U.S. health care policy. Unlike other Western nations, which established systems of universal health care in response to rapid social and economic change, the United States rejected national health insurance. Instead, it pursued a path of voluntary employment-based insurance.

The Welfare State in the United States

Why has the United States taken a different approach to health policy than other industrialized nations have (Quadagno, 1994)? Why, as a nation, have we been unable to ensure access to health care for everyone? This is clearly a complex question. It can best be answered by looking at the development of our nation's social welfare system, or welfare state. The term *welfare state* refers to the role and responsibility of the national government to ensure access to essential needs (economic, educational, health, social) for all citizens through its public policies and services. Systems of social welfare developed throughout the twentieth century in the Western world in response to social needs and continue to develop today. Health care policy in the United States developed within the framework of the nation's social welfare system.

Social scientists have identified some of the critical factors that shaped the development of welfare states among Western nations. Noble's (1997) work is particularly instructive. He identified three factors that played a central role:

- The conflict between working and capitalist classes that resulted from industrialization
- Racial and ethnic differences that compounded this conflict
- The structure of a nation's political or governmental institutions

Workers and their organizations in many countries, such as England and France, played a central role in advocating for expanded social welfare programs. Although employer groups also supported social welfare programs, they tended

1

to do so to a lesser degree than labor organizations. Racial and ethnic differences, or social heterogeneity, were also a factor. In environments in which racial and ethnic differences gave rise to social conflict, as they did in the United States, they created divisions among workers and, thereby, weakened efforts for social reform.

Finally, the structure of a nation's political institutions also play a role. In countries, such as Germany and Britain, where it took a long time to establish democracy, power became concentrated in centralized bureaucracies (Skocpol, 1992; Sanderson, 1995). This political structure facilitated the establishment of relatively generous social welfare programs. In contrast, in the United States, democracy (at least for white males) came early in the nation's development, and power was diffused. In the political system in the United States, competition takes place not only among the three branches of the federal government (executive, legislative, and judicial) but also between the federal government and the states. This fragmented structure made it much more difficult to establish national social welfare programs. The United States has not had the institutional capacity, or capability, to introduce a centralized, or European-style, welfare state easily (Skocpol, 1992).

Noble's (1997) framework helps us understand why social welfare programs have developed to varying degrees in different countries. By applying Noble's analysis to the United States we are better able to understand why this country "has been unusually inhospitable to social reformers" (Noble, 1997) or why the United States has a "reluctant welfare state" (Jansson, 2001). The states' rights tradition, which is tied to the period of white supremacy that followed the Civil War, has been a critical factor in the development of the U.S. welfare state. This was a dominant doctrine until the New Deal of the 1930s, and white supremacy lasted until the 1960s when it was legally eradicated by the passage and enforcement of the Civil Rights Act of 1965.

However, the influence of the states' rights tradition reemerged in the 1980s with the Reagan administration and again in 2000 with the Bush administration. This political tug of war between the states' rights and federalist approaches to social policy helps us understand the nation's reluctance to develop a universal system of health care. The white supremacist attitude toward people of color, particularly African Americans, also helps us to understand the disparities in health we still see today among people of color.

Historical Determinants

Economic and Racial Conflicts

During the late 1800s, the United States had all of the prerequisite characteristics shared by other industrialized nations that were developing strong welfare states—a capitalist economy, a democratic system of government, competing political parties, and an organized working class (represented by the American Federation of Labor founded in 1886). However, the United States also had a curious economic "dualism" (Quadagno, 1988). Industrialization and organized labor was concentrated in the North, while agriculture dominated the Southern economy. More importantly, the economy of the South was based on plantation-owner and slave relations and thus lacked a "working class," let alone an organized working class pushing for employment rights and benefits.

After the Civil War ended in 1865, the federal government sent troops to the South to restore order, enforce the Civil Rights Act of 1865, and oversee its policy of Reconstruction (1867–1876). For this brief period of time, African Americans in the South, assisted by the Freedmen's Bureau in the U.S. War Department, were granted civil rights. However, to counter the policy of Reconstruction, plantation owners organized to terrorize freed slaves and dismantle the newly formed governments established in the South. The conservative ideology of the southern Democrats took hold once again, and Jim Crow laws mandated rigid separation of the races in everything from public accommodations, trains, streetcars, and hospitals to telephone booths and water fountains (Rabinowitz, 1991).

White supremacy was not limited to the South, however. In the North, leading newspapers, periodicals, and academicians openly mocked and proclaimed the inferiority of African Americans (Kluger, 1975). Both political parties participated in the degradation of African Americans. Democratic President Woodrow Wilson (1856–1924), a former president of Princeton University, extended segregation to federal agencies and departments, including the civil service (Weiss, 1970). Republican President Warren G. Harding was inducted into the Ku Klux Klan in a ceremony held at the White House (Loewen, 1995).

White supremacy had a particularly adverse impact on the development of the labor movement in the United States. W. E. B. Du Bois (1975, p. 700), a prominent African American social scientist, described how, in exchange for low wages, white workers received a "public and psychological wage" in the form of "public deference and titles of courtesy." Unlike African Americans, poor whites were "admitted freely...to public functions, public parks, and the best schools." Politicians solicited their votes, and the courts "treated them with such leniency as to encourage lawlessness." This "carefully planned and slowly evolved" strategy of white privilege "drove...a wedge" between poor whites and African Americans.

During the 1880s and 1890s, the American Federation of Labor (AFL), which represented skilled workers, sanctioned segregated locals and denied African Americans "any effective voice in union policy" (Saxton, 1970, p. 107). Samuel Gompers, head of the AFL, went as far as to blame African Americans themselves for the unions' hostility (Saxton, 1970). In 1924, the National Association for the Advancement of Colored People (NAACP), a leading African American organization, warned, "'Negro labor in the main is outside the ranks of organized labor'" (Foner, 1974, p. 170). The primary reason for this was that "'white union labor does not want black labor'" (Foner, 1974, p. 170). The AFL's policy of "racial exclusion and segregation" lasted through the 1950s (Quadagno, 1994, p. 23).

During the mid-1930s, several unions broke with the AFL to create the Congress of Industrial Organizations (CIO). The CIO sought to organize unskilled workers in the automobile, steel, and other mass production industries (Brody, 1991), in which African Americans often made up a significant share of the workforce. Unlike the AFL, the CIO recognized the necessity of organizing all workers—whatever their skin color. "There were no constitutional bars, no segregation of blacks into separate locals, no Jim Crow rituals" (Foner, 1974, p. 216). Thurgood Marshall, the NAACP's chief attorney, and later a Supreme Court Justice, described the "program of the CIO" as "a Bill of Rights for Negro labor in America" (Foner, 1974, p. 237).

The relationship between African Americans and the CIO benefited both parties. For the CIO, the recruitment of African Americans helped bridge divisions in the working class and increase membership. For African Americans, particularly workers, the CIO brought a powerful new ally to the struggle for racial equality. The AFL and the CIO shared a broader goal as well. Since the 1930s, civil rights organizations had pursued both a "race-specific" and a "social welfare" agenda. The race-specific agenda targeted "*legal* segregation and discrimination" for reform (Hamilton and Hamilton, 1997, p. 2). The social welfare agenda transcended race and aimed at creating "policies and programs for *all* people with low-incomes" (p. 2). As such, the social welfare agenda dovetailed with labor's agenda, which has long included "universal" social insurance, full employment, and federal control of social welfare programs (Hamilton and Hamilton, 1997).

After World War II, the CIO lost momentum. The turning point was the defeat of Operation Dixie, which the AFL and CIO launched in 1946 to organize southern workers (Goldfield, 1997). Operation Dixie was important for two reasons. First, the South was the last, largely nonunionized section of the country, and wages there were lower than in any other region. Northern industrialists used the threat of moving south as a way to intimidate workers elsewhere (Patterson, 1996).

Second, the southern Democrats (along with their Republican allies) were the chief obstacles to enactment of the CIO's legislative agenda. Unionizing the South would strengthen the hand of labor, bring workers into that region's political process, and threaten the conservatives' base of power. The failure to unionize the South strengthened the influence of the southern conservatives in Congress who opposed a strong central government.

Political Conflicts and the Rise of the Conservative Coalition

The South was less democratic in its political structure than the North. The Republicans were the party of Lincoln and the North and drew support from farmers, skilled craftsmen, and other "upwardly mobile" groups (McPherson, 1988). After the Civil War, Republicans increasingly became the party of big business and grew more conservative (Rae, 1991; Hicks, 1960). Southern Democrats, on the other hand, represented the largely white plantation owners and their merchant–banker allies, who dominated a labor force of African American sharecroppers and tenant farmers. According to V. O. Key, a noted political scientist,

> The hard core of the political South—and the backbone of southern political unity—is made up of those counties and sections of the southern states in which

> Negroes constitute a substantial proportion of the population. In these areas a real problem of politics broadly considered, is the maintenance of control by a white minority... (Key, 1984, pp. 5–6).

To ensure "control" by the "white minority" during the 1890s, the Democrats enacted legislation prohibiting most African Americans, and many poor whites, from voting and turned the South into a one-party region (Litwak, 1998; Bloom, 1987).

Facing minimal opposition, southern Democrats easily won reelection to office. This gave southerners positions of seniority, and thus authority, on important congressional committees. In the House of Representatives, southerners chaired the two most important committees, Ways and Means and Rules, with little exception, from 1877 to 1963 (Quadagno, 1988). Because a bill must be reported out of committee before being voted on by the full House, the southern chairs were able to control the flow of legislation by refusing to schedule votes on bills they opposed. As a result, the southern Democrats exerted "a negative, controlling influence on national politics" (Quadagno, 1994, p. 17). Southerners also wielded great influence in the Senate. "The powerful Committee on Finance, for example, remained under southern control for seventy-three years" during this same period (Quadagno, 1988, p. 17). The presidency was also controlled by the South for fifty-eight years from 1875 to 1933, when President Roosevelt was elected (Quadagno, 1988, p. 17).

Finally, the courts, which were also dominated by conservatives during this period, contributed to the decentralization of our political structure. During the late nineteenth and early twentieth centuries, the Supreme Court imposed severe restrictions on the ability of government to interfere with private property and state laws (Hoffer, 1991). For example, in 1905, when some people worked as many as one hundred hours a week, the Court threw out a New York law limiting the workweek to sixty hours (Kens, 1992). This decision was not reversed until 1937. In 1896, in *Plessy v. Ferguson*, the Court upheld a Louisiana law requiring the segregation of the "white and colored races," a decision that stood until 1954 (Pratt, 1992, p. 637).

Franklin D. Roosevelt was elected president in 1932 in response to the economic chaos created by the Great Depression of 1929. For the first time since the late 1880s, the southern Democrats lost their control of national politics. In response, southern Democrats and conservative Republicans developed a strategic, "informal" working alliance, referred to as the conservative coalition (Freidel, 1990; Jansson, 2001; Leuchtenburg, 1963). Although these groups did not agree on everything, they did share two fundamental beliefs.

First, they both opposed independent unions and made every effort to thwart legislation that would help workers. One of the catalysts for the conservative coalition was the National Labor Relations (or Wagner) Act, which Congress enacted in 1935 to give workers the right to organize unions (Gorin, 1983). Although some companies accepted the Wagner Act and allowed their workers to organize, others, such as Ford and General Motors, resisted, sometimes violently (Gorin, 1983). A congressional committee found that the National Association of Manufacturers had "'blanketed the country with...propaganda'" to prevent implementation of the Wagner Act (Gorin, 1983, p. 197). In 1947, the conservative coalition passed the

Taft-Hartley Act, which aimed at "roll[ing] back the gains made by labor during the New Deal" (Foner and Garraty, 1991, p. 1057).

A second point on which southern Democrats and conservative Republicans agreed was the need for limited government, particularly at the federal level. For Republicans, limited government meant limited interference with the rights of property owners; for southern Democrats, it meant the right of states to ignore federal civil rights laws. These groups often cooperated in efforts to weaken the federal government and enhance the power of corporations and state governments (Patterson, 1996; Jansson, 2001). These efforts helped prevent the emergence of a strong, central government, which, as noted earlier, facilitates the development of a strong welfare state.

Early Efforts to Establish National Health and Mental Health Care Reforms: 1865–1912

The Beginnings of Social Work

After the Civil War ended in 1865, the nation entered into an era (1865–1920) of enormous industrial growth and expansion. This period brought rapid social and economic change to the United States, including massive immigration from Europe and severe poverty among the poor and working classes.

> On the one hand, it enhanced the national wealth, raised the general standard of living, speeded up urbanization, and had many other constructive effects. On the other hand, it produced, among other things, periodic cycles of depression and unemployment, a small group of men who controlled the nation's resources and modes of production, wretched living and working conditions, a high incidence of industrial accidents and fatalities, and numerous other unfortunate results that affected every segment of American society (Trattner, 1999, p. 82).

Both social work and the public health movement emerged in the United States in response to these social conditions and human needs. In a period fueled by Herbert Spencer's ideology of Social Darwinism ("survival of the fittest"), the government played little role in meeting the needs of children and families ravaged by the severe economic depression of 1870. Voluntary charity was acceptable, while public relief was discouraged.

> Orthodox Social Darwinists found no place in their general scheme of things for public support of education, or for sanitary regulation, a public mail system, regulation of business or trade, or, least of all, for public assistance to the needy (Trattner, 1999, p. 88).

Charity organization societies (COS) and settlement houses took on the role of providing assistance to poor and needy children and families. Charity organization societies originated in England and were replicated in the United States during the 1870s. As the name implies, the COS aimed at organizing, or rationalizing, the delivery of private charities. These societies wanted to deter the fraudulent receipt of aid and the duplication of private, charitable services offered by churches and other religious groups, labor unions, mutual aid societies, women's clubs, fraternal associations, ethnic/immigrant associations and clubs, and other philanthropic groups.

England gave birth to the settlement house movement during this period, which also spread quickly to the United States. Settlement houses brought together "people of different socioeconomic and cultural backgrounds to share knowledge, skills and values for their mutual benefit" (Barker, 1999, p. 436). From the beginning, settlement house workers focused on the relationship between poverty—including poor sanitation, substandard housing, malnutrition, disease and illness, and high mortality rates—and poor work conditions, crowded and unsafe housing, low wages, child labor, and industrial accidents. Initially, settlement house workers tried to improve neighborhood conditions by working to improve sanitation, garbage collection, and public health facilities. However, as Trattner (1999) states, they soon realized that to improve living and work conditions they would have to become involved in reforms at the local, state, and national level.

Although the COS and settlement house movements are often depicted as representing opposing, conservative and liberal, approaches to poverty, their differences should not be exaggerated. According to Brieland (1995), settlement house workers "often" worked "in COS programs," and "some" COS workers "lived in settlement(s)." Bertha C. Reynolds (1963), an influential social work pioneer and a self-described Marxist, credited the Boston COS with playing "a major part in creating the responsiveness to human need for which the city was famous" (p. 28).

In 1905, Jane Addams, founder of Hull House in Chicago, perhaps the most famous of the settlement houses, became the first president of the National Conference of Charities and Correction. The National Conference of Charities and Correction had been established in 1874 by the State Boards of Charities, but it quickly came under the control of the COS movement (Axinn and Levin, 1997). Between 1905 and 1914, activists from the charity organization society and settlement house movements increasingly became allies in efforts for social reform. As noted by Trattner (1999), reformers in both movements seemed in agreement that "poor people were...an oppressed lot...and that social reform was more important than the elevation of personal morality" (p. 183).

However, both groups had white European immigrants in mind in their social reform efforts. Charity organization societies and settlement houses generally ignored the needs of people of color. Some settlement leaders, such as Jane Addams and Lillian Wald, cofounder of New York's Henry Street Settlement, did help establish settlements for African Americans. They were also instrumental in founding the NAACP, a lobbying group for African Americans (Iglehart and Becerra, 2000). On the other hand, Addams does seem to have underestimated the significance of white supremacy as a barrier to social reform. Like many, she urged reformers to postpone confronting white supremacy until they had a broader following (Lasch, 1982). Others, such as W. E. B. Du Bois, argued that until reformers directly challenged white supremacy, they would not have a broader following (Lewis, 1993).

The National Conference of Charities and Correction proposed and advocated for legislation to establish fair standards of employment and workers' compensation, prohibit child labor, and improve public health. In 1912, the Conference's "platform of 'minimum standards' for well-being...included a federal system of accident, old-age, and unemployment insurance" (Trattner, 1999, p. 226 n. 5). The Conference worked with the American Association for Labor Legislation (AALL) to support and establish a system of social insurance in the United States (Trattner, 1999). The AALL, which had been established in 1906 by economists from the University of Wisconsin, represented a broad group of social reformers and progressives including "social workers," physicians, lawyers, political scientists, historians, labor leaders, business leaders, and politicians (Feingold, 1966).

Social workers were also instrumental in the creation of the U.S. Children's Bureau, which played a central role in promoting maternal and child health (Jaros and Evans, 1995). During the early 1900s, Florence Kelley (1859–1932), Lillian Wald (1867–1940), and Edward Devine (1867–1948) raised concerns about the condition of children in the United States (Trattner, 1999). In 1906, the National Child Labor Committee, whose board included Wald and Kelley, arranged for a bill to establish a Children's Bureau to be introduced in Congress. Three years later, in 1909, President Theodore Roosevelt hosted the first White House Conference on Dependent Children.

At the request of the conference delegates, Roosevelt urged Congress to enact the bill to create a Children's Bureau. In public hearings, reformers noted that the federal government devoted more resources to the study of animals than children, and "young animals" had a "lower mortality rate" than "young children" (Trattner, 1999). In 1912, Congress established the Children's Bureau to "'investigate and report'" on "'all matters'" concerning "the welfare of children and child life among the classes of our people" (U.S. Children's Bureau, 1914, p. 2). The bureau's first director was Julia Lathrop (1858–1932), a settlement house worker from Illinois and the first woman to run a federal agency (Edwards, 1995; Trattner, 1999).

The Need for Public Health Services

Industrialization and urbanization created sanitation and health issues in all of the major industrial cities. As urban centers grew rapidly with poor controls for water quality and sewage disposal, they exposed families and neighbors to the risk of communicable diseases. Increased trade between seaports contributed to the spread of disease from one region of the country to another. Overcrowded, unsanitary living conditions made it easy for infectious diseases to spread easily. For example, in 1849, cholera spread from New Orleans to Chicago, killing almost 3 percent of Chicago's population (Turnock, 1997).

The Chadwick and Shattuck reports of the 1840–1850 period documented the relationship of poverty, bad sanitation, housing, and working conditions with high mortality, and ushered in the idea of social epidemiology (Tulchinsky and Varavik-ova, 2000, p. 62).

In 1848, Britain's Parliament enacted the Health of Towns Act and the Public Health Act based on the work of Edwin Chadwick. This legislation established state and local health departments responsible for sanitation efforts, control of communicable diseases, data collection on vital statistics, and maternal and child health services. In the United States, Lemuel Shattuck replicated Chadwick's work, which led to the development of state boards of health, most of which were created after 1870. However, unlike Britain, boards of health in the United States initially limited their role to the control of infectious diseases (Turnock, 1997).

Although members of the upper class could escape overcrowded cities by moving to rural areas, members of the emerging urban middle class did not enjoy this luxury (Baltzell, 1964). They "paid taxes, supported cleanliness and public education, recognized and abhorred corruption, and, as home owners, had an investment in their cities" (Garrett, 2000, p. 284). Thus, the middle class took the lead in advocating a wide range of reforms, including the enactment of health and safety regulations (Garrett, 2000). During the 1890s, many cities "instituted new public works sanitation projects (such as piped water, sewer systems, filtration and chlorination of water) and public health administration" (Haines, 1991, p. 105).

Until the end of the nineteenth century, the sanitation movement in Britain and the United States was driven by the theory that disease was caused by "infectious mists or noxious vapors emanating from filth in the towns" and that the best way to prevent the spread of disease was "to clean the streets of garbage, sewage, animal carcasses, and wastes that were features of urban living" (Tulchinsky and Varavik-ova, 2000, p. 27). By the turn of the twentieth century, however, it was scientifically proven that miscroscopic germs were responsible for communicable diseases.

With the development of vaccines against rabies and diphtheria, many communities, particularly in the East, required their citizens to become immunized (Garrett, 2000). In New York City, Hermann Biggs, a leading public health figure, asserted that health authorities could resort to any measure that was "designed for the public good" and "beneficent" in its "effects" (cited in Garrett, 2000, p. 297). Authorities "routinely deployed police officers and zealous nurses or physicians to the homes of those suspected of carrying disease.... In some cases, police officers pinned the arm of those who refused while a city nurse jabbed it with a vaccination needle" (p. 299). These efforts seemed to pay off. Between 1900 and 1915, death rates (among children) from measles, whooping cough, scarlet fever, and diphtheria declined in the United States (Garrett, 2000).

The Mental Hygiene Movement

Public hospitals for the mentally ill also emerged during this period of industrial and urban change. Since the early 1800s, hospitalization served as the primary means of caring for people with problems of mental health. The approach used was known as "moral treatment" or "moral management" and was based on the work of a French theorist, Philippe Pinel (Grob, 1994). Pinel opposed the common practice of confining the "insane" to asylums and relying on seclusion and physical restraint to control deviant social behaviors. Pinel believed that the hospital could employ psychological treatments to help patients recover from their mental disease. In fact, Pinel's use of the French word *moral* did not refer to ethical or moral reforms, but rather to an institutional setting that could create order and promote recovery through psychological therapy (Grob, 1994).

From 1800 to roughly 1825, small privately funded hospitals were established in wealthy urban communities. Examples of these hospitals include the McLean Asylum in Boston (1818), the Hartford Retreat (1824), and the Friends Asylum in Philadelphia (1817). Initially, these institutions were designed to serve the entire community, yet they accepted few patients and remained rather exclusive. With patients expected to pay for their own treatment, these new hospitals found it increasingly difficult to live up to their ideal of serving everyone in the community (Grob, 1994).

Attention shifted to the need to establish and fund public hospitals for the mentally ill. According to Grob (1994), public hospitals emerged first in the rural South. These hospitals did not adopt the new therapeutic approach of moral treatment; they were essentially custodial in nature. The pioneer of the public mental health hospital movement was Worcester State Hospital, established in 1830 in Massachusetts. As noted by Mechanic (1999), in its early history, Worcester State Hospital "practiced moral treatment and offered its patients an optimistic and humanitarian climate" (p. 90). Reformers, such as Dorothea Dix, encouraged state legislatures to build new hospitals for the mentally ill.

However, with the huge wave of immigration that occurred between 1830 and 1850, and the industrial and urban growth that followed, Worcester State Hospital and others began to retreat to custodial care. "In densely populated areas insane people were more visible, and public concern about security increased" (Grob, 1994, p. 24). Overcrowding, insufficient funding, and other problems made it impossible to provide humane care.

The mental hygiene movement was a response to the inhumane treatment of patients in public hospitals and, initially, an effort to improve conditions. The National Conference of Charities and Corrections challenged asylum psychiatry and suggested the need for alternatives to institutional care. The National Association for the Protection of the Insane and the Prevention of Insanity was formed in 1880, and asylum physicians found it difficult to defend their practices. The bond between psychiatry and asylums began to break as younger psychiatrists turned away from asylums and wanted to be viewed as general practitioners. Some psychiatrists took up the task of redefining mental illness, while others joined the mental hygiene movement (Grob, 1994). Clifford W. Beers, a former mental patient diagnosed with manic depression, wrote an exposé of his hospitalization, titled *A Mind That Found Itself* in 1908 and became the leader of the mental hygiene movement.

Initially, Beers was concerned with the deplorable conditions of mental hospitals, but by the early 1900s the mental hygiene movement had shifted its attention to outpatient care and the prevention of mental illness (Grob, 1994). During this period, social workers participated in educational campaigns to broaden public understanding of mental illness and participated in the development of "free child guidance clinics, dispensaries, outpatient centers, and hospitals for early detection, diagnosis, and treatment of mental disorders" (Trattner, 1999, p. 198).

Compulsory Health Insurance Efforts: 1912–1920

By 1912, Germany, Austria, Hungary, Norway, Britain, and Russia had all created compulsory health insurance programs. The United States, in keeping with its decentralized government and its limited role in regulating the economy or social welfare, had not pursued this path. However, between 1912 and 1920, social and political events made compulsory health insurance an issue for public debate, both on the national level and in many of the states. Workers' compensation laws were enacted in forty-two states between 1910 and 1920 (Skocpol, 1992). During this period, advocates for health care reform were encouraged by this step toward social insurance.

Presidential candidate Theodore Roosevelt advocated compulsory health insurance in 1912 as part of a broad package of social insurance programs (Rolde, 1992; Starr, 1982). Jane Addams and other social workers active in the settlement house movement played leading roles in Roosevelt's campaign (Jansson, 2001). That same year, AALL (the American Association for Labor Legislation) established a Social-Insurance Committee to study various proposals for health care reform.

American Association for Labor Legislation

AALL leaders from the business and private insurance industry visited Europe to study the national health insurance systems in Germany and England. Their findings were discussed at social work meetings and conferences amid optimism for reform (Mizrahi, 1995). AALL developed model legislation that mandated health care coverage for workers and their dependents. Proposed benefits included physician, nurse, and hospital services; pay for sick days; maternity benefits; and death benefits. AALL proposed shared financing for the program from employers, employees, and state governments (Starr, 1982).

Between 1916 and 1919, believing that a movement for health insurance would prove as successful as the drive for workers' compensation, AALL launched a major campaign to enact its model legislation in the states. AALL leaders had identified a strong relationship between work-related accidents, sickness, and dependence on workers' compensation. Providing coverage for medical expenses, they argued, would help eliminate the poverty caused by sickness and injury, and help reduce employers' costs for compensation.

The reformers' optimism soon waned, however. With the entry of the United States into World War I, social insurance, which had originated in Germany, fell into disrepute (Rolde, 1992). The Bolshevik Revolution, and the subsequent "red scare," also placed reformers on the defensive. "Superpatriots" accused the National Welfare Council and the Federation for Social Service of the Methodist Church of "leaning towards Bolshevism," while Jane Addams and others faced blacklisting (Levin, 1971). At a "social work conference" held in 1917, a leading insurance executive described compulsory health insurance as a "'communistic system...repugnant to American minds and destructive of American initiative and individuality'" (Rolde, 1992, p. 20).

Opposition from labor leaders was also damaging to their cause. Samuel Gompers, and other prominent labor leaders, opposed compulsory health insurance. In 1920, the American Medical Association (AMA), which initially had supported compulsory health insurance, reversed its position and launched its opposition to reform (Rolde, 1992). Fifteen states introduced compulsory health insurance bills, and nine created commissions to study the problem of access to health insurance. However, no state actually enacted health insurance legislation (Rolde, 1992). After the failure of these efforts, compulsory health insurance was not considered again until the 1930s.

Establishment of the U.S. Public Health Service

The public health movement, on the other hand, continued to gain strength between 1912 and 1920. Despite the success of vaccines and treatments in lowering death rates from communicable diseases, a number of diseases, including tuberculosis, were still a serious threat to public health. Poor children and families in urban settings were particularly vulnerable. In the early 1900s, city health departments began the practice of sending public health nurses into communities to conduct home visits, and local schools began to establish health clinics. By 1915, there were more than a thousand health clinics administered by city health departments for the treatment of tuberculosis and to address the problem of infant mortality (Institute of Medicine, 1988).

In 1912, the Marine Hospital Service, established by the federal government, was renamed the U.S. Public Health Service. When the Marine Hospital Service was first established in 1798, it created a network of hospitals along the eastern and southern seaboard to treat merchant seamen and, thereby, prevent the spread of infectious diseases. By the end of the nineteenth century, the Marine Hospital Service was responsible for public quarantines and the health inspection of immigrants to the United States (Moroney, 1995). In 1912, the surgeon general of the U.S. Public Health Service was granted more authority and the agency took steps to address rural health and the control of venereal diseases (Institute of Medicine, 1988), but the "federal government [still] could not act directly in health matters; it could only act through states as the primary delivery system" (Turnock, 1997, p. 123).

Federal–State Reforms and Private Insurance: 1920–1932

Despite the opposition to compulsory health insurance, Congress did address the problem of maternal and child health care in 1921. Julia Lathrop and Grace Abbott, both of whom had worked at Hull House, the Chicago settlement house founded by Jane Addams, were advocates of this reform (Simon, 1994). Under

Lathrop's direction, the Children's Bureau had studied the problem of infant mortality; the findings were sobering. The United States had "a shockingly high infant mortality rate" and one of the highest maternal death rates in the world (Trattner, 1999, p. 219). Poverty and lack of prenatal care were identified as primary causes.

Sheppard-Towner Infancy and Maternity Bill

At Lathrop's urging, Jeanette Rankin, a former social worker and the first female member of Congress, introduced the Sheppard-Towner Infancy and Maternity Bill (or Act) in 1921. The legislation was designed to provide grants-in-aid to the states for prenatal and child health centers to help reduce maternal and infant death rates (Trattner, 1999; Starr, 1982). The Sheppard-Towner Act was passed in 1922 and was administered by the Children's Bureau, which disseminated more than 20 million pieces of literature, sponsored more than 100,000 conferences, created thousands of prenatal care centers, and facilitated millions of home visits between 1922 and 1929 (Skocpol, 1995). Sheppard-Towner established the Federal Board of Maternity and Infant Hygiene and was the first federal legislation to give funds to the states to establish programs in nursing, home care, health education, and maternal care (Institute of Medicine, 1988).

Sheppard-Towner was also the catalyst for government involvement in the establishment of federal guidelines for public health programs administered by the states. The expansion of federal–state efforts to improve public health increased the demand for public health experts and leaders (Institute of Medicine, 1988). As early as 1916, the Rockefeller Foundation, which had played a central role in the development of medical education, expressed concern that "insufficient attention was being paid to environmental and social factors in disease" (White, 1991, p. 2). To rectify this imbalance, the foundation advocated the creation of independent schools of public health, which would address "the determinants of health and disease in populations" (White, 1991, p. 2).

Whatever the foundation's intentions, the creation of schools of public health reinforced, indeed codified, a growing separation between efforts to prevent disease and efforts to cure it, and the Sheppard-Towner Act faced growing opposition from political conservatives and the medical profession. Physicians were particularly alarmed by the expansion of public health, viewing it as a threat to their authority. After New York City required physicians to report the names of patients who had been diagnosed with tuberculosis, the president of the County Medical Society accused the city of overstepping its bounds (Starr, 1982). Similarly, when the city health department started manufacturing and distributing serum for diphtheria and rabies, it was accused of engaging in "'municipal socialism' and unfair competition with private business" (Starr, 1982, p. 186).

The AMA called Sheppard-Towner "'a form of federal bureaucratic interference with the sacred rights of the American home'" (Rolde, 1992). The Illinois Medical Society published a pamphlet referring to the staff of the Children's Bureau as "'endocrine perverts [and] derailed menopausics'" and warning that Sheppard-Towner would make the bureau "'the ruling power in the United States'" (Trattner, 1999, p. 220). A prominent senator asserted that, under Sheppard-Towner, "'female celibates would instruct mothers on how to bring up their babies'" (p. 220). In 1929, Congress discontinued funding for Sheppard-Towner. A number of factors, including opposition from the Hoover administration and the stock market crash and economic crisis of 1929, led to its demise. However, the most significant factor was the concerted opposition by organized medicine (Trattner, 1999).

Efforts to establish compulsory health insurance were also waning. In 1928, a group of professionals, with funding from several foundations, established the Committee on the Costs of Medical Care (CCMC). The committee engaged in a comprehensive study of the economics of compulsory health insurance and in 1932 released a final report, which opposed compulsory health insurance (Abbott, 1966). The CCMC recommended a group practice and payment system, and the use of private insurance and local revenues to establish group health plans for low-income consumers. However, the AMA opposed the idea of group practices and any form of government involvement (Starr, 1982).

Given the political and economic obstacles facing advocates of prevention and public health, it is not surprising that physicians increasingly focused on biomedical research and clinical practice. By the 1930s, public health had been relegated to "a secondary status: less prestigious than clinical medicine, less amply financed, and blocked from assuming the higher-level functions of coordination and direction that might have developed had it not been banished from medical care" (Starr, 1982, p. 197).

The Creation of Blue Cross and Blue Shield

The Great Depression made it even more difficult for individuals and families to pay for hospital care and medical services, however, and sustained the social pressure to reform the health care system. In 1927, the president of the American Hospital Association (AHA) noted the difficulty faced by "'the great bulk of people of moderate means'" in meeting hospital bills (Kotelchuck, 1976, p. 84). With hospital occupancy rates falling and deficits spiraling, hospitals began to develop their own insurance plans under the name of Blue Cross (Kotelchuck, 1976). In 1932, the AHA sanctioned prepaid group hospital plans, as long as they were nonprofit, covered hospital care only, did not interfere with private practitioners, and allowed patients a free choice of hospitals. In 1939, Blue Shield, which offered coverage for physicians' services, was created (Edinburg and Cottler, 1995), and by 1940, thirty-nine Blue Cross plans were providing group hospital services to more than 6 million people (Starr, 1982). The establishment of Blue Cross and Blue Shield insurance plans laid the foundation for a third-party payment system, completely changed health care financing, and led the way for employment-based insurance.

The New Deal Reforms: 1932–1940

As hospitals and physicians struggled to control the medical system, President Franklin D. Roosevelt, elected in 1932, began to develop his administration's program for economic and social reform, the New Deal. Among Roosevelt's advisers was a social worker named Harry L. Hopkins. Hopkins's first job out of college had been as a camp counselor for Christadora House, a New York settlement. Radicalized by this experience, he "plunged into social work on the lower East Side" (Schlesinger, 1959, p. 265). Hopkins later worked for the Association for Improving the Condition of the Poor, the Board for Child Welfare, the (New Orleans) Red Cross, and the New York Tuberculosis and Health Association.

In 1931, when Roosevelt was governor of New York, he made Hopkins director of New York's Temporary Emergency Relief Administration (TERA) (Freidel, 1990). TERA spent millions of dollars to assist unemployed New Yorkers and provided both "a model" and "personnel for New Deal programs and agencies" (Trattner, 1999, p. 280). Hopkins was a friend of Roosevelt's wife, Eleanor, who was also "strongly influenced" by the settlement house movement. Eleanor Roosevelt was a tireless advocate for the Children's Bureau, Sheppard-Towner, and other progressive causes, including the rights of African Americans (Davis, 1991; Goodwin, 1994; Cook, 1992).

In 1933, Hopkins, along with William Hodson, a former president of the American Association of Social Workers, met with Frances Perkins, Roosevelt's secretary of labor, to discuss plans for a federal relief program (Schlesinger, 1959). Perkins, known as "Madam Secretary," was another veteran of the settlement house movement and the first social worker appointed to a federal cabinet position. Perkins arranged for Hopkins to meet with Roosevelt, who hired Hopkins to run the newly established Federal Emergency Relief Administration (FERA) (Schlesinger, 1959). By 1936, Hopkins, a strong supporter of compulsory health insurance (Starr, 1982), had become a close adviser and confidante of Roosevelt's (Goodwin, 1994).

In 1934, Perkins became chair of the Committee on Economic Security, which was given the task of developing a plan for old-age retirement, unemployment, and health care insurance. When Perkins suggested that the committee consider compulsory health insurance, the AMA organized physicians to flood Congress with telegrams and letters of protest (Marmor, 1973). Roosevelt feared that this controversy would doom plans for retirement and unemployment insurance. On advice from close advisers, including Hopkins, Roosevelt removed health insurance from the final version of the bill (Moniz, 1990).

Maternal and Child Health Services

When Congress enacted the Social Security Act in 1935, it chose not to introduce compulsory health insurance. However, it did enact Title V, which established Maternal and Child Health Services, a federal–state program administered by the Children's Bureau "to extend and improve" maternal and child health, and other services, particularly in rural and other underserved areas (Axinn and Levin, 1997). When the Sheppard-Towner Act was discontinued in 1929, the states struggled to continue their health promotion activities and infant mortality began to rise again (Jaros and Evans, 1995). Title V also provided funds for services for crippled children, and child welfare services, and gave the states resources to establish "prenatal care, well baby clinics, school health services, immunization, public health nursing and nutrition services, and health education" (Lesser, 1985, p. 1683).

The Failure to Enact Compulsory Insurance

Compulsory health insurance was excluded from the Social Security Act, but it remained a focus of public debate. In 1935, Roosevelt established an Interdepartmental Committee to Coordinate Health and Welfare Activities to monitor the programs enacted by the Social Security Act and to study the feasibility of compulsory health insurance (Abbott, 1966). That same year, the first large-scale study of health conditions, the National Health Survey, was conducted. In 1937, a subcommittee of the Interdepartmental Committee, the Technical Committee on Medical Care, recommended a National Health Program, including the possibility of compulsory insurance. But Roosevelt, again fearing opposition from conservatives, offered only lukewarm support for its plan (Starr, 1982). Frustrated by Roosevelt's ambivalence, Senator Robert Wagner (D-NY) introduced his own proposal for a national health plan in 1939 (Dewhurst and Associates, 1947). The AMA, the AHA, and the American Dental Association testified in opposition to Wagner's bill, and as the nation's attention shifted toward the start of World War II, interest in national health insurance waned.

Most historians and policy analysts agree that the New Deal launched the welfare state in the United States. The Social Security Act of 1935 established a strong role for federal government and laid the foundation for national social insurance programs. However, as noted by Trattner (1999) and others, it also had many shortcomings, particularly the failure to include national health insurance. Moreover, Social Security and other New Deal programs primarily benefited white people. Social Security's insurance programs excluded farmworkers and domestic servants, positions largely held by African Americans (Quadagno, 1994). Although African Americans were, in theory, eligible for Aid to Dependent Children (ADC) and other public assistance programs, given the racism of southern officials, they were highly unlikely to receive the same benefits as whites. With good reason, many African Americans were ambivalent about the New Deal (Hamilton and Hamilton, 1997).

The exclusion of African Americans during this period should be placed in social and political context, however. To enact his legislative agenda, FDR needed support from the southern Democrats, who strongly opposed extending rights and benefits to African Americans (Goldfield, 1997). Roosevelt's wife, Eleanor, was a strong advocate for African Americans, and through her, he helped "convey to blacks that the administration was on their side" (Goodwin, 1994, p. 165). She also helped convince him to issue an executive order banning discrimination in the Works Progress Administration, an important New Deal program. African American social workers were hopeful that the federal government was starting to "care" about "Negro men and women" (p. 163).

Federal Health and Mental Health Policy and Services: 1941–1946

World War II (WWII) (1941–1945) provided a major catalyst to efforts to expand and reform the health care system in the United States. The system's deficiencies were brought to light when men from across the country were recruited to join the military. Between 1940 and 1941, half of the potential inductees were found to be physically or mentally unfit to serve. Although the military later eased its standards, 8 million to 9 million young males were still deemed unfit for service. "Mental and nervous disorders" accounted for almost a third of the rejections; moreover, studies suggested that early intervention "might have prevented or remedied" half "the disqualifying defects" (Dewhurst and Associates, 1947, p. 247). Other studies found similarly high, and preventable, rates of illness and debilitation in other segments of the population.

Not surprisingly, the health of African Americans was much worse than that of whites. For example, in 1940, the infant mortality rate for African Americans was almost twice the infant mortality rate for whites (Newman et al., 1978). In addition, African Americans had a far greater likelihood of dying from diabetes, flu and pneumonia, hypertension, and tuberculosis than did whites. African Americans also faced discrimination in the health professions. In the late 1940s, a third of the nation's medical schools refused to admit African Americans, and only fourteen hospitals admitted African American patients (Newman et al., 1978).

Emergency Maternal and Infant Care Program

In an effort to address the nation's pressing health care needs, Congress, in 1943, created the Emergency Maternal and Infant Care Program (EMIC), a federal–state program to provide free health care and social services to the wives and infants of servicemen (Simon, 1994; Axinn and Levin, 1997). Before the war, most of these women and children had had limited access to care. Katherine Fredrica Lenroot (1891–1982), head of the Children's Bureau and former president of the National Council of Social Work, was a major catalyst for EMIC (Syers, 1995). During its two years of existence, EMIC provided care to 1.25 million women and 230,000 children (Simon, 1994). At the end of the war, the federal government established the Veterans Administration, which provided health care to millions of veterans through a network of hospitals.

Public Health Services Act

WWII also gave impetus to medical research (Starr, 1982). In 1944, Congress enacted the Public Health Services Act, which gave the Public Health Service (PHS) responsibility for the National Institute of Health (NIH). The NIH had been created in 1930 as successor to the National Hygienic Laboratory. In 1937, it was expanded to include the National Cancer Institute (Starr, 1982). Although the 1937 legislation also allowed the NIH "to make grants to outside researchers," funds for this purpose remained "quite limited" (p. 340).

With the advent of the war, however, the importance of research became abundantly clear. In 1941, the Roosevelt administration established an Office of Scientific Research and Development to address war-related medical problems. Roosevelt also commissioned a report on postwar government aid to science, "including what could be done to aid 'the war of science against disease'" (Starr, 1982, p. 341). Between 1945 and 1947, NIH research funding increased dramatically (Starr, 1982). Even "[o]pponents of national health insurance could display their deep concern for health by voting generous appropriations for medical research" (p. 343).

National Mental Health Act

The most significant contribution of the mental hygiene movement occurred during the early years of World War II. Selective service boards throughout the country tried to evaluate the mental health status of millions of draftees but were forced to rely on an insufficient supply of psychiatrists and inadequate screening tools. Psychiatrists were supposed to spend at least fifteen minutes conducting individual examinations, yet reports indicated that an average evaluation lasted only two minutes and an individual psychiatrist might examine two hundred men in a single day (Mechanic, 1999). To assist selective service boards, State Committees on Mental Hygiene across the country enlisted thousands of volunteer social workers from 1941 to 1946 to conduct social case histories of men drafted for the war effort (Trattner, 1999).

During this period, conventional beliefs about the hereditary nature of mental "disease" were being challenged by the impact of environmental stress. Combat and the "realities of war," not personality, seemed to be the defining cause of mental breakdown and illness for many soldiers. To treat nightmares, sleep disturbances, anxiety, and other conditions that soldiers experienced, psychiatrists experimented with "rest periods, rotation policies, and measures encouraging group cohesion and social relationships" at battalion aid stations. From these experiments they found that the alleviation of stress brought positive results (Grob, 1994).

This finding led psychiatrists to the belief that similar approaches could help other mental patients and that government and other social institutions could play a role in reducing mental health problems. To help realize this goal, in 1946 Congress passed the National Mental Health Act, which established a Mental Hygiene Division in the U.S. Public Health Service, and a research center, which, in 1949, became the National Institute of Mental Health (NIMH). The purpose of NIMH was to pursue research on war-related problems such as "battle fatigue," as well as "child development, juvenile delinquency, suicide prevention, alcoholism, and television violence" (Starr, 1982, p. 346). It was the first national effort supported by federal funding to promote mental health through research, education, and training.

The NIMH encouraged each state to find supplements and alternatives to hospitalization for mental health care. It explicitly promoted the development of a broader scope of services to a wider population of consumers that included children and adults with both acute and chronic needs. It also encouraged the development of follow-up clinics to serve patients as they left the hospital and to assist with reintroduction to the community. By the 1950s, community-based programs could be found in every state (Grob, 1994).

The mental hygiene movement had little impact on the prevention of mental illness, but it was influential in decreasing the central role of hospitals in the delivery of mental health care. Other contributing factors to this change were the discovery of pharmaceutical drugs, which allowed individuals to function independently in the community, and the expanded role of the federal government. As noted by Grob (1994), the NIMH not only funded the establishment of community clinics, it also established close ties between the government and mental health professionals. NIMH established regional offices across the country and employed consultants in psychiatry, psychology, social work, and nursing.

Hill-Burton Hospital Survey and Construction Act

In 1946, in an effort to expand access to care, Congress enacted the Hospital Survey and Construction Act of 1946. This legislation, also known as Hill-Burton, enjoyed support from both the AMA and the AHA (Mizrahi, 1995). Hill-Burton provided federal grants and loans (approximately $4 billion between 1946 and 1975) for the construction of hospitals (Patterson, 1996). The policy encouraged states to survey their medical facilities and develop plans to ensure an adequate number of hospital beds, particularly in low-income areas (Starr, 1982).

Although funds from Hill-Burton were used to increase the number of hospital beds available in the poorer states, the policy did not have the impact many of its supporters intended. "Within states…funds went disproportionately to middle-income communities" (Starr, 1982, p. 350). Hill-Burton also failed to protect African Americans. In 1949, a federal official noted that out of 218 new hospitals, only 4 were not "'operated on a policy of segregation'" (Newman et al., 1978, p. 198). The courts did not prohibit "separate but equal" hospitals until 1963 (Starr, 1982). Although Hill-Burton did require hospitals to offer "a reasonable volume of…service to persons unable to pay," it created no mechanism to enforce this (Starr, 1982, p. 350). It also created no mechanism for cost control and thus contributed to subsequent health care inflation (Kotelchuck, 1976).

Highlights

■ Unlike other industrialized nations, the United States has not established a national health care system that guarantees access to health care services for all of its citizens. The political tension between states' rights and federalist approaches to social welfare policy provides a framework to examine the nation's reluctance to develop universal health insurance. Efforts to achieve compulsory health insurance failed to survive ideological and political opposition.

■ From 1912 to 1920, the American Association for Labor Legislation (AALL), supported by the National Conference of Charities and Correction, led the initial drive for compulsory health insurance. It advocated a broad system of social insurance programs that included public health, and proposed legislation for mandatory health insurance. By 1920, however, prominent labor leaders and organized medicine (American Medical Association) opposed compulsory insurance and played a key role in defeating reform efforts underway in many of the states. On the other hand, efforts to establish a system of public health during this period were more successful. The U.S. Public Health Service was established in 1912.

■ The Children's Bureau, also established in 1912, was highly influential in the promotion of maternal and child health and was the catalyst for the Sheppard-Towner bill. Sheppard-Towner provided grants-in-aid to the states to establish child health centers to help reduce infant mortality. Sheppard-Towner also gave rise to the development of federal public health guidelines for the states, which once again incensed the AMA. Congress discontinued funding for Sheppard-Towner in 1929.

■ A final effort to establish compulsory health insurance during the 1920s was led by the Committee on the Costs of Medical Care (CCMC) in 1928 and was opposed by the AMA.

■ The Great Depression of 1929 and the 1932 New Deal administration of President Roosevelt were major turning points in the development of health and social welfare legislation. However, when Congress enacted the Social Security Act of 1935, it chose not to include compulsory health insurance. Instead, it enacted Title V, the Maternal and Child Health program, to reestablish funding to the states; Title V also created Child Welfare Services. In 1937, Roosevelt's administration considered the possibility of compulsory insurance but offered little support for it. Senator Robert Wagner introduced a bill in 1939, but the nation's attention had already shifted to WWII.

■ Entry into WWII highlighted the nation's pressing health care needs. Millions of young male potential inductees were physically or mentally unfit to serve. In 1943, Congress established a federal–state system of "free" health care and social services, the Emergency Maternal and Infant Care Program (EMIC), for the infants and wives of servicemen. It was clear from the recruitment process that many of these families had little or no access to health care.

■ At the end of the war, Congress established the Veterans Administration and a nationwide network of government hospitals to address the medical needs of returning veterans. In 1946, Congress also established a Mental Hygiene Division in the U.S. Public Health Service, and a research center, which became the National Institute of Mental Health (NIMH) in 1949. Many WWII veterans returned with battle fatigue and psychological disorders that challenged conventional beliefs about mental "disease." The NIMH was successful in promoting state-level community-based care as an alternative to mental asylums, while Congress enacted legislation, the Hill-Burton Act of 1946, to provide billions of dollars in funding for the construction of hospitals, particularly in poor, underserved areas.

■ The economic crisis of the 1930s and the demands of WWII dramatically increased the role of the federal government in health care policy. However, in both cases, the government addressed immediate, pressing needs that were created or exposed by these events, and it did so by providing funds to the states to establish facilities and services. By the end of WWII, the federal government had taken major steps to help build the nation's medical system and to expand access to care to segments of the population, but the nation was no closer to a social insurance model of health care.

REFERENCES

Abbott, Grace (1966). *From Relief to Social Security*. New York: Russell & Russell.

Axinn, J. and Levin, H. (1997). *Social Welfare: A History of the American Response to Need*, 4th ed. New York: Longman.

Baltzell, E. D. (1964). *The Protestant Establishment*. New York: Vintage Books.

Barker, R. L. (1999). *The Social Work Dictionary*, 4th ed. Washington, DC: National Association of Social Workers.

Bartley, N. V. (1995). *A History of the South*, Vol. XI, *The New South 1945–1980*. Baton Rouge: Louisiana State University Press.

Bloom, J. M. (1987). *Class, Race, and the Civil Rights Movement*. Bloomington: Indiana University Press.

Brieland, D. (1995). Social Work Practice: History and Evolution. In R. L. Edwards (Ed.-in-Chief), *Encyclopedia of Social Work*, 19th ed. (pp. 2247–2257). Washington, DC: National Association of Social Workers.

Brody, D. (1991). Labor. In E. Foner and J. A. Garraty (Eds.), *Readers Companion to American History* (pp. 627–630). Boston: Houghton Mifflin.

Cook, B. W. (1992). *Eleanor Roosevelt*, Vol. I, *1884–1933*. New York: Viking.

Davis, A. F. (1991). Settlement Houses. In E. Foner and J. A. Garraty (Eds.), *Readers Companion to American History* (pp. 983–984). Boston: Houghton Mifflin.

Dewhurst, J. F. and Associates. (1947). *America's Needs and Resources*. New York: Twentieth Century Fund.

Du Bois, W. E. B. (1975). *Black Reconstruction in American 1860–1880*. New York: Atheneum.

Edinburg, G. M. and Cottler, J. M. (1995). Managed Care. In R. L. Edwards (Ed.-in-Chief). *Encyclopedia of Social Work*, 19th ed. (pp. 1635–1642). Washington, DC: National Association of Social Workers.

Edwards, L. M. (1995). Lathrop, Julia Clifford (1858–1932). In R. L. Edwards (Ed.-in-Chief), *Encyclopedia of Social Work*, 19th ed. (pp. 2596–2597). Washington, DC: National Association of Social Workers.

Feingold, E. (1966). *Medicare: Policy and Politics*. San Francisco: Chandler.

Foner, E. and Garraty, J. A. (1991). The Taft-Hartley Act. In E. Foner and J. A. Garraty (Eds.), *Readers Companion to American History* (p. 1057). Boston: Houghton Mifflin.

Foner, P. S. (1974). *Organized Labor and the Black Worker 1619–1973.* New York: International.

Freidel, F. (1990). *Roosevelt.* Boston: Little, Brown.

Garrett, L. (2000). *Betrayal of Trust: The Collapse of Global Public Health.* New York: Hyperion.

Goldfield, M. (1997). *The Color of Politics.* New York: New Press.

Goodwin, D. K. (1994). *No Ordinary Time—Franklin and Eleanor Roosevelt: The Home Front in WWII.* New York: Simon & Schuster.

Gorin, S. (1983). *Labor–Management Relations and Democracy: The Wagner and Taft-Hartley Acts.* Ann Arbor: UMI Dissertation Services.

Grob, G. N. (1994). *The Mad Among Us, a History of the Care of America's Mentally Ill.* New York: Free Press.

Haines, M. R. (1991). Birthrate and Mortality. In E. Foner and J. A. Garraty (Eds.), *Readers Companion to American History* (p. 103–105). Boston: Houghton Mifflin.

Hamilton, C. D. and Hamilton, C. V. (1997). *The Dual Agenda—The African-American Struggle for Civil and Economic Equality.* New York: Columbia University Press.

Hicks, J. D. (1960). *Republican Ascendancy.* New York: Harper.

Hill, H. (1961). Racism within Organized Labor: A Report of the AFL-CIO. *Journal of Negro Education, 30,* 109–118.

Hoffer, P. C. (1991). Due Process, Substantive. In E. Foner and J. A. Garraty (Eds.), *Readers Companion to American History* (pp. 237–239). Boston: Houghton Mifflin.

Inglehart, A. P. and Becerra, R. M. (2000). *Social Services and the Ethnic Community.* Prospect Heights, IL: Waveland Press.

Institute of Medicine. (1988). *The Future of Public Health.* Washington, DC: National Academy Press.

Jansson, B. S. (2001). *The Reluctant Welfare State,* 4th ed. Belmont, CA: Wadsworth.

Jaros, K. J. and Evans, J. C. (1995). Maternal and Child Health. In R. L. Edwards (Ed.-in-Chief), *Encyclopedia of Social Work,* 19th ed. (pp. 1683–1689). Washington, DC: National Association of Social Workers.

Kens, P. (1992). Lochner v. New York. In K. L. Hall (Ed.), *The Oxford Companion to the Supreme Court* (pp. 508–511). New York: Oxford University Press.

Key, V. O. (1984). *Southern Politics in State and Nation.* Knoxville: University of Tennessee.

Kluger, R. (1975). *Simple Justice.* New York: Alfred A. Knopf.

Kotelchuch, D. (Ed.). (1976). *Prognosis Negative: Crisis in the Health Care System.* New York: Vintage Books.

Lasch, C. (Ed.). (1982). *The Social Thought of Jane Addams.* New York: Irvington.

Lesser, A. J. (1985). The Origin and Development of Maternal and Child Health Programs in the United States. *American Journal of Public Health, 76,* 590–598.

Leuchtenburg, W. E. (1963). *Franklin D. Roosevelt and the New Deal.* New York: Harper.

Levin, M. B. (1971). *Political Hysteria in America.* New York: Basic Books.

Lewis, D. L. (1993). *W. E. B. Du Bois, Biography of a Race.* New York: Henry Holt.

Litwak, L. F. (1998). *Trouble in Mind—Black Southerners in the Age of Jim Crow.* New York: Alfred A. Knopf.

Loewen, J. W. (1995). *Lies My Teacher Told Me.* New York: Touchstone (Simon & Schuster).

Lubell, S. (1965). *The Future of American Politics,* 3rd ed. New York: Harper.

Marmor, T. R. (1973). *The Politics of Medicare.* Chicago: Aldine.

Moroney, R. M. (1995). Public Health Services. In R. L. Edwards (Ed.-in-Chief), *Encyclopedia of Social Work,* 19th ed. (pp. 1967–1973). Washington, DC: National Association of Social Workers.

McPherson, J. M. (1988). *Battle Cry of Freedom—The Civil War Era.* New York: Oxford University Press.

Mechanic, D. (1999). *Mental Health and Social Policy, The Emergence of Mental Health,* 4th ed. Boston: Allyn & Bacon.

Mizrahi, T. (1995). Health Care: Reform Initiatives. In R. L. Edwards (Ed.-in-Chief), *Encyclopedia of Social Work,* 19th ed. (pp. 1185–1198). Washington, DC: National Association of Social Workers.

Moniz, C. M. (1990). *National Council of Senior Citizens: The Role of the Elderly in the Enactment of Medicare.* Ann Arbor: UMI Dissertation Services.

Newman, D. K. et al. (1978). *Protest, Politics, and Prosperity—Black Americans and White Institutions, 1940–75.* New York: Pantheon.

Noble, C. (1997). *Welfare As We Knew It.* New York: Oxford University Press.

Patterson, J. T. (1996). *Grand Expectations—The U.S. 1945–1974.* New York: Oxford University Press.

Pratt, W. F. (1992). *Plessy v. Ferguson.* In K. L. Hall (Ed.), *The Oxford Companion to the Supreme Court* (pp. 637–638). New York: Oxford University Press.

Quadagno, J. (1994). *The Color of Welfare.* New York: Oxford University Press.

Quadagno, J. (1988). *The Transformation of Old Age Security: Class and Politics in the American Welfare State.* Chicago: University of Chicago Press.

Rabinowitz, H. N. (1991). Segregation. In E. Foner and J. A. Garraty (Eds.), *Readers Companion to American History* (pp. 976–978). Boston: Houghton Mifflin.

Rae, N. C. (1991). Republican Party. In E. Foner and J. A. Garraty (Eds.), *Readers Companion to American History* (pp. 931–935). Boston: Houghton Mifflin.

Reynolds, B. (1963). *An Uncharted Journey: Fifty Years of Social Work by One of Its Great Teachers,* 2nd ed. Hebron, CT: Practitioners Press.

Rolde, N. (1992). *Your Money or Your Health.* New York: Paragon House.

Sanderson, S. K. (1995). *Macrosociology,* 3rd ed. New York: HarperCollins.

Saxton, A. (1970). Race and the House of Labor. In G. B. Nash and R. Weiss (Eds.), *The Great Fear* (pp. 98–120). New York: Holt, Rinehart and Winston.

Schlesinger, A. Jr. (1959). *The Age of Roosevelt—The Crisis of the Old Order.* Boston: Houghton Mifflin.

Simon, B. L. (1994). *The Empowerment Tradition in American Social Work—A History.* New York: Columbia University Press.

Skocpol, T. (1995). *Social Policy in the United States.* Princeton: Princeton University Press.

Skocpol, T. (1992). *Protecting Soldiers and Mothers.* Cambridge: Harvard University Press.

Starr, P. (1982). *The Social Transformation of American Medicine: The Rise of a Sovereign Profession and the Making of a Vast Industry.* New York: Basic Books.

Syers, M. (1995). Lenroot, Katherine Frederica (1891–1982). In R. L. Edwards (Ed.-in-Chief), *Encyclopedia Social Work,* 19th ed. (pp. 2596–2597). Washington, DC: National Association of Social Workers.

Trattner, W. I. (1999). *From Poor Law to Welfare State,* 6th ed. New York: Free Press.

Tulchinsky, T. H. and Varavikova, E. A. (2000). *The New Public Health.* San Diego, CA: Academic Press.

Turnock, B. J. (1997). *Public Health.* Gaithersburg, MD: Aspen Publishers.

U.S. Children's Bureau. (1914). *First Annual Report of the Chief, to the Secretary of Labor for Year Ended June 30, 1913.* Washington, DC: Government Printing Office.

U.S. Congress, House. (July and August 1961). Committee on Ways and Means Hearings, 87th Congress, 1st Session. *Health Services for the Aged under the Social Security Insurance System.* Washington, DC: U.S. Government Printing Office.

Weeks, L. and Berman, H. (1985). *Shapers of American Health Care Policy—An Oral History.* Ann Arbor: University of Michigan.

Weiss, R. (1970). Racism in the Era of Industrialization. In G. B. Nash and R. Weiss (Eds.), *The Great Fear* (pp. 121–143). New York: Holt, Rinehart and Winston.

Wencour, S. and Reisch, M. (1989). *From Charity to Enterprise: The Development of Social Work in a Market Economy.* Urbana: University of Illinois.

White, K. L. (1991). *Healing the Schism: Epidemiology, Medicine, and the Public's Health.* New York: Springer-Verlag.

2 The Emergence of Employment-Based Insurance and Managed Care: 1943–Present

Chapter 2 begins with the defeat of efforts to achieve national health insurance during the 1940s. It provides an overview of the significant reform efforts that followed, including the political battle for Medicare in 1965 and the Clinton administration's efforts to enact universal health care coverage in the early 1990s. Although federal legislation to establish a national health care system was defeated, two significant health insurance programs, Medicare and Medicaid, were enacted. By the early 1970s, however, it was clear that the United States had not adequately resolved the issues of access and coverage. Between 1965 and 1990, health care inflation grew dramatically and the number of people without coverage increased. At the root of these problems was the nation's embrace of voluntary, employment-based insurance.

Political Opposition to National Health Insurance: 1943–1950

During the 1940s, voluntary, employment-based coverage became the primary means of financing and accessing health care services. This occurred largely as a result of World War II. Facing a shortage of qualified workers, and government-imposed wage controls, some employers began offering health insurance to their employees (Starr, 1982). In 1943, the government's War Labor Board ruled that health insurance did not violate wage and price controls. After the war, workers "gained the right to bargain collectively for health benefits," and employment-based insurance emerged as a "functional substitute for social insurance" (p. 311).

The growth of employment-based insurance was accelerated by political developments within the labor movement and society. During the 1930s, in its efforts to organize workers, the Congress of Industrial Organizations (CIO) had pursued a "popular-front" (or center-left) strategy, which united moderates and radicals (Bartley, 1995). Between 1935 and 1940, Roosevelt also pursued a center-left strategy, uniting "radicals, liberals, and moderates in support of a broad reform program"

(Bartley, 1995, p. 45; Wencour and Reisch, 1989). Although most leftists felt that the New Deal reforms were limited, they also believed Roosevelt was preferable to the Republicans (Baltzell, 1966; Wencour and Reisch, 1989). This popular front was replicated internationally when the United States and the Soviet Union collaborated against the Axis powers during World War II.

As the war ended, and the alliance between the United States and the Soviet Union began to crumble, the domestic alliance also ended. In 1948, the popular front liberals broke with Truman over the Cold War and supported the presidential candidacy of Henry Wallace, the vice president during Roosevelt's third term (Patterson, 1996). Truman, and other conservative liberals, attacked Wallace and his supporters as Communist sympathizers and a threat to national security (Caute, 1978; Bartley, 1995). The struggle between Truman and Wallace put liberals at war with themselves, and by 1950, liberalism had "sharply narrowed" its focus and the energy and excitement of the 1930s had waned (Bartley, 1995).

In 1949, the CIO expelled its left-wing unions, which had been the strongest advocates of race and gender equality (Bartley, 1995). As it moved to the right, the CIO began to emulate the "job-conscious business unionism" of the American Federation of Labor (AFL). The prewar CIO had advocated for its members and workers as a whole (Bartley, 1995). The postwar CIO downplayed this broader, class perspective and increasingly focused on obtaining "contracts with welfare, health, and retirement provisions" (p. 44).

The split within the CIO also weakened progressives and strengthened conservatives. When the CIO embarked on Operation Dixie, a postwar effort to organize workers in the South, its efforts were hindered by the "absence of the dedicated and tireless organizers of the left who had contributed to so many previous drives" (Foner, 1974, p. 277). The failure of Operation Dixie, and a related effort by the AFL, ensured the continued dominance of the southern Democrats, who had played such a prominent role in blocking social welfare legislation, including national health insurance (NHI) (Bloom, 1987; Lubell, 1965; Quadagno, 1988). During the 1960s, the southern Democrats helped create the modern Republican Party, which continues to oppose NHI.

The Defeat of National Health Care Legislation: 1943–1949

In 1943, Senators Robert F. Wagner (D-NY) and James Murray (D-MT) and Representative John Dingell (D-NY) introduced a new national health care bill, which was more comprehensive than the one introduced by Wagner in 1939. The expanded bill included medical, hospital, dental, and nursing home provisions (Rolde, 1992; Starr, 1982). One of the authors of Wagner-Murray-Dingell was Wilbur Cohen (1913–1987) (Berkowitz, 1989). Well-known in social work circles, Cohen had helped write the Social Security Act and later played a central role in the development of Medicare and Medicaid. He also served as secretary of health, education, and welfare under President Lyndon Johnson (Guyotte, 1995).

African American organizations, such as the NAACP and the National Urban League, tried unsuccessfully to include antidiscrimination clauses in the Wagner-Murray-Dingell bill (Hamilton and Hamilton, 1997). They knew that even if Congress enacted the bill, its implementation in the South would be subject to segregationist policies. Although organized labor supported the Wagner-Murray-Dingell bill, the AMA opposed it, and like Wagner's original bill, it died in committee (Moniz, 1990). President Roosevelt did not support the Wagner-Murray-Dingell bill because he wanted to wait until the end of the war to seek compulsory insurance.

In 1944, Roosevelt proposed an "economic bill of rights" that included "a right to adequate medical care" (Starr, 1982, p. 280). However, Roosevelt died in 1945 before he could reveal his plan to campaign for compulsory insurance as part of his reelection platform. His successor, Harry Truman, took up the mantle and advocated "a single health insurance system that would include all classes of the society" (Starr, 1982, p. 281). Again conservatives reacted strongly (Ball, 1995). Senator Robert Taft (R-OH) derided Truman's bill as "'the most socialistic measure this Congress has ever had before it,'" and the AMA warned that it would turn doctors into "slaves" (Starr, 1982, pp. 282–283).

Although Truman denied that his plan was "'socialized medicine,'" which he defined as a system in which "'all doctors work as employees of the government,'" the Republicans were able to block the bill (Rolde, 1992, p. 25). When Truman tried unsuccessfully to resurrect it a few years later, the AMA and its allies engaged in a high-powered propaganda campaign that convinced many, including even some of the bill's supporters, that it would bring about "'socialized medicine'" (Starr, 1982, p. 285). Once again, NHI came to naught.

The Enactment of Medicare: 1950–1965

The defeat of Truman's proposal led many supporters of NHI to seek a more limited goal (Ball, 1995). During the early 1950s, the Truman administration, under the leadership of Wilbur Cohen and others, developed a plan to provide Social Security recipients with sixty days of hospital coverage (Marmor, 1973). This allowed the government to expand an existing program, as opposed to creating a new one, and to insure older adults against financial catastrophe (Moniz, 1990). However, the 1952 elections brought victory for the Republicans and derailed efforts to extend hospital coverage to older adults (Ball, 1995).

Although the Eisenhower administration acknowledged seniors faced difficulty in affording health care, it opposed compulsory insurance. AMA leaders and staff had figured prominently in Eisenhower's campaign, and as president, he relied on them for advice. Eisenhower encouraged state efforts, rather than national reforms, and recommended subsidies to private insurers to expand coverage for people with low incomes (Moniz, 1990).

During the 1950s, support for Medicare came largely from organized labor, which was concerned about its retirees. Through collective bargaining, unions had gained private health insurance benefits for their members while they were employed. However, these workers often lost this coverage when they retired (Moniz, 1990).

In 1955, the newly created AFL-CIO targeted disability insurance as its first legislative effort. According to Nelson Cruikshank, the labor federation's department of Social Security focused on disability insurance because it wanted a "'foot in the door'" toward compulsory health insurance (Moniz, 1990, p. 69). In 1956, with labor's encouragement, Congress amended the Social Security Act to provide income assistance to totally and permanently disabled workers over age 55. Wilbur Cohen worked actively to support this legislation (Marmor, 1973).

Between 1957 and 1959, Rep. Aime Forand (D-RI) introduced legislation for compulsory health insurance. This was the first legislative effort to build on the Social Security Act by providing health insurance to retired beneficiaries (Moniz, 1990). According to Marmor (1973), the Forand bill was motivated by a need to "resurrect health insurance in a dramatically new and narrower form" (p. 13). The Forand bill faced strong opposition from the AMA and the conservative coalition of southern Democrats and northern Republicans. In 1959, the House Ways and Means Committee held hearings across the country, raising awareness of the health care problems of older adults. Nevertheless, the committee rejected the social insurance approach to health care policy (Moniz, 1990).

The Democrats renewed their commitment to Medicare at their 1960 national convention, at which they endorsed a plan to expand Social Security by adding compulsory health insurance for older adults. In response, the Republicans proposed voluntary, state-administered programs that would be limited to low-income older adults. In 1960, as a compromise, Congress enacted the Kerr-Mills bill, a means-tested, optional grant-in-aid program to the states for poor elderly citizens (Trattner, 1999). Kerr-Mills did not adequately address the growing concern for reform, however; and by 1963, "only thirty-six states had 'joined' the system" and "only some (states) paid physician fees" (Trattner, 1999, p. 326).

With the election to the presidency of John Kennedy, a strong supporter of Medicare, the AMA launched a new effort against "'socialized medicine'" (Bernstein, 1991, p. 253). Despite this, Kennedy immediately appointed a task force on health and Social Security (chaired by Wilbur Cohen), which recommended expanding Social Security to provide hospital and nursing home coverage for older adults (Bernstein, 1991). Kennedy sent this proposal to Congress, where it was introduced as the King-Anderson bill (Feingold, 1966). After several days of hearings, the House Ways and Means Committee, headed by Wilbur Mills (D-AK), who was lukewarm about Medicare, decided not to act on the legislation (Marmor, 1973). Although Kennedy died before Medicare passed, Bernstein (1991) argues that, by the time of his assassination, Kennedy had come to an agreement with Mills that resulted in the bill's enactment in 1965.

To the surprise of many, Kennedy's successor, Lyndon Johnson, became a strong supporter of Medicare (David, 1985). Between 1963 and 1965, Johnson and the Democrats, along with the National Council of Senior Citizens (formed in 1961) and organized labor, mobilized support for the bill (Moniz, 1990). In the November 1964 elections, several congressional opponents of Medicare, including three members of the House Ways and Means Committee, were defeated (Moniz, 1990).

Despite a final effort by the AMA to enact a means-tested plan, Wilbur Mills recognized the need for a compromise. In March 1965, he proposed a "three-layer cake" comprised of compulsory insurance for hospital, nursing home, and home-health care (Medicare "Part A"); voluntary insurance for physicians' services (Medicare "Part B"); and a means-tested insurance plan for people with low incomes (Medicaid). In July 1965 the Senate approved Mills's proposal, and, with Harry Truman looking on, President Johnson signed Medicare and Medicaid into law as Titles XVIII and XIX of the Social Security Act of 1935 (Marmor, 1973).

Health Care Inflation and Strategies for Reform: 1970–1988

During the late 1960s, health care analysts and political leaders became concerned about a new phenomenon: health care inflation (Rolde, 1992). Inflation was not *completely* new, of course. "But what had been a steady rise during the 1950s and early 1960s took a sharp turn upward after 1966" (Kotelchuck, 1976, p. 17). During the 1970s, national health expenditures increased by 238 percent, and during the 1980s, they grew by 177 percent (Levit et al., 1994). Between 1970 and 1993, the share of gross domestic product (GDP) accounted for by health expenditures increased from 7.4 percent to 13.9 percent (Levit et al., 1994). Health care inflation played a key role in accelerating change in the nation's health care system.

Renewed Struggle for National Health Insurance

One response to health care inflation was renewed interest in national health insurance. In 1970, Senator Edward M. Kennedy (D-MA) and Representative Martha W. Griffiths (R-MI) introduced the Health Security plan, which resembled the Canadian system of socialized insurance. It included universal coverage and a national health care budget (also called a global budget) and promoted the development of prepaid group practices (Starr, 1982). The Kennedy-Griffiths bill enjoyed strong support from organized labor.

A year later, President Richard Nixon proposed legislation that allowed employers to contribute to the cost of insuring their workers and created a federal plan "to provide a less generous package of benefits for low-income families" (Starr, 1982, p. 397). Critics objected that Nixon's plan would reduce spending for Medicare and "still leave uninsured 20 to 40 million people who fell outside its two programs" (Starr, 1982, p. 396). The AMA and other organizations also developed proposals to reform the health care system.

In 1974, Nixon introduced the Comprehensive Health Insurance Plan, which required employers to pay 65 percent of the cost of buying insurance for their workers (Kotelchuck, 1976). Individuals with low incomes, and those without jobs, would be eligible for subsidies from the government (Kotelchuck, 1976). The new proposal also offered a wider range of benefits than the earlier one. Critics argued that the new bill still burdened consumers with high copayments and deductibles, which discouraged "preventive care or early treatment," and would leave many older adults worse off then they were under Medicare (p. 461). Kennedy, in an effort to reach a compromise, abandoned the Kennedy-Griffiths bill and, with Wilbur Mills, introduced a bill similar to Nixon's (Kotelchuck, 1976). Ultimately, all these efforts failed. With Nixon under fire for the Watergate scandal, liberals anticipated the election of a "'veto-proof'" Congress; they rejected Kennedy's compromise, and a stalemate ensued (Starr, 1982).

NHI surfaced again, a few years later, during the Carter administration. In September 1979, Senator Edward Kennedy (D-MA) and Representative Henry Waxman (D-CA) introduced the Health Care for All Americans Act, which relied on a variety of mechanisms to achieve universal coverage and control costs (Rolde, 1992). Carter supported less ambitious legislation, which provided catastrophic coverage with a high deductible, to workers (Rolde, 1992). Senators Robert Dole (R-KS), John Danforth (R-MO), and Pete Domenici (R-NM) introduced a similar bill (Rolde, 1992). However, with Democrats fighting among themselves and conservatives strongly opposed to any legislation, these bills languished.

The election of Ronald Reagan in 1980 ended serious discussion of NHI. However, in 1988, Congress, with support from Reagan, enacted the Medicare Catastrophic Coverage Act, the "largest extension of health care benefits for Americans since Medicare and Medicaid" (Rolde, 1992, p. 40). The Catastrophic Coverage Act limited patients' responsibility for copayments under Medicare Part B (physician's coverage) and gradually introduced prescription drug coverage (Rice, Desmond, and Gabel, 1990). To pay for the act, Congress set "a new precedent" by imposing a tax solely on older adults (p. 77). The burden of this tax fell on individuals with high incomes, many of whom already had coverage for benefits provided by the act. This tax, along with the act's failure to significantly expand long-term care coverage, provoked widespread criticism and led Congress to repeal it in 1989 (Rice, Desmond, and Gabel, 1990).

The Rise of HMOs

Health care inflation also gave impetus to the development and spread of prepaid health care. According to Friedman (1996), the "roots" of prepaid health care may lie in mutual aid societies created by immigrants during the 1800s. Later, mining companies, railroads, and other corporations also offered health care services to their workers on a prepaid basis (Friedman, 1996).

The AMA strongly opposed prepaid heath care, and the approach spread slowly. In 1929, in California, physicians, working through the Ross-Loos Clinic, began providing medical services to public employees in exchange for "a fixed monthly payment" (Dranove, 2000, p. 37). Prepaid plans also developed in Texas, Oklahoma, Wisconsin, and elsewhere (Starr, 1982).

During the 1930s, Henry J. Kaiser, a noted industrialist, organized perhaps the best-known prepaid health plan when he contracted with a physician named Sidney Garfield to provide health care to Kaiser's employees engaged in building the Grand Coulee Dam (Starr, 1982). During World War II, Kaiser hired "prepaid physicians to provide medical care in group practice settings" to two hundred thousand workers in his West Coast shipyards (Dranove, 2000, p. 38). After the war, Kaiser's plan reopened as the Kaiser Foundation Health Plan and allowed members of the public to join. Prepaid health plans developed in other areas as well (Dranove, 2000).

In 1970, amid growing concern over health care inflation, officials of the Nixon administration began working with Paul Ellwood, Jr., a Minnesota physician and advocate of prepaid health care. They developed plans for a system of prepaid group practices, or "health maintenance organizations" (HMOs), as Ellwood called them (Starr, 1982, p. 395). The logic behind HMOs was simple. In exchange for a lump sum of money for each patient, physicians would assume responsibility for meeting the health care needs of these individuals. Because the provider would "share the financial risk of ill health with the consumer...both would have an interest in maintaining health" (Ellwood et al., 1976, p. 351). This, in turn, would hopefully encourage providers to address prevention as well as treatment and lead to lower health care costs. HMOs thus seemed a foolproof, market-driven approach to reforming the health care system (Kotelchuck, 1976).

In February 1971, Nixon urged Congress to approve funding to create a network of HMOs, which would eventually cover most of the population (Starr, 1982). By now, HMOs had been discovered and endorsed by governors (including Ronald Reagan), business groups, labor unions, and the media (Starr, 1982). With federal assistance, the number of HMOs tripled between 1970 and 1973, and Congress, in an amendment to the Public Health Service Act, eventually enacted the Health Maintenance Act (P.L. 93-222) of 1973 (Patel and Rushefsky, 1999).

In addition to providing funds for the development of HMOs, the act altered the definition of a prepaid group practice. Whereas the original prepaid group practices were nonprofit corporations, HMOs could be for-profit companies (Starr, 1982). Moreover, as Starr (1982) points out, the expression HMO "referred not only to prepaid group practice" but also to independent practice associations (IPAs), "which receive prepayments from subscribers and then reimburse independent physicians and hospitals on a fee basis" (p. 397). These changes were to have a dramatic impact on the development of the health care system (Mizrahi, 1995).

Regulatory Reform

The government also tried planning as a way of bringing costs under control. The assumption here was that there were too many "health care facilities and services—too many hospitals, too many hospital beds and too much medical equipment" (Patel and Rushefsky, 1999, p. 42). This surplus seemed to be fueling inflation. In 1966, Congress enacted the Comprehensive Health Planning Act to provide funds for communities and localities to create health-planning agencies (Patel and Rushefsky, 1999). Ultimately, these agencies failed to receive the support or funding they needed and the act had little impact (Starr, 1982).

Six years later, Congress created the Professional Standards Review Organization (PSRO), which required local physicians to review the decisions and practice patterns of colleagues in hospitals and nursing homes. "If PSROs denied payment for inappropriate care, the hospitals would lose reimbursement, even though a doctor authorized the treatment" (Starr, 1982, p. 402). The Reagan administration reduced funding for PSROs and narrowed their scope (Patel and Rushefsky, 1999).

In 1974, Congress combined the Comprehensive Health Planning Act, Hill-Burton, and other programs and enacted the National Health Planning and Resources Development Act (McKinney, 1995). This legislation required the states to enact certificate-of-need laws by 1980. "Certificate-of-need laws require hospitals to document 'community need' to obtain approval for major capital expenditures for expansion of physical plants, equipment, and services" (Patel and Rushefsky, 1999, p. 169). These efforts had minimal impact on health care inflation (Patel and Rushefsky, 1999).

During the late 1970s, regulation and planning fell into disrepute, and market-oriented solutions became the order of the day (McKinney, 1995). Under the Omnibus Budget Reconciliation Act of 1981 (P.L. 97-35), funding for planning was cut and states were allowed to dismantle health-planning agencies. Not surprisingly, the Reagan and Bush administrations made little effort to support health planning (McKinney, 1995).

Diagnosis-Related Groups (DRGS)

Despite its opposition to regulation, the Reagan administration did alter the means by which Medicare reimbursed hospitals. Under the new Prospective Payment System (PPS), the U.S. Department of Health and Human Services divided medical conditions into 468 diagnosis-related groups (DRGs) and calculated a reimbursement rate for each DRG (Patel and Rushefsky, 1999). As a result, hospitals knew in advance, that is, prospectively, how much they would receive for specific admissions. If a hospital treated a patient for less than its DRG reimbursement, it could keep the extra money (Garrett, 2000). To ensure that standards were not lowered, Peer Review Organizations (the old PSROs) were placed in charge of "monitoring the quality and appropriateness of care for Medicare patients" (Patel and Rushefsky, 1999, p. 176).

The impact of the PPS has been mixed. The system does seem to have slowed the rate of increase in hospital costs through fewer admissions, lower occupancy rates, and shorter lengths of stay (Patel and Rushefsky, 1999). However, hospitals in rural and inner-city areas and public hospitals have faced difficulty under the PPS (Garrett, 2000). Previously, these institutions were able to bill Medicare for the cost of treating poor and uninsured people. The PPS made this type of cost shifting impossible, and many hospitals curtailed uncompensated care or closed their doors. In contrast, "hospitals located in areas rife with wealthy Medicare patients …turned large profits and drove up the overall costs of medical care in America" (Garrett, 2000, p. 387). Reinhardt (1996) suggests that the DRGs, and other practices that encourage the transfer of patients from hospitals to subacute facilities and home care, may actually increase "total national health spending" (p. 152).

The Creation and Role of Community Mental Health Centers: 1963–1992

Although President Kennedy did not live to see Medicare enacted, he did succeed in transforming the nation's mental health policy. The president was sensitized to the issues of mental retardation and mental health through the experience of his sister, Rosemary. While hospitalized for mental retardation, Rosemary Kennedy received a lobotomy, which significantly worsened her condition. The reform of mental health services became one of Kennedy's personal legislative priorities.

The first efforts to provide community-based mental health services to hospitalized patients occurred in the states. New York led the way in 1954 by passing the Community Health Services Act. This bill allowed local communities to establish mental health boards, which could use state funds to partially support the delivery of community-based inpatient and outpatient care. Other states, including California, soon enacted similar legislation (Grob, 1994).

The structure and funding of state mental health services slowly began to shift from state mental hospitals to local community-based care (Grob, 1994). In 1955, Congress enacted the Mental Health Study Act, which established the Joint Commission on Mental Illness and Mental Health to examine effective approaches to treating mental illness. In 1961, the commission proposed a new community-based mental health system, which would come about through the gradual transformation of large state mental hospitals (over 1,000 beds) into chronic community care centers and the construction of new smaller hospitals. The community centers would facilitate access to social supports and reduce the need for hospitalization (Grob, 1994; Mechanic, 1999).

Mental Retardation and Community Mental Health Centers Construction Act

In 1963, after establishing several committees to study the needs of those with mental illness and mental retardation, Kennedy introduced a federal plan for the construction of comprehensive community mental health centers (Grob, 1994; Mechanic, 1999). The final bill, the Mental Retardation and Community Mental Health Centers Construction Act, was enacted in 1963. It provided funds for grants to the states between 1965 and 1967 to construct community mental health centers.

The Mental Retardation and Community Mental Health Centers Construction Act established approximately 2,000 catchment areas, with populations ranging in size from 75,000 to 200,000 (Karger and Stoesz, 1998). The intent was that a clinic, or mental health center, would serve each catchment area. By 1980, however, there were still only 754 centers, far short of the goal of 2,000 centers (Grob, 1994).

According to Grob (1994), the failure to establish community mental health centers was largely due to disagreement over their purpose. Some professionals believed the centers should focus on treatment whereas others argued that they should focus on *prevention*. A third group saw the centers as providing an opportunity to focus on larger social reforms that would promote *community mental health*. There was disagreement about the organizational structure and staffing of the centers and even the kind of clients they should serve (Grob, 1994).

The shift away from hospitalization toward community care also raised policy issues for planners and administrators given the lack of agreement on the mental health centers' purpose and function. Should the centers be substitutes for hospitals? If so, what should be the future of mental health hospitals? If not, what should be the relationship among hospitals, centers, and other community resources? Who should administer the mental health centers? How should they be staffed? How should the operating costs be financed? (Lin, 1995)

As mental health professionals grappled with these issues, mental health centers found it harder and harder to function as substitutes for mental hospitals and provide truly comprehensive care, as the legislation required. For example, how could mental health centers ensure food, clothing, housing, and safety for patients with severe and chronic mental illness? What kind of aftercare programs could they offer to support and maintain patient health?

Medicaid's Role in Deinstitutionalization

While community mental health centers struggled to become alternatives to mental hospitals, the passage of Medicaid in 1965 added to the growing trend to release patients from state mental hospitals. In fact, Medicaid played an even more significant role in the deinstitutionalization of mental hospitals during the 1960s and 1970s than did the community mental health center movement, and it fueled the growth of nursing homes (U.S. General Accounting Office, 1977). Medicaid extended coverage for psychiatric hospital care to poor people and created incentives for states to place elderly recipients with behavioral problems in nursing homes. The nursing home population doubled during the 1960s as a result of Medicaid (Grob, 1994). In addition, Medicaid provided support for community residential care for former mental patients who were eligible for Aid to the Permanently and Totally Disabled (which was changed to Supplemental Security Income/SSI in 1972) (Segal, 1995).

These Medicaid policies contributed to the decline of hospital admissions and the increase in patient discharges from mental hospitals during the 1960s. They also contributed to the emerging division of care in mental health services. Public mental health hospitals were becoming institutions for the treatment of severely and chronically mentally ill patients, whereas community mental health centers were becoming counseling and crisis intervention centers for individuals with acute problems.

Alcohol and Drug Abuse Services

In 1968, the Community Mental Health Centers Construction Act was amended to include funding for alcohol treatment and programs. This amendment came on the heels of congressional action in 1966 to expand NIMH to create the Center for the Studies of Narcotic Addiction and Drug Abuse and the National Center for the Prevention and Control of Alcoholism. With national attention shifting toward alcohol and drug abuse, and much needed additional funding, community mental health centers began to focus on alcohol and drug abuse counseling.

President Nixon advocated curtailing the federal government's role in mental health policy. Between 1970 and 1972, Nixon considered serious reductions in funding for NIMH programs, and in 1973, he recommended the termination of federal funding for community mental health centers. The Watergate scandal prevented Nixon from implementing these proposals.

Nevertheless, the Nixon administration set the stage for Congress to examine the problems of community-based mental health care and reconsider the federal role in mental health policy. In 1973, Congress reorganized the Public Health Service (PHS) and moved NIMH back to the National Institutes of Health (NIH). Congress also created the Alcohol, Drug Abuse, and Mental Health Administration (ADAMHA) as an umbrella organization to administer the Public Health Service, NIMH, the National Institute on Alcoholism and Alcohol Abuse (NIAAA), and the National Institute on Drug Abuse (NIDA). NIDA had been created in 1972 in response to increased concern about substance abuse (Grob, 1994).

In 1975, Congress decided against termination of funding for community mental health centers. Instead, it required the delivery of seven new services, including screening and aftercare, which were considered essential to a comprehensive continuum of community-based care. However, mental health centers across the country were already struggling to meet the needs of patients discharged from mental hospitals that had been closed or reduced in size. Most centers were unprepared to expand their services (Grob, 1994).

Consumer Protection Efforts: Patients' Rights

In the 1970s, states also faced the need to protect the civil rights of people identified as mentally ill. For example, in *Wyatt v. Stickney,* a district court required the state of Alabama to treat patients still living in state hospitals (Karger and Stoesz, 1998). The Supreme Court *(Donaldson v. O'Connor)* ruled that states could not "'confine'" individuals unless they were a danger to themselves or to the community or were being treated during confinement (Karger and Stoesz, 2002, p. 363). These rulings led the states to accelerate efforts to empty hospitals and, as much as possible, limit new hospitalizations. "Thus, legal decisions favoring the mentally ill often proved illusory," in many instances, offering "nothing more than the right to be insane" (Karger and Stoesz, 2002, p. 363).

A few years later, President Jimmy Carter established a Commission on Mental Health, which developed recommendations for coordinating existing federal, state, and local services, and protecting the rights of patients (Grob, 1994). In 1979, families of the mentally ill founded the National Alliance for the Mentally Ill to advocate these protections. In 1980, Congress enacted the Mental Health Systems Act, which included a model bill of rights for patients that the states were expected to enact (Grob, 1994; Mental Health Policy Resource Center, 1996). As noted by Mechanic (1999), the process was "long and tortuous" and "substantially modified" to satisfy opponents of the legislation. By the time the bill was signed by President Carter, Ronald Reagan was only a month away from winning the 1980 presidential election and embarking on a new direction of mental health policy.

Community Support Program

In 1977, the NIMH established a new Community Support Program in an effort to respond to policy issues that surfaced during the congressional review of mental health centers. The purpose was to facilitate a federal–state partnership that would encourage state initiatives to target the needs of people with severe mental illness. The program focused on issues of daily living, such as housing, income, and a host of support services needed to sustain community-based care for the mentally ill, especially those with severe or chronic disorders. The "Madison Model," or Programs of Assertive Community Treatment (PACT) pioneered by Marx, Test, and Stein (1973) at the Mendota State Hospital in Madison, Wisconsin, served as the model for the Community Support Program. PACT was designed to teach life skills to patients in the community rather than in a state hospital (Hughes, 1999).

The Community Support Program also recognized the need to integrate the funding and delivery of services provided by Medicare, Medicaid, Supplemental Security Income (SSI), and Social Security Disability Insurance (SSDI) with community-based services provided by the mental health centers. During the late 1970s, NIMH promoted changes that enabled recipients of public assistance and entitlement programs to receive community-based care. For example, changes in Medicaid allowed for reimbursement of specialized case management services and services offered by the mental health centers (Grob, 1994).

The community service programs initiated by NIMH had a positive effect on the lives of many severely and chronically mentally ill patients (Grob, 1994). However, these improvements received little public attention in light of the emerging problems of homelessness that dominated the social landscape of the 1980s. For example, between 1980 and 1990 the size of the homeless population increased fivefold (Jencks, 1994). Many of those living on the streets and in shelters were severely mentally ill, substance abusers, or both.

The Decline of Community Mental Health: 1980–1992

The Reagan administration was determined to reverse the expanding federal welfare state that first emerged during the New Deal in the mid-1930s. In 1981, the Omnibus Budget Reconciliation Act (OBRA) was passed as a way to reduce the federal role in social welfare and federal funding for social programs. One of the primary strategies used to achieve this was the creation of block grants, which shifted the responsibility for many social programs from the federal government to the states.

OBRA collapsed fifty-seven separate programs and their funding into seven block grants. Federal funding appropriated for specific legislated programs within a given policy area was consolidated, reduced by 20 percent, and then granted to the states to spend as they saw fit. In doing this, the federal government relinquished its responsibility for regulating and monitoring these individual categorical programs. Instead, each state was given the freedom to decide on its priorities. Many states struggled to find ways to maintain the same programs and services with reduced funds; some succeeded, but many failed.

Mental health programs were not spared from this process. Several NIMH categorical programs for mental health and substance abuse were collapsed into one Alcohol, Drug Abuse, and Mental Health block grant available to the states and, like other block grants, overall funding was reduced by 20 percent. By making these changes, the Reagan administration in essence repealed the provisions of the Mental Health Systems Act (1980) and the Community Mental Health Centers Construction Act (1963).

In addition to the block grants, the Reagan administration used OBRA to make changes in a number of public assistance programs. These changes were designed to reduce eligibility and thereby decrease the number of recipients. By redefining disability, thousands of disabled SSI and SSDI recipients were denied coverage by the Social Security Administration. Many of these recipients were mentally ill and their benefits were denied until 1983 when the Supreme Court reinstated their benefits (see Chapter 5). To make matters worse, other programs that served low-income mentally ill individuals, such as Medicaid, housing, and social services, were also reduced by OBRA.

The NIMH role in directing national mental health policy was clearly altered during the Reagan/Bush era (1980–1992). In fact, by 1992, Congress no longer provided funding to NIMH for direct services; instead, NIMH was reorganized to focus primarily on research. A new agency, the Substance Abuse and Mental Health Services Administration (SAMSHA), was created and made responsible for training and services. SAMSHA managed three separate centers—the Center for Substance Abuse Treatment (CSAT), the Center for Substance Abuse Prevention (CSAP), and the Center for Mental Health Services (CMHS).

State Comprehensive Mental Health Services Plan Act

However, the Community Support Program did gain legislative support from Congress in 1984 during the Reagan administration, and in 1986, Congress encouraged the federal–state partnership approach by enacting the State Comprehensive Mental Health Services Plan Act. This legislation allowed states to use federal block grant funds to expand their community-based mental health services, and as noted earlier, these efforts did have a positive impact on the recipients of these services (Grob, 1994).

Stewart B. McKinney Homeless Assistance Act

In 1987, Congress passed the Stewart B. McKinney Homeless Assistance Act. This bill established a new federal block grant available to the states to provide assistance and services to homeless individuals, including emergency food and shelter, housing, health and mental health services, alcohol and drug abuse treatment, and prevention services such as education and job training. The programs were "inadequately funded, fragmented, and extremely diverse," however (Johnson, 1995, p. 1343). Most of the funds were spent on building emergency shelters, and little was done to provide outreach to mentally ill people and others who avoided shelters (Jansson, 2001).

The Rise and Fall of the Health Security Act: 1988–1996

During the late 1980s, as health care costs continued to accelerate, NHI reemerged as an issue. In 1988, as part of the Medicare Catastrophic Coverage Act, Congress created a Bipartisan Commission on Comprehensive Health Care (Rolde, 1992). The chair of the commission was Representative Claude Pepper (D-FL), a long-time advocate for older adults. When Pepper died, Senator Jay Rockefeller (D-WVA) became chair and the commission was renamed the Pepper Commission.

In its final report, released in September 1990, the Pepper Commission warned that the "American health system" was "approaching a breaking point" (The Pepper Commission, 1990, p. 2). Thirty-two million people (including nine million children) lacked any health care coverage, and 20 million more had inadequate coverage. Moreover, due to "continuously escalating health care costs," anyone relying "on job-based coverage face[d] an increasing risk of joining the ranks of the uninsured" (The Pepper Commission, 1990, p. 5). The commission also called attention to the need for long-term care coverage, noting that between 9 million and 11 million people "of all ages" had chronic disabilities, and 4 million were "so severely disabled that they cannot survive without substantial help from others" (p. 10).

The Pepper Commission went beyond analysis and considered ways of expanding coverage for health and long-term care. By a narrow vote, the commission recommended a step-by-step approach that would eventually require all employers to provide coverage to their workers (The Pepper Commission, 1990). Unemployed people and individuals in poverty would receive coverage through a public plan. The commission also endorsed managed care to reduce costs and the enactment of legislation that would prevent insurers from refusing to cover high-risk individuals (The Pepper Commission, 1990). Finally, the commission recommended *"social insurance for home and community-based care and...three months of nursing home care, for all Americans, regardless of income"* (emphasis in original) (The Pepper Commission, 1990, p. 120).

Although Congress largely ignored the Pepper Commission's report, the commission's work strengthened the hand of reformers and helped frame debate in years ahead. The commission's employment-based model of universal coverage was refined into the "play or pay" approach, which required employers to insure their workers (play) or contribute to a national plan (pay) for individuals without coverage (Marmor, 1994). A play or pay bill was introduced by George Mitchell (D-ME), the Senate majority leader, and enjoyed broad support (Rolde, 1992).

Proposals for a Single-Payer Plan

The Pepper Commission also considered, and eventually rejected, a Canadian-style, single-payer plan. Under a single-payer plan, "health insurance is paid for by the government, out of funds it collects from individuals (and, possibly, employers)" (Marmor, 1994, p. 11). With such a plan, Canada succeeded in covering its entire population at much less cost than the United States could (Rachlis and Kushner, 1994). In the early 1970s, Senator Edward Kennedy had proposed a plan based on the Canadian system (Marmor, 1994). During the late 1980s and early 1990s, the single-payer plan was resurrected as a possible model for the United States by labor unions, advocacy groups, and others, including Lee Iacocca of Chrysler (Marmor, 1994). David Himmelstein and Steffie Woolhandler (1989), from Physicians for a National Health Plan, published numerous articles demonstrating the relative efficiency of the Canadian health care system and arguing in favor of a single-payer plan.

The National Association of Social Workers (NASW) also supported a single-payer plan. As noted previously, social workers have long played a leading role in struggling for NHI. In 1979, NASW formally went on record in favor of NHI (National Association of Social Workers, 1991). The 1990 Delegate Assembly identified NHI as the profession's chief policy priority (National Association of Social Workers, 1990a). In 1993, Senator Daniel Inouye (D-HI) introduced the National Health Care Act (S. 684), NASW's proposal for a single-payer system (Mizrahi, 1995).

By 1990, national health expenditures amounted to 12.1 percent of GDP (up from 8.9 percent in 1980), and per capita health expenditures stood at $2,686 (versus $1,068 in 1980) (Levit et al., 1994). Backing for reform now reached a forty-year high (Skocpol, 1995). A year later, with the unexpected election of Harris Wofford, an advocate of NHI, to the Senate, health care reform assumed center stage (Smith et al., 1992). Despite this, President George Bush adamantly opposed fundamental reform. Although the Democratic presidential candidates criticized Bush, they hesitated to propose solutions of their own. When Senator Bob Kerrey (D-NE) announced support for a single-payer system, the other candidates also faced pressure to become more specific (Johnson and Broder, 1996).

Bill Clinton, then the governor of Arkansas, promised to reform "the healthcare system to control costs, improve quality, expand preventive and long-term care, maintain consumer choice, and cover everybody" (cited in Skocpol, 1997, p. 37). Clinton developed a plan that required employers to contribute to the cost of insuring their employees; the government would cover individuals without jobs (Starr and Zelman, 1993). To control costs, Clinton advocated "'competition within a budget'" (cited in Starr and Zelman, 1993, p. 9).

An Election Day exit poll showed that voters preferred Clinton's approach to health care to George Bush's by a wide margin (www.ropercenter.uconn.edu/cgibin/hsrun.exe/roperweb/HPOLL/StateId/BgRTk6FQWrrXp7aGOrkszYDJx/HAHTpage/SetWhereClause). A quarter of Clinton's supporters identified his position on health care as the chief reason that they had voted for him. When the pollsters asked voters to choose among Clinton's plan, Bush's plan (which relied on tax incentives and HMOs), and a single-payer proposal, Clinton's plan finished last (www.ropercenter.uconn.edu/cgibin/hsrun.exe/roperweb/HPOLL/StateId/BgRTk6FQWrrXp7aGOrkszYDJx/HAHTpage/SetWhereClause). According to Robert Blendon, an expert on public opinion, these findings showed that although Clinton had support for a plan to "'expand coverage and contain costs,'" he did not "have a mandate for a particular plan" (cited in Johnson and Broder, 1996, p. 91).

Clinton's Proposal: The Health Security Act of 1993

Bill Clinton introduced the Health Security Act (HSA) (H.R. 3600, 103d Congress, 1st Session) on September 22, 1993. The fundamental goals of the act were to ensure universal coverage and control costs (Zelman, 1994). To achieve universal coverage, the HSA required employers to pay 80 percent of the cost of insuring their employees; the government guaranteed coverage for low-income and unemployed people (Zelman, 1994). To control costs, the HSA relied on a combination of competition and regulation (Zelman, 1994).

The HSA built on the work of several theorists, particularly Alain Enthoven, a Stanford economist (Starr, 1994; Reinhardt, 1994). The RAND Health Insurance Experiment found that staff-model health maintenance organizations (HMOs) could deliver high-quality, low-cost care (Newhouse et al., 1993). Enthoven and Kronick (1991) proposed a system of managed, or government-regulated, competition among prepaid plans. Small businesses and self-employed people would join purchasing cooperatives, which would negotiate with HMOs for discounted prices (Roberts and Clyde, 1993). Consumers, who annually would choose the group they wished to belong to, would drive this system (Starr, 1994). As rational actors, they would presumably opt for the best combination of cost and quality (Enthoven and Kronick, 1991).

Managed competition did not go unchallenged (Starr, 1994). Some observers questioned whether it would really contain costs (Schwartz and Mendelson, 1992; Aaron and Schwartz, 1993; Schwartz and Mendelson, 1994). Others worried that managed care would have an adverse impact on the quality of health care (Davis, Collins, and Morris, 1994). Even supporters of managed competition acknowledged that it would not work in areas with few providers (Kronick et al., 1993).

In response to this criticism, the Clinton administration expanded Enthoven's framework (Starr, 1994). The most significant change was around cost control. As a "backstop," in case competition did not reduce costs, the administration proposed capping the rate of growth of insurance premiums (Zelman, 1994; Enthoven and Singer, 1994; Kronick, 1994). The act also included a comprehensive benefit package, which would force providers to compete based on quality, not withholding care, and prevent cost shifting (Zelman, 1994). Comprehensive benefits would prevent development of a two-tiered system.

Mental Health Parity. The HSA also addressed mental health needs. Tipper Gore, the wife of the vice president, and a leading advocate for people with mental illness, headed a Working Group on Mental Health and Substance Abuse. No other specialty area received this level of attention. As a result of the group's work, the Health Security Act offered a wide range of mental health and substance abuse services, including hospitalization and nonresidential care, prescription drug coverage, therapy and counseling, and case management (Arons et al., 1994). Copayments and deductibles were similar to those for other health services. Although Congress failed to pass the HSA, the act's emphasis on parity, or equity between health and mental health treatment, helped set the stage for more limited reforms.

Why the Act Failed

Clinton's speech introducing the HSA received wide acclaim, and for a time, it seemed possible that the United States might finally achieve universal coverage. Before long, however, public opinion turned against the act (Johnson and Broder, 1996; Skocpol, 1997). In July of 1994, leading Democrats declared the HSA "officially dead" and attempted to develop a proposal of their own (Johnson and Broder, 1996). On September 26, a year and four days after Clinton's original speech, George Mitchell (D-ME), the Senate majority leader, announced an end to efforts for "comprehensive" reform (Johnson and Broder, 1996). In assessing why the HSA failed, several factors stand out.

Political Weakness of Reformers. One was the political weakness of reformers. Although the electorate clearly wanted to end the Reagan-Bush era in 1992, many voters had doubts about Clinton, who received only 43 percent of the vote (Johnson and Broder, 1996). This narrow margin gave the administration little room for maneuver. To gain support for his first budget, Clinton had to make an embarrassing public appeal to Bob Kerrey, a former rival. The administration also faced controversial issues, such as allowing gay men and lesbians in the military, Somalia, and Whitewater. These prevented Clinton from focusing on the HSA (Skocpol, 1997; Johnson and Broder, 1996).

Clinton's difficulties were compounded by the failure of many Democrats to support the act (Skocpol, 1997). Although the congressional Democrats had enough votes to enact the HSA, they failed to do so. In the House, liberals supported Representative Jim McDermott's (D-WA) single-payer bill (H.R. 3960, 103d Congress, 2d Session), which would have nationalized the insurance industry. Conservatives supported Representative Jim Cooper's (D-TN) Managed Competition Act (H.R. 3222, 103 Congress, 2d Session), which did not guarantee universal coverage (Johnson and Broder, 1996). In the Senate, influential figures, including Bob Kerrey and Daniel Moynihan (D-NY), openly criticized the act (Starr, 1995;

Skocpol, 1997). The Democratic Party also failed to mobilize support for the HSA (Johnson and Broder, 1996).

Many progressives advocated a single-payer system and also refused to support the act (Skocpol, 1997). The enthusiastic reaction to Clinton's speech introducing the HSA led many to believe that reform was inevitable (Starr, 1995). Progressives continually pressured Clinton to revise the act, threatening to withhold support if he did not meet their demands. Single-payer supporters focused on Proposition 186, California's single-payer ballot initiative (Brodie and Blendon, 1995). They failed to object when Senator Dianne Feinstein (D-CA) reneged on her commitment to universal coverage. Yet, Feinstein's action undermined Senator George Mitchell's (D-ME) effort to salvage the HSA (Rothstein, 1995).

Social workers were also ambivalent about the act (Mizrahi, 1995). In October 1993, the association noted that the act came close to meeting NASW's principles for reform (National Association of Social Workers, 1993). The NASW Board praised Clinton's efforts and noted that his bill was consistent with "many of the principles of the single-payer approach" (National Association of Social Workers, 1993). Despite this, the association did not urge the act's enactment or mobilize social workers to work for it and continued to express support for a single-payer plan. As a result, the profession as a whole was largely uninvolved in the battle over the act.

Some progressives believe that Clinton would have received more support if he had advocated a less conservative approach (Navarro, 1996; Skocpol, 1997). Navarro (1995) has argued that Clinton "moved so far to the right" that he could not "mobilize...the grass roots of the Democratic Party" (p. 461). According to Navarro (1995), if Clinton had introduced a single-payer plan, he might have rallied working- and middle-class people and, in turn, forced conservatives to compromise on "a center position as the final outcome" (p. 461).

This view is questionable, however. As noted earlier, the HSA initially enjoyed support (Yankelovich, 1995). Moreover, it was far from conservative—it did establish a right to health care. Clinton himself later noted that his "greatest blunder" was refusing to compromise this position, even after political support for it had "wan[ed] alarmingly" (Johnson and Broder, 1996). In addition, much of the criticism of the HSA was applicable to the single-payer proposals (Enthoven and Singer, 1994). For example, a central problem for the administration was convincing Congress that the act would not increase taxes (Mognan, 1995; Johnson and Broder, 1996; Skocpol, 1997). The single-payer proposals required a sizable tax increase (Newhouse, 1995). Although this would likely have paid for itself, defending it would have been difficult in the heated environment of 1994 (Mognan, 1995; Skocpol, 1997). Single-payer supporters would also have had to answer for the problems, real and imagined, of the Canadian single-payer system (Skocpol, 1997; Rachlis and Kushner, 1994). In short, Clinton would likely have had no greater success with a single-payer proposal than with the HSA (Skocpol, 1997). On the other hand, if supporters of a single-payer plan had joined forces with supporters of the HSA, they might have isolated opponents of universal coverage and forced a compromise.

Strong Opposition. A second factor was the intransigence of opponents, particularly conservatives, who made every effort to "demonize" and distort the HSA (Johnson and Broder, 1996; Skocpol, 1997; Reinhardt, 1995; Swartz, 1994). William Kristol, a prominent conservative analyst, warned that the HSA would refurbish the Democrats' image as defenders of the middle class and urged Republicans to "'kill'" it (Johnson and Broder, 1996). The act's opponents spent a fortune to disseminate a "largely false" view of the HSA (Johnson and Broder, 1996; Altman, 1995). Members of Congress "heard constantly…from anti-reform groups, but almost never from advocates of reform" (Altman, 1995, p. 25). Conservatives succeeded particularly in intimidating moderates, whom the administration had counted on to work toward a compromise (Skocpol, 1997; Johnson and Broder, 1996).

Public Ambivalence and Confusion. A third factor was public ambivalence about the role of government (Blendon, Brodie, and Benson, 1995). Although people supported universal coverage, they doubted the government's ability to implement it (Jacobs and Shapiro, 1995; Yankelovich, 1995). This skepticism had deep roots. Jimenez (1997) notes that "[b]elief in individual responsibility for health" has long been a dominant theme in American thought. At the same time, distrust of government had grown. Between 1984 and 1994, the fraction of the population believing that the "government in Washington" could be trusted to do "what is right" fell by half, to around 20 percent (Skocpol, 1997).

One root of this distrust was the puncturing of the nation's "grand expectations" (Patterson, 1996). During the early postwar years, median family income doubled; since then, however, incomes have stagnated and the gap between rich and poor has widened. In addition, the federal tax structure has become more regressive (Patterson, 1996; Marmor, Mashaw, and Harvey, 1992). These and other changes fueled discontent with government and turned opinion against the welfare state (Marmor, Mashaw, and Harvey, 1992). This antigovernment sentiment worked to the advantage of the HSA's opponents (Blendon et al., 1995).

A fourth factor was public confusion about the act. The extent of this confusion was revealed in a March 1994 poll, which found 45 percent of the population opposing the "the Clinton plan" and 37 percent backing it. On the other hand, 76 percent supported an unnamed plan that included essential components of the HSA (Stout 1994). The unidentified plan was more popular than "four other Congressional proposals," including the McDermott and Cooper bills (Stout, 1994). In short, without the name Clinton attached, the act enjoyed broad support. This suggests that, for many people, opposition to the HSA had more to do with emotion and misconception than reasoned analysis.

The public also misunderstood the implications of Congress's failure to enact the HSA. Many people, particularly those with coverage, feared that the act would force consumers into "low-quality managed care plans" (Skocpol, 1997; Johnson and Broder, 1996). The HSA's opponents played on this fear, warning that the act would "limit choice of doctors" and access to care (Yankelovich, 1995; Blendon, Brodie, and Benson, 1995). The debate thus seemed between rationing and unlimited choice (Aaron, 1998).

For most people, however, unlimited choice was no longer an option. By 1993, only 5 percent of insured workers belonged to unmanaged fee-for-service plans (Starr, 1994). In one form or another, managed care was clearly the wave of the future. The real issue was who would regulate this emerging system—government or industry. The HSA included "safeguards to ensure that managed-care medicine would be of high quality" (Skocpol, 1997). By rejecting the HSA, the public opened the door to an unregulated system, without consumer protections (Johnson and Broder, 1996). This may explain why, in 1996, with the benefit of hindsight, 58 percent of the population said they would have been "better off" had the HSA been enacted (Skocpol, 1997).

Confusion about the HSA was linked in part to the act's complexity (Skocpol, 1997). Even the act's supporters had difficulty understanding and explaining it. Yet, it is hard to see how it could have been otherwise. If the HSA had been less complex, critics would likely have labeled it simplistic. In 1992, Clinton was criticized "for being too vague about health care reform" (Rothstein, 1995). The act's complexity was shaped in part by political considerations. In light of Clinton's narrow political base, the administration needed to develop a plan that could win support from diverse constituencies (e.g., older adults, union members, and primary care providers) and divide opponents. The HSA's complexity also mirrored the complexity of the health care system: Changes in one part of this system have consequences for the whole. Although the act's complexity may have played a role in its defeat, the administration seems to have had little choice in the matter (Skocpol, 1997).

A fifth factor was the easing of health care inflation (White, 1995). As noted above, during the late 1980s and early 1990s, health care costs increased rapidly. By 1993, inflation had begun to moderate (Aaron, 1994; Huskamp and Newhouse, 1995). Although the reasons for this were unclear, the slowing of inflation made reform seem less urgent (Levit, Lazenby, and Sivarajan, 1996).

The Aftermath of the Health Security Act

The failure of the HSA contributed to the Republican sweep of Congress in 1994 (Johnson and Broder, 1996). For many voters, the act represented both the threat of government bureaucracy and the inability of the Democratic Congress to govern effectively. According to Bill McInturff, a leading Republican pollster, "the collapse of the health care plan…fed the voters' sense that Washington was in gridlock and that the Democrats…were to blame" (cited in Toner, 1994).

Health Insurance Portability and Accountability Act

The election led many observers to conclude that NHI was dead (Aaron, 1998). Attention increasingly focused on incremental reform as a path to universal coverage (Gorin, 1997). In 1996, in an effort to demonstrate their commitment to compromise, Republicans joined the Democrats and Clinton in supporting P.L. 104-191, the Health Insurance Portability and Accountability Act (HIPAA) (Atchison and

Fox, 1997). The primary aim of HIPAA was to "eliminate health status from health insurance consideration" (Patel and Rushefsky, 1999, p. 296). In a sense, it was the culmination of the 1993–1994 effort for health care reform. An evaluation of HIPAA by Pollitz and associates (2000) concluded that despite "early implementation challenges, HIPAA's successes have been significant, although limited by the law's incremental nature" (p. 8). Although HIPAA had expanded protections for individuals belonging to group plans, it had done little to help people with individual coverage (Pollitz et al., 2000).

State Children's Health Insurance Program (S-CHIP)

Congress and the White House also addressed the problem of children without insurance (Rosenbaum et al., 1998). The Balanced Budget Act of 1997 created Title XXI of Social Security, also known as the State Children's Health Insurance Program (S-CHIP). Title XXI provides funds for the state to expand coverage for children, by either expanding Medicaid or creating new programs (see Chapter 5) (Rosenbaum et al., 1998).

Mental Health Parity Act

In addition to HIPAA and S-CHIP, Congress also enacted the Mental Health Parity Act in 1996 (Frank, Koyanagi, and McGuire, 1997). This act, which went into effect on January 1, 1998, and expired on September 30, 2001, "imposed new federal standards on mental health coverage offered under most employer-sponsored group health plans" (U.S. General Accounting Office, 2000, p. 3) and is currently under review for reauthorization. Under the act, employers who offer mental health benefits to their workers cannot "impose annual or lifetime dollar limits on mental health benefits that are less than those applied to medical/surgical benefits" (Hennessy and Goldman, 2001, pp. 59–60). The National Association of Social Workers (1996) called the act a "significant [legislative] win" and a "first step" toward mental health parity.

Although the aim of this legislation was to address long-standing discrimination against people with mental health disorders, its impact has been relatively limited. The act does not require employers to provide mental health benefits, and it does not prevent plans from imposing other restrictions, "such as differential cost sharing or day and visit limits," on mental health benefits (Hennessy and Goldman, 2001, p. 60). It also does not apply to benefits for treating substance abuse.

Despite its limits, the act did raise parity as an issue and gave impetus to state efforts to enact "more-comprehensive parity provisions" (Gitterman, Sturm, and Scheffler, 2001, p. 68). As a result, in a majority of states, plans may not "place a greater financial burden on access to diagnosis or treatment for mental health conditions than for other health conditions" (Gitterman, Sturm, and Scheffler, 2001, p. 69). Yet, as Gitterman, Sturm, and Scheffler (2001) note, these state laws are limited by the federal Employment Retirement Income Security Act (ERISA), which prevents states from regulating health plans financed by employers. This suggests that further action is needed at the federal level. Senators Paul Wellstone

(D-MN) and Pete Domenici (R-NM) have introduced legislation that would expand the original act as another "step toward full parity" (Gitterman, Sturm, and Scheffler, 2001, p. 70).

Highlights

■ Although the federal government's role in the delivery of health and mental health services grew substantially during the 1940s, efforts to establish national health insurance were unsuccessful. From 1943 to 1950, the Congress of Industrialized Organizations (CIO) became increasingly narrow in its goals and significantly undermined earlier efforts by organized labor to legislate national health insurance. At the same time, the American Medical Association (AMA) escalated its opposition to national health insurance and lobbied against government intervention in health care.

■ With the defeat of the Wagner-Murray-Dingell bill in 1943 and President Truman's efforts in 1949, many advocates of national health care concluded that compulsory insurance could be achieved in the United States only in stages (Ball, 1995). Accordingly, they turned their attention to one of the most needy segments of the population, older adults over age 65 (Ball, 1995).

■ Between 1900 and 1950, the number of older adults in the United States quadrupled; only one in eight had private health insurance (Bernstein, 1991). The Democratic Party supported Medicare and introduced legislation as early as 1952, but the bill languished in Congress until 1960. The political battle for Medicare was tedious and costly, but it was finally enacted in 1965.

■ Medicare established a mandatory, federal health insurance system for retired adults. Congress also enacted Medicaid in 1965, a voluntary federal–state system of health insurance for poor adults and children. Today, these are still at the core of the nation's health care system and health care policy.

■ Health care inflation in the 1970s and 1980s exacerbated the problem of health insurance coverage and renewed national interest in universal health insurance. President Nixon, Senator Edward Kennedy (D-MA), Senator Henry Waxman (D-CA), the AMA, and other organizations proposed national reforms during the 1970s, none of which were really taken seriously by Congress. Instead, regulatory reforms, such as certificate-of-need laws and a Prospective Payment System for Medicare reimbursement to hospitals, were introduced.

■ Health maintenance organizations (HMOs) also emerged, supported by the Health Maintenance Act of 1973. These reforms did little to reduce the nation's growing health care costs, but the introduction of HMOs had a significant impact on the private system of health care delivery.

■ Significant mental health legislation was enacted between 1963 and 1992. The Mental Retardation and Community Mental Health Centers Construction Act of 1963 provided funds to the states to close psychiatric hospitals and replace them with community-based services. This shift in policy led to problems of dein-stitutionalization with insufficient care at the community level. Congress was increasingly disheartened by the approach and threatened to terminate funding in 1975, but introduced new regulations in an effort to improve the system. During the Reagan administration in the 1980s, funds were dramatically reduced, however, and the system underwent further decline.

■ The only significant effort to establish a national system of health insurance since 1950 was the Clinton administration's Health Security Act of 1993. This bill was designed to expand coverage to low-income and unemployed adults and their families, but it too failed to be enacted.

■ In the aftermath of this failed attempt to achieve universal health care, the nation's will to address the issue of national insurance was depleted. Incremental reforms were supported. Congress passed the Health Insurance Portability and Accountability Act, the State Children's Health Insurance Program (S-CHIP), and the Mental Health Parity Act.

REFERENCES

Aaron, H. J. (1998). Less Is More: After the Clinton Plan, Let's Think Small. In S. H. Altman, U. E. Reinhardt, and A. E. Shields (Eds.), *The Future U.S. Healthcare System: Who Will Care for the Poor and Uninsured?* (pp. 233–246). Chicago: Health Administration Press.

Aaron, H. J. (1994, Winter). Thinking Straight about Medical Costs. *Health Affairs, 13,* 5, 7–13.

Aaron, H. J. and Schwartz, W. B. (1993, Supplement). Managed Competition: Little Cost Containment without Budget Limits. *Health Affairs, 12,* 204–215.

Altman, D. E. (1995, Spring). The Realities Behind the Polls. *Health Affairs, 14,* 24–26.

Arons, B. S., Frank, R. G., Goldman, H. H., McGuire, T. G., and Stephens, S. (1994, Spring [I]). *Health Affairs, 13,* no. 1, 192–205.

Atchinson, B. K. and Fox, D. M. (1997, May/June). The Politics of the Health Insurance Portability and Accountability Act. *Health Affairs, 16,* 3, 146–150.

Ball, R. M. (1995, Winter). Perspectives on Medicare: What Medicare's Architects Had in Mind. *Health Affairs, 14,* 4, 62–73.

Baltzell, E. D. (1966). *The Protestant Establishment: Aristocracy and Caste in America.* New York: Vintage Books.

Bartley, N. V. (1995). *A History of the South,* Vol. XI, *The New South 1945–1980.* Baton Rouge: Louisiana State University Press.

Berkowitz, E. D. (1989). Wilbur Cohen and American Social Reform. *Social Work, 34,* 4, 293–303.

Bernstein, I. (1991). *Promises Kept: JFK's New Frontier.* New York: Oxford University Press.

Blendon, R. J., Brodie, M., and Benson, J. (1995, Summer). What Happened to America's Support for the Clinton Health Plan? *Health Affairs, 14,* 2, 7–23.

Bloom, J. M. (1987). *Class, Race, and the Civil Rights Movement.* Bloomington: Indiana University Press.

Brodie, M. and Blendon, R. J. (1995, Summer). The Public's Contribution to Congressional Gridlock on Health Care Reform. *Journal of Health Politics, Policy and Law, 20,* 2, 403–409.

Caute, D. (1978). *The Great Fear: The Anti-Communist Purge Under Truman and Eisenhower.* New York: Simon & Schuster.

Corning, P. (1969). *Evolution of Medicare...From Idea to Law.* U.S. Deptment of Health, Education, and Welfare, Social Security Administration, Office of Research and Statistics, Report #29. Washington, DC: U.S. Government Printing Office.

David, S. I. (1985). *With Dignity: The Search for Medicare and Medicaid.* Westport, CT: Greenwood.

Davis, K., Collins, K. S., and Morris, C. (1994, Fall). Managed Care: Promise and Concerns. *Health Affairs, 13,* 4, 178–185.

Dranove, D. (2000). *The Economic Evolution of American Health Care: From Marcus Welby to Managed Care.* Princeton: Princeton University Press.

Ellwood, P. M. Jr., Anderson, N., Billings, J. E., Carlson, R. J., Hoagberg, E. J., and McClure, W. (1976). Health Maintenance Strategy. In *Prognosis Negative: Crisis in the Health Care System* (pp. 347–352). New York: Vintage Books.

Enthoven, A. C. and Kronick, R. (1991, May 15). Universal Health Insurance Through Incentives Reform. *Journal of the American Medical Association 265,* 19, 2532–2536.

Enthoven, A. C. and Singer, S. J. (1994, Spring [I]). A Single-Payer in Jackson Hole Clothing. *Health Affairs, 13,* 1, 81–95.

Feingold, E. (1966). *Medicare: Policy and Politics.* San Francisco: Chandler.

Foner, P. S. (1974). *Organized Labor and the Black Worker 1619–1973.* New York: International.

Frank, R. G., Koyanagi, C., and McGuire, T. G. (1997, July/August). Politics and Economics of Mental Health "Parity" Laws. *Health Affairs, 16,* 4, 108–119.

Friedman, E. (1996). Capitation, Integration, and Managed Care. *JAMA, 275,* 12, 957–963.

Garrett, L. (2000). *Betrayal of Trust: The Collapse of Global Public Health.* New York: Hyperion.

Gitterman, D. P., Sturm, R., and Scheffler, R. M. (2001, July–August). Toward Full Mental Health Parity and Beyond. *Health Affairs, 20,* 4, 68–76.

Gorin, S. (1997, August). Universal Health Care Coverage in the United States. *Health and Social Work, 22,* 3, 223–230.

Grob, G. N. (1994). *The Mad Among Us, a History of the Care of America's Mentally Ill.* New York: Free Press.

Guyotte, R. L. (1995). Cohen, Wilbur (1913–1987). In R. L. Edwards (Ed.-in-Chief), *Encyclopedia of Social Work,* 19th ed. (p. 2579). Washington, DC: National Association of Social Workers.

Hamilton, C. D. and Hamilton, C. V. (1997). *The Dual Agenda: The African-American Struggle for Civil and Economic Equality.* New York: Columbia University Press.

Hennessy, K. D. and Goldman, H. H. (2001, July–August). Full Parity: Steps Toward Treatment Equity for Mental and Addictive Disorders. *Health Affairs, 20,* 4, 58–67.

Himmelstein, D. and Woolhandler, S. (1989). A National Health Program for the U.S. *New England Journal of Medicine, 320,* 102–108.

Hughes, W. C. (1999). Managed Care, Meet Community Support: Ten Reasons to Include Direct Support Services in Every Behavioral Health Plan. *Health and Social Work, 24,* 103–111.

Huskamp, H. A. and Newhouse, J. P. (1995, Winter). Is Health Spending Slowing Down? *Health Affairs, 13,* 5, 32–38.

Jacobs, L. R. and Shapiro, R. Y. (1995, Summer). Don't Blame the Public for Failed Health Care Reform. *Journal Health Politics, Policy and Law, 20,* 2, 410–423.

Jansson, B. S. (2001). *The Reluctant Welfare State,* 4th ed. Belmont, CA: Wadsworth.

Jencks, C. (1994). *The Homeless.* Cambridge, MA: Harvard University Press.

Jimenez, M. A. (1997, March). Concepts of Health and National Health Care Policy: A View from American History. *Social Service Review,* 35–50.

Johnson, A. K. (1995). Homelessness. In R. L. Edwards (Ed.-in-Chief), *Encyclopedia of Social Work,* 19th ed. (pp. 1705–1711). Washington, DC: National Association of Social Workers.

Johnson, H. and Broder, D. S. (1996). *The System: The American Way of Politics at the Breaking Point.* Boston: Little, Brown.

Kaiser/Harvard/KRC. (1994, November 15). *National Election Night Survey,* 2, 148–152.

Karger, H. J. and Stoesz, D. (2002). *American Social Welfare Policy,* 4th ed. New York: Longman.

Kotelchuck, D., ed. (1976). *Prognosis Negative: Crisis in the Health Care System.* New York: Vintage Books.

Kronick, R. (1994, Spring). A Helping Hand for the Invisible Hand. *Health Affairs, 13,* 1, 96–101.

Kronick, R., Goodman, D. C., Wennberg, J., and Wagner, E. (1993, January 14). The Marketplace in Health Care Reform: The Demographic Limitations of Managed Competition. *New England Journal of Medicine, 328,* 2, 145–148.

Levit, K. R., Cowan, C. A., Lazenby, H. C., McDonnell, P. A., Sensenig, A. L., Stiller, J. M., and Won, D. K. (1994, Winter). National Health Spending Trends, 1960–1993. *Health Affairs, 13,* 5, 14–31.

Levit, K. R., Lazenby, H. C., and Sivarajan, L. (1996, Summer). Health Care Spending in 1994: Slowest in Decades. *Health Affairs, 15,* 2, 130–144.

Lin, A. M. P. (1995). Mental Health Overview. In R. L. Edwards (Ed.-in-Chief), *Encyclopedia of Social Work,* 19th ed. (pp. 1705–1711). Washington, DC: National Association of Social Workers.

Lubell, S. (1965). *The Future of American Politics,* 3rd ed., rev. New York: Harper.

Manchester, W. (1974). *The Glory and the Dream—A Narrative of American History 1932–1972.* Boston: Little, Brown.

Marmor, T. R. (1994). *Understanding Health Care Reform.* New Haven: Yale University Press.

Marmor, T. R. (1976). Origins of the Government Health Insurance Issue. In D. Kotelchuck (Ed.), *Prognosis Negative: Crisis in the Health Care System.* New York: Vintage Books. (pp. 292–303).

Marmor, T. R. (1973). *The Politics of Medicare.* Chicago: Aldine.

Marmor, T. R., Mashaw, J. L. and Harvey, P. L. (1992). *America's Misunderstood Welfare State: Persistent Myths, Enduring Realities.* New York: Basic Books.

Marx, A. J., Test, M. A., and Stein, L. J. (1973). Extrohospital Management of Severe Mental Illness. *Archives of General Psychiatry, 29,* 505–511.

McKinney, E. A. (1995). Health Planning. In R. L. Edwards (Ed.-in-Chief), *Encyclopedia of Social Work,* 19th ed. (pp. 1199–1205). Washington, DC: National Association of Social Workers.

Mechanic, D. (1999). *Mental Health and Social Policy, The Emergence of Mental Health,* 4th ed. Boston: Allyn & Bacon.

Mental Health Policy Resource Center. (1996, April). Themes and Variations: Mental Health and Substance Abuse Policy in the Making. *Policy in Perspective.* Washington, DC: Mental Health Resource Center.

Mizrahi, T. (1995). Health Care: Reform Initiatives. In R. L. Edwards (Ed.-in-Chief), *Encyclopedia of Social Work,* 19th ed. (pp. 1185–1198). Washington, DC: National Association of Social Workers.

Mognan, J. J. (1995, Spring). Anatomy and Physiology of Health Reform's Failure. *Health Affairs, 14,* 1, 99–101.

Moniz, C. M. (1990). *National Council of Senior Citizens: The Role of the Elderly in the Enactment of Medicare.* AnnArbor: UMI Dissertation Services.

National Association of Social Workers. (2000, April). Behavioral Healthcare Parity. *Social Work Practice Update.* Washington, DC: National Association of Social Workers.

National Association of Social Workers. (1996, October 4). Health Insurance Portability and Accountability Act, Mental Health Parity. *Government Relations Update.* Washington, DC: National Association of Social Workers.

National Association of Social Workers. (1993, October 1). *An Analysis of the Clinton Health Care [sic] in Relation to the Five Basic Principles of Health Care Reform* [Issue Brief]. Washington, DC: National Association of Social Workers.

National Association of Social Workers. (1991). National Health. In *Social Work Speaks: NASW Policy Statements* (pp. 178–180). Silver Spring, MD: NASW Press.

Navarro, V. (1995, Summer). Why Congress Did Not Enact Health Care Reform. *Journal of Health Politics, Policy and Law, 20,* 2, 455–461.

Newhouse, J. P. (1995, Spring). Economists, Policy Entrepreneurs, and Health Care Reform. *Health Affairs, 14,* 1, 182–199.

Newhouse, J. P. (1993, Supplement). An Iconoclastic View of Health Cost Containment. *Health Affairs, 12,* 152–171.

Newhouse, J. P. and the Insurance Experiment Group. (1993). *Free for All? Lessons from the RAND Health Insurance Experiment.* Cambridge, MA: Harvard University Press.

Patel, K. and Rushefsky, M. E. (1999). *Health Care Politics and Policy in America.* 2nd ed. Armonk, NY: M. E. Sharpe.

Patterson, J. T. (1996). *Grand Expectations—The U.S. 1945–1974.* New York: Oxford University Press.

The Pepper Commission (U.S. Bipartisan Commission on Comprehensive Health Care). (1990, September). *A Call for Action.* Washington, DC: U.S. Government Printing Office.

Pollitz, K., Tapay, N., Hadley, E., and Specht, J. (2000, July–August). Early Experience with "New Federalism" in Health Insurance Regulation. *Health Affairs, 19,* 4, 7–22.

Quadagno, J. (1988). *The Transformation of Old Age Security: Class and Politics in the American Welfare State.* Chicago: University of Chicago Press.

Rachlis, M. and Kushner, C. (1994). *Strong Medicine: How to Save Canada's Health Care System.* Toronto: HarperCollins.

Reinhardt, U. E. (1995, Spring). Turning Our Gaze from Bread and Circus Games. *Health Affairs, 14,* 1, 33–36.

Reinhardt, U. E. (1996, Summer). Spending More through "Cost Control": Our Obsessive Quest to Gut the Hospital. *Health Affairs, 15,* 2, 145–154.

Reinhardt, U. E. (1994, Spring [II]). Lineage of Managed Competition. *Health Affairs, 13,* 12, 290.

Rice, T., Desmond, K., and Gabel, J. (1990). The Medicare Catastrophic Coverage Act: A Post-Mortem. *Health Affairs, 9,* 3, 75–87.

Roberts, M. J. and Clyde, A. (1993). *Your Money or Your Life: The Health Care Crisis Explained.* New York: Doubleday.

Rolde, N. (1992). *Your Money or Your Health.* New York: Paragon House.

Rosenbaum, S., Johnson, K., Sonosky, C., Markus, A., and DeGraw, C. (1998, January–February). The Children's Hour: The State Children's Health Insurance Program. *Health Affairs, 17,* 1, 75–89.

Rothstein, R. (1995, Winter). Friends of Bill? Why Liberals Should Let Up on Clinton. *The American Prospect, 20,* 32–41.

Schwartz, W. B. and Mendelson, D. N. (1994, Spring [I]). Eliminating Waste and Inefficiency Can Do Little to Contain Costs. *Health Affairs, 13,* 1, 224–238.

Schwartz, W. B. and Mendelson, D. N. (1992, Summer). Why Managed Care Cannot Contain Hospital Costs—Without Rationing. *Health Affairs, 11,* 2, 100–107.

Segal, S. P. (1995). Deinstitutionalization. In R. L. Edwards (Ed.-in-Chief), *Encyclopedia of Social Work,* 19th ed. (pp. 704–712). Washington, DC: National Association of Social Workers.

Short, P. F. et al. (1995, October 25). New Estimates of the Underinsured Younger Than 65 Years. *Journal of the American Medical Association, 274,* 16, 1302–1306.

Skocpol, T. (1997). *Boomerang: Health Care Reform and the Turn Against Government.* New York: W. W. Norton.

Skocpol, T. (1995, Spring). The Rise and Resounding Demise of the Clinton Plan. *Health Affairs, 14,* 1, 66–85.

Smith, M. D., Altman, D. E., Leitman, R., Moloney, T. W., and Taylor, H. (1992, Winter). Taking the Public's Pulse on Health System Reform. *Health Affairs, 11,* 2, 124–133.

Starr, P. (1995, Winter). What Happened to Health Care Reform? *The American Prospect, 20,* 1–31.

Starr, P. (1994). *The Logic of Health Care Reform: Why and How the President's Plan Will Work.* New York: Whittle Books in association with Penguin Books.

Starr, P. (1982). *The Social Transformation of American Medicine: The Rise of a Sovereign Profession and the Making of a Vast Industry.* New York: Basic Books.

Starr, P. and Zelman, W. (1993, Supplement). Bridge to Compromise: Competition under a Budget. *Health Affairs,* 7–23.

Stout, H. (1994, March 10). Many Don't Realize It's Clinton's Plan They Like. *Wall Street Journal,* p. B1, B6.

Swartz, K. (1994, January 5). Dynamics of People Without Health Insurance: Don't Let the Numbers Fool You. *Journal of the American Medical Association, 271,* 1, 64–66.

Toner, R. (1994, November 16). Pollsters See a Silent Storm That Swept Away Democrats. *New York Times,* p. 12.

Trattner, W. I. (1999). *From Poor Law to Welfare State,* 6th ed. New York: Free Press.

U.S. General Accounting Office. (2000). *Mental Health Parity Act: Despite New Federal Standards, Mental Health Benefits Remain Limited* (HEHS-00-95). Washington, DC: U.S. Government Printing Office.

U.S. General Accounting Office. (1977). *Returning the Mentally Disabled to the Community: Government Needs to Do More.* Washington, DC: U.S. Government Printing Office.

Wencour, S. and Reisch, M. (1989). *From Charity to Enterprise: The Development of Social Work in a Market Economy.* Urbana: University of Illinois.

White, J. (1995, Summer). The Horses and the Jumps: Comments on the Health Care Reform Steeplechase. *Journal of Health Politics, Policy and Law, 20,* 2, 373–383.

Yankelovich, D. (1995, Spring). The Debate That Wasn't: The Public and the Clinton Plan. *Health Affairs, 14,* 1, 7–23.

Zelman, W. A. (1994, Spring [I]). The Rationale behind the Clinton Health Reform Plan. *Health Affairs, 13,* 1, 9–29.

3 Access to Care

When Congress failed to pass the Health Security Act of 1993, it ushered in a period of disillusionment and concern about the nation's willingness to reform the health care system and expand access to the uninsured. The Clinton administration's proposal provided a momentous opportunity to transform the system and achieve universal coverage. The failure to seize this moment was "most devastating" (Altman, Reinhardt, and Shields, 1998), and advocates of reform felt that the nation's "commitment...seemed to collapse...as if the problem of the uninsured had disappeared" (p. 1). In reality, the number of people without insurance was growing and was projected to reach 60 million by 2007 (Health Insurance Association of America, 1999).

Today, the size of the uninsured population in the United States is a major public policy issue. As noted by Rhoades and Chu (2000), there are several reasons for concern. First, people who lack insurance are more likely to lack a usual source or provider of care, to spend more on health care services, and to experience more problems with treatment, quality of care, and continuity of care. The uninsured population is not adequately protected from the medical and financial risks of illness and injury. Second, the composition of the uninsured population raises concerns about equity in the health care system. The uninsured population is predominantly of lower income, and people of color are disproportionately poor. Third, the magnitude of the uninsured population raises doubts about the efficiency of the current structure and the adequacy of the private and public sectors in financing and managing access to care.

Studies of health insurance coverage in the United States reveal three disturbing profiles. First, many people (15.5 percent of the population in 1999) have no medical insurance at all (U.S. Census Bureau, 2000). This is particularly troublesome for a society that is the richest nation in the world and prides itself on having the best medical care system. Second, the percent of the U.S. population without health insurance grew steadily from 12.9 percent in 1987 to 16.3 percent in 1998 (U.S. Census Bureau, 1987–2000). Third, the size of the uninsured population rises and falls with changes in the economy. In 1999, the percent of the U.S. population without insurance declined for the first time since 1987, but this was due to an unusually strong economy and low unemployment (Mills, 1999). During the 1990s, when health care costs increased dramatically, the size of the uninsured population increased as private employers and insurers reduced their commit-ment to the provision of health insurance benefits.

This chapter provides an overview of these trends in coverage. It also ad-dresses broader public policy issues concerning access, coverage, and financing. The uninsured population as a whole and groups at greater risk for lack of cover-age are examined. Finally, the role of insurance is discussed. Does health insur-ance really matter? How does it affect the utilization of health care services?

Health Insurance Coverage in the United States

In the early 1990s, during the debate on universal health insurance, about 35 mil-lion people (14 percent of the population) lacked health insurance coverage. Ac-cording to the federal government's Current Population Survey (see Figure 3.1), the number of uninsured in the United States increased to 44.3 million people (16.3 percent of the population) in 1998; in 1999, the number had decreased to 42.6 million people (15.5 percent) (U.S. Census Bureau, 2000).

These figures may not provide a complete depiction of the scope of the prob-lem, however. Some analysts believe the Census Bureau underestimates the number of uninsured people (Weinick and Drilea, 1998) because its data do not in-clude people who lose their insurance coverage for *part of a year*. For example, the Medical Expenditure Panel Survey (MEPS), which is conducted by the Agency for Healthcare Research and Quality (AHRQ) at the U.S. Public Health Services (Rhoades and Chu, 2000), shows a higher estimate for 1999; it reports that 42.8 mil-lion people (15.8 percent of the population) were uninsured during the first half of 1999. Other surveys identify the number of people uninsured for at least one month during the course of a year or a given period of time. For example, the Kaiser Family Foundation found that 66.6 million people were uninsured for at least a month during one twenty-eight-month period in the early 1990s (Kaiser Family Foundation, 1998).

FIGURE 3.1   Uninsured Population, 1989–1999

Year	Total (number in thousands)	Percent of Total Population
1999	42,554	15.5
1997	43,448	16.1
1995	40,582	15.4
1993	39,713	15.3
1991	35,445	14.1
1989	33,385	13.6

Sources: U.S. Census Bureau, March Demographic Profiles, Current Population Surveys, 1990, 1992, 1994, 1996, 1998, 2000.

In addition, although millions lack insurance, millions more have insurance that is *inadequate* to cover their medical needs and expenses. Inadequate coverage, or *under*insurance, is typically defined as out-of-pocket costs, such as insurance deductibles, copayments, and noncovered expenses that exceed 10 percent of personal income. This kind of financial burden often results from a catastrophic illness or a serious accident or injury. A study by the Centers for Disease Control and Prevention (1998) found that one in five people between the ages of 18 and 64 was uninsured or underinsured in the late 1990s. Shearer (1998) estimated that 33 million people (12 million elderly and 11 million nonelderly) incurred expenses that exceeded 10 percent of their income in 1996.

Individuals who need expensive long-term care because of chronic illness or permanent disability are also at risk for *under*insurance. Studies have shown, for example, that Medicare recipients spend on average about 20 percent of their income on medical expenses. This is a disturbing finding. Elderly individuals actually spent on average less than this before Medicare was enacted (Himmelstein and Woolhandler, 1994).

Declining Coverage

Residents of the United States obtain health insurance in one of two primary ways. The first is through *government-sponsored* health insurance programs, primarily Medicaid and Medicare (see Figures 3.2 and 3.3). About one of every four members of the population relies on government-sponsored programs for health insurance. The second and most important means of coverage is *employment-based* insurance. Nearly two out of every three members of the population receive health insurance through their employers (U.S. Census Bureau, 1999).

The decline of employment-based insurance during the past decade has had a dramatic effect on insurance coverage, however. Between 1987 and 1998, the percentage of *nonelderly adults* (ages 18–64) without health insurance increased from 15.6 percent to an alarming 19.6 percent; in 1999, as mentioned earlier, the number decreased to 19 percent. The percentage of *children* without coverage increased from 1987 to 1992, but then began to decline. For the total population, the number of uninsured increased dramatically between 1991 and 1992, continued to climb until 1998, and then declined substantially between 1998 and 1999 (U.S. Census Bureau, 1987–2000).

The primary cause of the decline in coverage, particularly between 1987 and 1992, was the increase in the cost of private insurance, which triggered reductions in employment-based coverage. Between 1987 and 1995, the fraction of the nonelderly population insured by employers fell from 69.2 percent to 63.8 percent (Employee Benefit Research Institute, 1997). With rising costs, many employers seemed to feel that "their contribution…should be even less" than it had been in the past (Rovner, 1997, p. 56). Between 1998 and 1999, employment-based insurance did expand as the economy grew stronger and unemployment declined. In addition, children in near-poor families (above the federal poverty level) were able to receive insurance through expansions in the State Children's Health Insurance Program (S-CHIP) promoted by the Clinton administration.

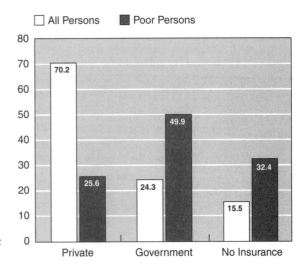

FIGURE 3.2   Health Insurance, 1999 (all persons)

Source: U.S. Census Bureau, March Demographic Profiles, Current Population Survey, 2000.

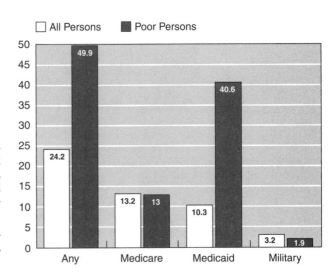

FIGURE 3.3   Government Insurance, 1999 (all persons)

Note: Military health care includes CHAM-PUS (Comprehensive Health and Medical Plan for Uniformed Services)/Tricare, CHAMPVA (Civilian Health and Medical Program of the Department of Veterans Affairs), and veterans and military health care.

Source: U.S. Census Bureau, March Demographic Profiles, Current Population Survey, 2000.

Overall, however, the erosion of employment-based coverage has adversely impacted family dependents, especially young people under age 18 (Newacheck, Huges, and Cisternas, 1995). In 1995, only 66 percent of children had private insurance compared to 73 percent in 1989 (U.S. General Accounting Office, 1995). In 1999, between 65.1 percent (Rhoades and Chu, 2000) and 68.9 percent of children (U.S. Census Bureau, 2000) had private insurance. As the percentage of young people with private coverage has declined, the importance of Medicaid has grown. Without Medicaid at least 4 million additional pregnant women and children would have been uninsured during the late 1980s and early 1990s (Holahan, 1997).

There are, however, concerns about the coverage provided by Medicaid because it does not offer "the same level of access to care" (Newacheck et al., 1995, p. 252) as private insurance. In addition, due to changes in Aid to Families with Dependent Children (AFDC) and Supplemental Security Income (SSI) (discussed later in this chapter), many children risk loss of their Medicaid coverage (Newacheck et al., 1995; Iglehart, 1997).

Rising Costs.   Health care costs rose rapidly in the late 1980s and early 1990s, far outpacing wages, family incomes, and consumer prices. Between 1988 and 1996, the average premium for family coverage rose almost 10 percent (Kaiser Commission on Medicaid and the Uninsured, 1998b). Businesses and employers, especially small businesses, began to shift these costs to their employees. In fact, in 1988, employees paid 11 percent of the cost of single coverage; by 1996, they were paying 21 percent of the cost (Kaiser Family Foundation, 2000a). In 1998, the average employee share of premiums increased to 27 percent (Kaiser Commission on Medicaid and the Uninsured, 2000a).

Since the late 1980s, employers have raised the premium share paid by *employees* and, in doing so, have made health insurance unaffordable for many families. In 1998, according to Gabel and associates (1999), workers in small businesses with fewer than 200 employees paid on average 44 percent of the premium for family coverage; in 1988, they paid only 34 percent. In larger firms, in 1998, employees paid on average 28 percent of the premiums for family coverage.

The financial burden of paying an increasing share of the cost of health insurance has proved to be too great for many families. An increasing number of employees are eligible for benefits, yet they decline coverage because they cannot afford to pay their premium share. Cooper and Schone (1997) show that fewer employees accepted coverage from their employers in 1996 than in 1987. In 1996, 15 percent of workers declined coverage (75.4 percent were offered insurance, but only 60.4 percent had coverage); in 1987, 8.5 percent of workers declined coverage (72.4 percent were offered insurance, but only 63.9 percent had coverage).

Carrasquillo and colleagues (1999) challenge the view that most health insurance today is provided by the private sector. They argue that the drop in employer-based coverage created by these cost shifts has actually diminished the role of the private sector and increased the role of the public sector. If the government's roles as employer and health insurance provider are combined, their findings show that, in 1996, only 43 percent of the population had their coverage paid by private employers. Fifty percent received coverage through local, state, or federal employment or government-sponsored health plans, such as Medicare. The remaining 7 percent purchased insurance on their own. Thus, from this perspective, government actually plays a far greater role than commonly thought.

Jobs without Coverage.   A separate, but related problem, in health insurance coverage is the *decline in jobs that provide insurance coverage.* Service-sector jobs, which are less likely to provide insurance benefits, continue to increase in relation to manufacturing jobs. As discussed earlier in Chapter 1, labor unions played a major role in the development of employer-based insurance, particularly in manufacturing, and today, unionized workers are far more likely to receive coverage. In 1995, according to Thorpe (1997), 16.8 percent of nonunion workers did not receive coverage compared to only 5.9 percent of union workers. However, the number of workers in unionized jobs has also decreased.

Changing Workforce.   The *structure of the workforce* has also changed in recent decades. The number of "contingent" or "alternative" jobs, including part-time, temporary, contractual, and self-employed positions, has increased; these jobs are less likely to provide coverage. Thorpe (1999) estimates that employees in these categories make up 25 percent of the workforce. In 1997, according to Thorpe (1999), 53.3 percent of employees ineligible for coverage were either part-time or partial-year employees. Workers who do not receive employment-based insurance and do not purchase it on their own cite *cost* as the primary reason for lack of insurance. In a Harvard survey (1995), 55 percent of the uninsured said they did not have coverage because it was too expensive.

Reductions in Coverage.   Finally, in response to the rising cost of health insurance, *some employers have reduced their commitment to workers' spouses and other family members.* Some employers have begun to deny coverage to spouses if they choose to decline the coverage provided by their own employers. Most employers have not gone this far, but they have increased the portion or cost of the dependent care coverage that is paid by the employee (Gabel, 1999).

Low- and middle-income workers are affected most by these employer practices, which lead to a decline in coverage. As premiums rise and workers are forced to spend more and more of their earnings on family coverage, they are more likely to decline the coverage provided by their employers.

The Uninsured Population in the United States

Who are the uninsured? Most of the uninsured in the United States are *working adults with moderate incomes and their dependent family members.* More than a third of the individuals who were uninsured in 1999 lived in families with incomes below 150 percent of the federal poverty level (see Figure 3.4). However, the size of the uninsured group living in families with incomes between 150 and 300 percent of the federal poverty level was nearly as large. Within these groups, low-income *men* are at even greater risk for lack of coverage than are low-income women because Medicaid provides coverage for eligible pregnant women.

Health insurance coverage in the United States varies not only by employment status and income level but also by employer size and type of employment. Regional differences in employment patterns play a role in access to coverage, and age, race, and ethnicity play a considerable role in insurance patterns. Latina/os (34.2 percent) and African Americans (21.1 percent) experience the highest uninsured rates, whereas young adults (ages 19–24) (31.4 percent) are the age group at greatest risk for lack of coverage.

FIGURE 3.4 Uninsured in U.S. Population by Family Income,* 1999 (numbers in thousands)

As Percent of Total Population in Income Category					
< 150% FPL: $25,000 or less	15,577	24.1	300–450% FPL: $50,000–75,000	6,706	11.8
150–300% FPL: $25,000–49,999	13,996	18.2	>450% FPL: $75,000 or more	6,275	8.3
			TOTAL	42,554	15.5

*Federal Poverty Level (FPL) for a family of four was $16,700 in 1999.

Source: U.S. Census Bureau, March Demographic Profiles, Current Population Survey, 2000.

Uninsured Workers. Employees in unionized and manufacturing jobs are most likely to receive health insurance coverage. Large employers are able to negotiate with insurance companies for group coverage for their workers. Small employers have a much harder time providing coverage because they have too few employees to be able to negotiate *group* rates; they often find themselves priced out of the insurance market. Some employers choose not to offer coverage at all. Thus, some employees find themselves at greater risk for lack of coverage because of the size of their employers.

Although full-time employees are far more likely than temporary or part-time workers to have coverage, not all *full-time* workers receive health insurance benefits. In 1999, 16.4 percent of full-time workers had no health insurance (see Figure 3.5). Because most of the workforce consists of full-time workers, it is also true that most of the uninsured population consists of full-time workers and their dependents. The Kaiser Family Foundation (1998) estimates that eight out of ten uninsured people are full-time workers or their dependents.

FIGURE 3.5 Employment Status of Uninsured Workers (ages 18–64), 1999 (numbers in thousands)

	Total Number of Workers	Number of Uninsured Workers	Percent of Uninsured Workers
Unemployed	29,923	7,921	26.5
Employed PT	23,245	5,204	22.4
Employed FT	115,973	18,984	16.4

Note: PT = Part-time, FT = Full-time

Source: U.S. Census Bureau, March Demographic Profiles, Current Population Survey, 2000.

Employers also vary in their policies regarding coverage for family dependents. Some employee health plans restrict dependents from preventive care or acute care, and provide protections for hospitalization and surgical services only. Other plans may provide coverage for dependents only if they have no other coverage options. Another area of concern for dependent coverage is the definition of "eligible dependents." Historically, dependents have included spouses and children. However, family composition has changed dramatically since the 1960s. Increasingly, employers are faced with the need to decide whether to extend coverage to unmarried partners, gay partners, adopted or foster children, parents, or other family members residing in the employer's household.

In 1995, about 14 million people lived in households with nonrelatives. Yet, only a few employers extend coverage to same-sex partners, and even fewer have been willing to consider coverage for unmarried heterosexual partners. Employers are least likely to extend coverage to the parents of employees or to other relatives. Yet, many working middle-aged adults find themselves caring for aging and elderly parents and for other relatives as well. As people in the United States continue to live longer, the financial and emotional burden of providing custodial, long-term care has fallen on their children. Some employers are beginning to provide employees with the opportunity to purchase long-term-care insurance (Wiatrowski, 1995).

Occupation also plays an important role in access to health insurance. Employees who work in private households are least likely to have health insurance, whereas executives, administrators, managers, and professionals are most likely to have coverage (see Figure 3.6).

Regional and State Differences. Lack of health insurance is a problem in every state and region of the country, but varies from location to location depending on

FIGURE 3.6 **Uninsured Workers by Occupation, 1997, As Percent of Total Population in Occupation Category**

Professional specialty	8.3
Executive, administration, and managerial	9.9
Technicians and related support	10.0
Protective services*	13.1
Sales	18.0
Machine operators, assemblers, and inspectors	21.4
Transportation and material moving	23.6
Precision production, craft, and repair	23.8
Services, excluding protective and household	29.7
Handlers, equipment cleaners, helpers, laborers	32.1
Farming, forestry, and fishing	35.7
Private household	42.8

(*More than two-thirds are government employees.)

Source: U.S. Census Bureau, March Demographic Profiles, Current Population Survey, 1998.

differences in employment patterns and state Medicaid policies. As shown in Figure 3.7, in 1999, the percentage of a state's population that lacked health insurance coverage ranged from a high of 25.8 percent in New Mexico to a low of 6.9 percent in Rhode Island, followed by Hawaii with 7.5 percent.

FIGURE 3.7   **Uninsured Population by Region and State, 1999, As Percent of Total Population in State**

Midwest		Northeast	
Illinois	14.1	Connecticut	9.8
Indiana	10.8	Delaware	11.4
Iowa	8.3	District of Columbia	15.4
Kansas	12.1	Maine	11.9
Michigan	11.2	Maryland	11.8
Minnesota	8.0	Massachusetts	10.5
Missouri	8.6	New Hampshire	10.2.
Nebraska	10.8	New Jersey	13.4
North Dakota	11.8	New York	16.4
Ohio	11.0	Pennsylvania	9.4
South Dakota	11.0	Rhode Island	6.9
Wisconsin	11.0	Vermont	12.3

South		West	
Alabama	14.3	**Arizona**	**21.2**
Arkansas	14.7	**California**	**20.3**
Florida	19.2	Colorado	16.8
Georgia	16.1	Idaho	19.1
Kentucky	14.5	Montana	18.6
Louisiana	**22.5**	**Nevada**	**20.7**
Mississippi	16.6	**New Mexico**	**25.8**
North Carolina	15.4	Oregon	14.6
Oklahoma	17.5	Utah	14.2
South Carolina	17.6	Washington	15.8
Tennessee	11.5	Wyoming	16.1
Texas	**23.3**		
Virginia	14.1		
West Virginia	17.1		

Alaska and Hawaii	
Alaska	18.1
Hawaii	7.5

Note: Bold type shows states with uninsured rates higher than 20 percent.

Source: U.S. Census Bureau, March Demographic Profiles, Current Population Survey, 2000.

Southern and western states have more workers employed by small firms that do not provide coverage (Rowland, 1994). In addition, many states in the South extend Medicaid coverage to *fewer* children. Between 1989 and 1993, the South had more poor, uninsured children than any other region in the country (U.S. General Accounting Office, 1995). In 1999, almost one-fifth of the people who lived in the West and South were uninsured, while less than 13 percent of people living in the Northeast or Midwest lacked coverage (Rhoades and Chu, 2000).

Age.   Young adults 18 to 24 years old are at greater risk than any other age group to lack health insurance. In 1999, almost a third of young adult workers lacked coverage (see Figure 3.8). Many young adults are employed in jobs that do not offer health insurance benefits. If their parents are unable to provide them with benefits as family dependents, there is no public insurance program they can turn to. The Medicaid program does not cover young adults over the age of 18 unless they have children or are disabled and meet the income criteria for eligibility.

On the other hand, the Medicaid program is a true safety net for low-income children under age 18. Although young adults older than 18 are at greatest risk for lack of coverage, infants, children, and youth between the ages of 0 and 18 far out-number this age group; in 1999, 10,023 children (0–18 years of age) were unin-sured, while 7,688 young adults (18–24 years of age) were uninsured (U.S. Census Bureau, 2000). If the Medicaid program did not exist, the number as well as the proportion of uninsured children would be much higher than the current figures.

Medicaid expansions in the 1980s and 1990s played a significant role in re-ducing the size of the population of uninsured children. Between 1989 and 1993, changes made in the Medicaid program increased the number of insured children by 4.8 million. Although this increase did not offset the increase in the number of children who lost employment-based insurance during this same period, the number of children who lacked insurance would have been even greater without these reforms (U.S. General Accounting Office, 1995).

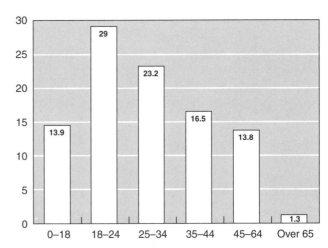

FIGURE 3.8 Uninsured Population by Age, 1999, As Percent of Total Population in Age Group

Source: U.S. Census Bureau, March Demo-graphic Profiles, Current Population Survey, 2000.

In 1997, the State Children's Health Insurance Plan (S-CHIP) allowed further expansions of the Medicaid program by extending coverage to more families who were unable to afford insurance. Unemployed parents, parents in transition between jobs, and employed parents without coverage were targeted. However, the Personal Responsibility and Work Opportunity Act of 1996 delinked Medicaid and the Temporary Assistance for Needy Families (TANF) program, which replaced Aid to Families with Dependent Children (AFDC).

Prior to 1996, families eligible for AFDC were automatically eligible for Medicaid; the Personal Responsibility Act changed this. As an "unintended consequence" of the new legislation, "in 1997, an estimated 675,000 low-income people became uninsured...[and] more than three out of five (62 percent) were children" (Families USA, 1999, p. 2). Moreover, the Families USA (1999) study found that most of these children should not have lost their coverage because they were still eligible for Medicaid.

Race and Ethnicity.   People of color (see Terminology Box) in the United States continue to experience inequality in their social and economic well-being. Compared to whites, a disproportionate number of people of color live in poverty and experience unemployment and inadequate education. These conditions are of concern in and of themselves. However, they also have a significant impact on health status, access to health care, and insurance coverage.

People of color represent 24 percent of the nation's population, yet 46 percent of the uninsured population in the United States is comprised of people of color (Levan et al., 1998). As shown in Figure 3.10, Latina/os (Hispanics) are more likely than any other racial/ethnic group to be uninsured. People of color are particularly susceptible to the lack or loss of employment-based insurance described earlier. They have higher rates of unemployment than whites, and they are more likely to have low-wage jobs and "contingent" jobs.

Income and socioeconomic status certainly play an important role in access to coverage. The fact that people of color are disproportionately employed in low-income jobs increases the likelihood that they will not have employment-based insurance. However, studies show that people of color in high-income jobs are also at greater risk for lack of coverage than whites. For example, Hall, Collins, and Glied (1999) found that, in 1997, 70 percent of Latina/o executives compared to 83 percent of white executives had employment-based coverage. The reasons for the disparity are not clear, but the fact that people of color have fewer family or reserve assets is a likely factor. They may be in a weaker financial position than whites to pay their share of the premiums and thus more likely to decline the coverage.

Latinas/os.   The Hispanic or Latina/o population in the United States includes people with Mexican, Puerto Rican, Cuban, Central American, South American, and other Spanish-speaking origins; they are the second-largest and fastest-growing population in the United States. In 1999, one of every three (nonelderly) Latina/os lacked insurance coverage (see Figure 3.10). Mexican Americans or Chicana/os, the largest subgroup, are affected most. In 1994, 37.2 percent of Mexican Americans, 7.4

TERMINOLOGY BOX

People of Color

The term *people of color* is used in this text in lieu of the term *minorities,* which was used by sociologists for decades to describe the majority (dominant)–minority (subordinate) patterns of social relationships that exist between whites (majority) and oppressed racial groups in the United States (Doob, 1996). However, it is important to note that "race" is a social construction. Sociologists have discredited the biological concept of race; they have shown that it is impossible to classify distinct groups of people based on physical characteristics or genes (Kottak, 1994). Most scientists today accept the finding that all humans are more similar than different (Jaret, 1995); we are essentially all the same.

Nonetheless, four groups in the United States continue to be treated as distinct "racial" groups: Native Americans, African Americans, Hispanics or Latina/os, and Asian Americans. Our cultural belief that race exists allows us to act as if it is real, even as our definitions and classifications of racial groups continue to evolve and change. For example, historically, individuals in the United States with "one drop" of black African blood in their heritage were legally and socially defined as African American. However, to be defined legally as Native American has required at least one-eighth Native American heritage. Until 1962, the U.S. Census defined only three races—White, Black/Negro, and Indian—when it added two new racial classifications, Spanish American and Oriental. In 1977, in an effort to include "Hispanic" groups, the U.S. Census Bureau established four racial categories—non-Hispanic White, non-Hispanic Black, Asian or Pacific Islander, and Native American—and two ethnic classifications, Hispanic and non-Hispanic. In 2000, the U.S. Census separated Asian and Pacific Islanders into two racial categories (see Figure 3.9) and created a multiracial classification, "Two or More Races," which can result in fifty-seven combinations of race (U.S. Census Bureau, 2000).

The U.S. Census defines Spanish-speaking people (Hispanic or Latino) as an ethnic group, not a racial group, because Spanish-speaking people can be of any race. In fact, for Census 2000 Hispanics were asked to identify their race (U.S. Census Bureau, 2000). This distinction makes the term *people of color* somewhat confusing. However, Latina/os have been treated as a minority group in our society. For this reason, the term *people of color* has included Latina/os. In this text, we will continue this practice.

FIGURE 3.9   Classification of Federal Data on Race and Ethnicity

Race (five categories)	Ethnicity (two categories)
American Indian or Alaska Native	Hispanic or Latino
Asian	Not Hispanic or Latino
Black or African American	
Native Hawaiian or Other Pacific Islander	
White	

Source: U.S. Census Bureau, 2000.

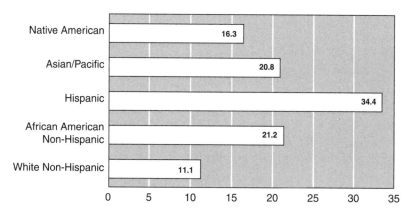

**FIGURE 3.10   Racial and Ethnic Status of Uninsured, 1999, As Percent of
Total Population in Racial/Ethnic Group**

Source: U.S. Census Bureau, March Demographic Profiles, Current Population Survey,
2000, Native American data, 1996.

percent of Cuban Americans, and 17.4 percent of Puerto Rican Americans lacked
health insurance (Kass et al., 1996).

Latina/os are also less likely to have employment-based insurance than are
other people of color in the United States. In 1996, only half of Latino (male) workers received coverage through their employers, compared to two-thirds of African
American male workers and three-fourths of white male workers. Working Latinas (women) were at less risk than working Latinos; over 60 percent of Latina
workers had employer-based insurance in 1996 (Kass et al., 1996).

These figures are a reflection of larger socioeconomic conditions. According to
1999 census data, Hispanic students have the highest high school dropout rates of
any group in the United States and lower rates of college attendance than non-His-
panics (see Figure 3.11). In 1995, the poverty rate for Hispanics exceeded that of African Americans for the first time and remained higher until 1998 (see Figure 3.12).

Latina/o workers, especially recent immigrants with little education and
poor English-speaking skills, are more likely to work in low-skill service-sector
jobs, such as gardeners, nannies, and restaurant workers, or low-skill manufacturing jobs with no or few health benefits. Chicana/o workers in California, for example, are concentrated in the clothing and furniture manufacturing industries;
between 1970 and 1990 real wages declined significantly for Chicana/o workers in
these jobs. Many researchers blame discrimination in employment practices and
culturally insensitive, inadequate education for the condition of many Latina/os
in the United States (Goldberg, 1997; U.S. General Accounting Office, 1992).

African Americans.   African Americans have greater access to health insurance
coverage than do Latina/os in the United States, but are more than twice as likely
as whites to go without health insurance (see Figure 3.10). African Americans
have better access to employment-based insurance than do Hispanics. However,

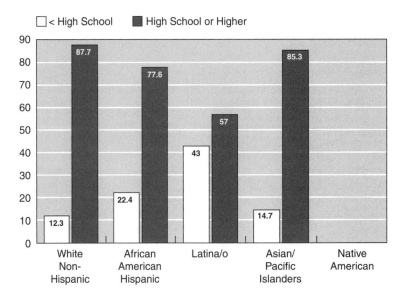

FIGURE 3.11 **Educational Attainment of Population 18 Years and Older by Race and Ethnicity, 1999, As Percent of Total Population in Racial/Ethnic Group**

Note: Native American data not available.

Source: U.S. Census Bureau, March Demographic Profiles, Current Population Survey, 2000.

they have less access than whites, even though they are more likely than whites to work in large businesses. Rates of employment-based coverage for African American female and male workers are the same. However, African Americans are more likely than either whites or Latina/os to have government insurance (Medicaid or Medicare) and to lack access to private insurance (Kass et al., 1996).

FIGURE 3.12 **Poverty Status by Race and Ethnicity, 1995–1999, As Percent of Total Population in Racial/Ethnic Group**

	1995	1996	1997	1998	1999
White Non-Hispanic	8.5	8.6	8.6	8.2	7.7
African American Non-Hispanic	29.3	28.4	26.5	26.1	23.6
Hispanic	30.3	29.4	27.1	25.6	22.8
Asian/ Pacific Islander	14.6	14.5	14.0	12.5	10.7
Native American	*	*	*	*	*

Note: Native American data not available.

Source: U.S. Census Bureau, March Demographic Profiles, Current Population Survey, 2000.

The fact that African Americans have greater access to insurance coverage than Latina/os do, yet are less likely to have private insurance, may be a reflection of the widening economic gap among African Americans. The civil rights and affirmative action legislation of the 1960s provided unprecedented opportunities for African Americans and led to the development of an African American middle class. Since the 1960s, the number of affluent African Americans who are married, are college-educated, have annual incomes over $50,000, own homes, and live in the suburbs has grown substantially (O'Hare et al., 1991).

At the same time, however, African Americans overall have lower rates of participation in the job market, higher rates of unemployment, and more single female–headed families. At the low end of the economic ladder, poor inner-city African Americans experience extreme economic hardship and have been described as a permanent "underclass" (Wilson, 1987). Although African Americans who have achieved middle-class status have gained access to employment-based health insurance, a disproportionate number of poor women and their children are more likely to receive Medicaid than other groups (see Figure 3.13).

Asian Americans. African Americans and Latina/os are the largest racial/ethnic groups in the United States; together they make up almost one-quarter (24.3 percent) of the U.S. population. Asian Americans and Native Americans, on the other hand, comprise only 4.9 percent of the population (U.S. Census Bureau, 2000). As a result, most studies of health and access to care by race or ethnicity have focused on whites, African Americans, and Latina/os. Much less research has been done to study Asian Americans (Jang et al., 1998) and Native Americans.

Access to health insurance for Asian Americans is nearly the same as it is for African Americans (see Figure 3.10); approximately 21 percent of Asian Americans are uninsured. However, in 1999, Asian American workers ages 18–64 were more likely to be insured than were their African American or Latina/o counterparts

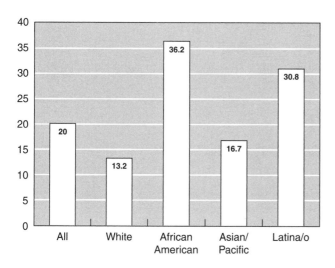

FIGURE 3.13   Children Insured by Medicaid by Race and Ethnicity, 1999

Source: U.S. Census Bureau, March Demographic Profiles, Current Population Survey, 2000.

(see Figure 3.14); this is also a reflection of the socioeconomic status of Asian Americans compared to African Americans and Latina/os.

As a group, Asian Americans have achieved high academic standing. In 1999, 85.3 percent of Asians/Pacific Islanders had attained more than a high school education compared to 87.7 percent of whites (U.S. Census Bureau, 2000). The poverty rate for Asian Americans is higher than for whites, but significantly lower than that of other groups of color; in 1999, the poverty rate for Asians/Pacific Islanders was 10.7 percent (see Figure 3.12) (U.S. Census Bureau, 2000). However, these data can be misleading.

Asian Americans are part of an extremely diverse group that includes individuals with Chinese, Japanese, Filipino, Korean, Asian Indian (India, Pakistan, Bangladesh, Sri Lanka, Nepal), and Southeast Asian (Vietnam, Cambodia, Thailand, Laos, Hmong tribe) origins. Asian Americans are an

> economically stratified group with a highly visible and successful layer of professionals—doctors, engineers, and scientists—a strong commercial middle class that includes grocers, nurses, and government workers, and a less visible group of immigrants, many still on welfare (Zaldivar, 1991).

Despite their academic achievements, the U.S. Census Bureau found that Asian Americans had a harder time than whites using their high levels of education to achieve high earnings. Asian Americans earn less than their white college-educated counterparts and have a harder time rising to administrative and managerial positions (Bovee, 1992).

Poverty rates also vary enormously among Asian American groups. For example, at the high end of the economic scale, Japanese Americans have a lower poverty rate than whites. But at the low end, most Hmong immigrants, who began their emigration to the United States in 1973, "are still on welfare" and "80

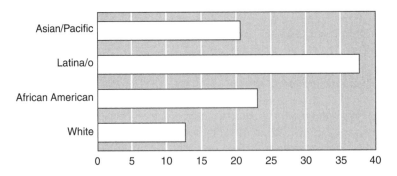

FIGURE 3.14   Uninsured Workers (ages 18–64) by Race and Ethnicity, 1999, As Percent of Total Population in Racial/Ethnic Group (numbers in thousands)

Source: U.S. Census Bureau, March Demographic Profiles, Current Population Survey, 2000.

percent speak little or no English and few have job skills" (Deane, 1998). Other Southeast Asian Americans from Vietnam, Cambodia, Thailand, and Laos lack functional English-speaking skills, which makes it extremely difficult for them to obtain jobs and pursue training or education.

Jang and associates (1998), in a study of 1,800 Chinese American residents of San Francisco, found a clear link between education and income and health insurance coverage. People with higher levels of education and income were more likely to have health insurance. They also found a negative link between levels of acculturation and rates of insurance; the less acculturated (ranging from noncitizens to naturalized citizens to U.S.-born citizens) the residents were, the more likely they were to be uninsured.

Native Hawaiians and Pacific Islanders. Approximately half a million (Ross, 2000) Native Hawaiians and Pacific Islanders (see Figure 3.15) live in the very rural state of Hawaii and on 104 other islands in the Pacific that are under United States jurisdiction, including Guam and American Samoa. Hawaii is a racially and ethnically diverse island, but 60 percent of the residents are Native Hawaiians (Jiang, 2000). Native Hawaiians are Polynesians; other Pacific Islanders are Polynesians, Micronesians, and Melanesians (Ross, 2000). Federal officials and health policy analysts have mostly overlooked this population. In an effort to gather more accurate data and address the specific health needs of this group, the U.S. Census Bureau created a new category (see Figure 3.19) in 2000 for Native Hawaiians and Pacific Islanders. Prior to this date, ethnic data were collected for Asians and Pacific Islanders as one category.

In "Correcting the Visions of Paradise," Jiang (2000) provides a realistic image of Hawaii (the "most remote land mass in the world," [p. 4], 2,500 miles from the California coast) and dispels some of the stereotyped images of the island created by the media and vacation travel advertising. Most visitors to Hawaii travel to Honolulu, O'ahu, the most populated area and only urban center in the state, but the vast majority of O'ahu (almost 90 percent) and all of the other Hawaiian islands are extremely rural. The only means of transportation between the islands is by plane, which makes access to health care services both difficult and

FIGURE 3.15 The U.S.-Associated Pacific

"Flag Territories" Nations Originally under U.S. Jurisdiction under the United Nations Trusteeship of 1947 (now independent nations)	Freely Associated States
American Samoa	Federated States of Micronesia (Truk, Kosrae, Pohnpei, Yap)
Territory of Guam	Republic of Palau
Commonwealth of the Northern Mariana Islands	Republic of the Marshall Islands

Source: National Institute of Medicine Pacific Partnerships for Health, 1998.

expensive. For Pacific Islanders, who live in an area larger than the continental United States, transportation and issues of isolation are of even greater concern (Ross, 2000).

Compared to other states, Hawaii has fewer uninsured people; this is because Hawaii is the only state that has an Employee Retirement Income Security Act (ERISA) waiver that mandates employer-based health insurance for employees who work at least twenty hours a week. However, Native Hawaiians "tend to be both unemployed and uninsured" (Aiu, 2000, p. 8). The uninsured rate is higher among Native Hawaiians and Pacific Islanders (about 17 percent) than the national rate. In addition, the uninsured rate is higher for Native Hawaiians than it is for other people of color who reside in Hawaii (Aiu, 2000).

Senator Daniel Inouye (D-HI) was instrumental in the passage of the Native Hawaiian Health Care Act, which was extended in 1988, was reauthorized in 1992, and created an umbrella health care service organization, Papa Ola Lokahi (POC) and the Native Hawaiian Health Care Systems (NHHCS). POC is the research and administrative arm of the system, whereas NHHCS delivers services through five health centers (Ross, 2000).

Native Americans.   In 1995, according to the U.S. Census Bureau, Native Americans had a higher rate of health insurance coverage than did African Americans, Hispanics, or Asian Americans (see Figure 3.10); only 16.3 percent of Native Americans lacked insurance compared to 12.3 percent of whites. The reason for this unlikely status is the unique social, political, and cultural position of Native Americans in the United States. Since the 1800s, the federal government has had a special obligation to provide health care and improve the health status of Native American people. The Indian Health Service (IHS), an agency of the Public Health Service, U.S. Department of Health and Human Services, was established in 1955 and is responsible for health care services for federally recognized Native American tribes (U.S. Government Accounting Office, 1993).

Approximately 2.4 million Native Americans from 554 recognized tribes (half in Alaska) make up less than 1 percent of the U.S. population (U.S. Census Bureau, 2000). To be *eligible* for direct care services, including hospitals and outpatient clinics operated directly by the IHS or indirectly by the tribal governments, tribal members must live on or near a reservation with designated services, or be an eligible student, foster child, or transient person (U.S. General Accounting Office, 1993).

Because the majority of Native Americans (60 to 70 percent) live in urban areas, access to these services is actually quite limited. To receive care, an individual must travel to the IHS located on or near the tribal reservation. Tribal members who do live on reservations may also have difficulty with "access" to IHS medical care depending on where they live, given the geographic size of many reservations. A Kaiser (2000) study found that only 20 percent of eligible residents reported access to services. In addition, as discussed later, the quality of services is of serious concern.

The IHS has not successfully provided services to meet the health care needs of Native Americans, and like other people of color in the United States, Native

Americans have been unable to access employment-based or private health insurance adequately. Less than half of Native Americans have employment-based coverage. Until the 1990s, when gaming and casinos developed on some reservations, employment opportunities were scarce. For example, in 1995, the unemployment rate on the Pine Ridge Reservation in South Dakota was 75 percent (Brooke, 1995). Native Americans who live in urban settings have lower rates of unemployment comparable to those of African Americans (McLemore and Romo, 1998).

Historically, Native Americans have been the most severely and consistently disadvantaged racial group in the nation. Poverty is a major concern; almost one out of every four Native Americans relies on Medicaid as the primary source of insurance (Kaiser, 2000). Available data on health insurance coverage and access to care are very limited, but a Kaiser survey (2000) found that that over a third of Native Americans are uninsured.

Figure 3.16 provides a summary of relative risk factors that influence access to health insurance. These factors includes income, employment status, occupation, locality, age, race and ethnicity, and gender.

Health Insurance and Utilization of Services

Some have argued that uninsured "citizens are not denied care" (Stelzer, 1994). It is true that not every uninsured person goes without care. Donelan and colleagues (1996) found that 47 percent of uninsured adults had no trouble getting medical care. Government-sponsored clinics and public hospitals offer reduced-cost or "free" care, and government programs sometimes offer care such as vaccinations and cancer screenings.

Despite this, evidence suggests that many individuals without insurance have a difficult time obtaining the care they need. Medical facilities that offer reduced-cost or free care are not geographically accessible to all who need them, particularly those who live in rural areas. Hospital emergency rooms have become increasingly overcrowded, and many hospitals increasingly view "free" or "charity care" as an "unaffordable option" (Preston, 1996; Rosenthal, 1995). Moreover, as Donelan and colleagues (1996) found, half of uninsured adults have trouble obtaining care, and for many these difficulties lead to serious consequences.

Differences in Access among the Insured and Uninsured

People who lack health insurance find it more difficult to access health care services and therefore are less likely to seek the care they need. This is especially true for early and preventive care. Studies show that those who lack insurance consistently use physician services at lower rates than those who have insurance. In 1997, a survey conducted by the Kaiser Family Foundation (1997) found that only 58 percent of *uninsured* (nonelderly) adults compared to 83 percent of *insured* (nonelderly) adults received physician care. Similar results were found for children; 61 percent

FIGURE 3.16 **Summary of Relative Risk Factors: Lack of Health Insurance**

Socioeconomic Factors	Higher Risk	Lower Risk
Income	Poor Near Poor (100–300% FPL)	Nonpoor (> 300% FPL)
Employment status	Unemployed Self-Employed	Employed
	Temporary, part-time employed	Full-time employed
Occupation	Nonunionized	Unionized

	Services
	Manufacturing
	    (blue-collar jobs)
		Administrative
		Professional
		Technical
		    (white-collar jobs)

Locality	South West	Northeast Midwest Hawaii
Age	Young adults (19–24) Middle-age adults (25–54)	Senior adults (over 65) Infants, children, and adolescents Older adults (55–64)
Race and ethnicity	People of color Latina/os African Americans Asian Americans Native Americans Native Hawaiians	Whites
Gender*	Women	Men

*Gender risk factors are related to income, employment, and occupational status.

of *uninsured* children compared to 80 percent of *insured* children visited a physician. The differences found in the use of preventive services were especially disturbing. The Kaiser study (1997) found that uninsured persons were far less likely to receive mammograms, pap smears, prostate exams, or routine physical checkups.

The Kaiser survey (1997) also showed that uninsured persons were more likely to postpone care or avoid medical care because they could not afford to pay for the services. Thirty percent of those *uninsured* (compared to 7 percent of those *insured*) did not receive *necessary* medical care. Fifty-five percent of the *uninsured* in the study (compared to 14 percent of the *insured*) *postponed necessary* medical care, and 24 percent of those *uninsured* (compared to 6 percent of those *insured*) *did not fill a prescription*. In 1996, the U.S. Public Health Service (Krauss et al., 1999) obtained similar findings. Approximately 75 percent of those *with insurance* used ambulatory medical services compared to only 50 percent of those who were *uninsured*. Forty-three percent of the uninsured population obtained prescribed medicine compared to 65 percent of the insured population.

The lack of preventive care and the tendency to delay treatment among the uninsured often leads to the onset of more serious conditions that are also more difficult and expensive to treat once care is finally sought. As a consequence, people who are uninsured are also at greater risk for hospitalization for conditions that generally do not require hospital care. The same is true for people with low incomes (Billings et al., 1996). The uninsured population is twice as likely to be hospitalized for diabetes, hypertension, and other problems that are often treated with ambulatory care (Weissman et al., 1992).

Use Patterns by People of Color.   Finally, surveys also show differences in use patterns by race and ethnicity. The U.S. Public Health Service (Krauss et al., 1999) found that Latina/os (60 percent) and African Americans (62 percent) were less likely to use ambulatory medical care than whites (75 percent). Latina/os were less likely than African Americans or whites to have a usual source of hospital-based and office-based care. Given their socioeconomic status, Latina/os were also more likely than other groups to be unable to afford and therefore access health care services (Kass et al., 1996). For example, in 1996 only 70 percent of Latinas in California received prenatal care in their first trimester of pregnancy. In comparison, 82 percent of white and Asian American women and 74 percent of African American women received prenatal care (Latino Coalition for a Healthy California, 1996).

People of color also have different utilization patterns for mental health services. The surgeon general's 2001 report on mental health, culture, and race shows that people of color are disproportionately represented among the large population of individuals (two out of three) who are in need of mental health services, but fail to receive treatment. For Latina/os, who have the lowest rate of health insurance among people of color, language barriers further reduce access. For all people of color, the stigma of mental illness is a "further shame" that may be too much to bear (U.S. Department of Health and Human Services, 2001).

U.S. Indian Health Service.   The IHS administers medical care through twelve area offices across the country. Health care services are provided directly by IHS staff or tribal groups, or indirectly through contracts with private providers. In 1996, the IHS operated thirty-six hospitals, sixty-one health centers, four school health centers, and forty-eight health stations (Indian Health Service, 1998). The IHS covers fees for services that are not reimbursed by third-party payers, including Medicare, Medicaid, and private insurers.

In a 1993 study of five IHS areas, the U.S. General Accounting Office (1993) found that "basic clinical services" delivered in hospitals and clinics were more available than were preventive and dental care. Treatment services, such as prenatal care and intensive care were generally available to approximately 90 percent of the population. Diagnostic services such as biopsies, radiology, and laboratory tests were also generally available to about 80 percent of the population. Preventive services, such as family planning, cancer screening, and diabetes education and services, were far more limited, however, and available to only 60 percent of the population. The least available service identified by the study was dental care. Both adults and children found it difficult to access dental care in all five of the IHS service areas. Untreated cases were backlogged and few staff members were available.

The GAO study identified a number of factors to explain the lack of access to preventive care. First, contract care was more difficult to access than direct care. Patients were required to seek alternative sources of payment, such as Medicaid, and many found the enrollment procedures to be unwieldy and confusing. In addition, physicians were often unwilling to accept the service fees offered by Medicaid. The more restrictive criteria for eligibility for contract-care services (described earlier) also created problems (U.S. General Accounting Office, 1993).

A second factor was geography. As mentioned earlier, many reservations are large and underdeveloped, and travel to health care facilities can be extremely difficult. For example, in Alaska, nearly half the population would need to travel by air to see a physician due to the lack of roadways and the distance. In addition, coverage of patient travel costs varies among the service areas and often depends on available funding.

The GAO also found that access to preventive services often depended on the existence of alternative health services, such as Medicaid. For example, the IHS in California had a large Medicaid population within its service area and could therefore afford to use more of its funding on diagnostic and preventive services (U.S. Government Accounting Service, 1993).

Community Benefits: The "Free Care" Safety Net

For most of the millions of people who are uninsured in the United States, medical care is simply unaffordable. For them, the only available health care is hospital "charity care." The continued existence of a "free" hospital care safety net is of growing concern, however. What is "free care" or "charity care," and why is it a growing concern? Essentially, charity care is hospital care provided at no cost to patients who cannot afford to pay for the services rendered. Hospitals may provide reduced-cost services to patients who can afford partial payment. In general, however, hospitals do not expect to be reimbursed for the free or charity care they provide to the community.

Although there are laws and legal obligations that require hospitals to provide free care, there are no standard rules, regulations, or laws that govern hospital practices across the country. For example, nonprofit hospitals are generally exempt from local, state, and federal taxes and, in return, are obliged to provide some form of service to the state or local community. Hospitals often meet this obligation by providing some degree of free or reduced-cost care.

States and communities have also expected community benefits from nonprofit insurers and health plans. For example, when Blue Cross Blue Shield was originally structured as a nonprofit institution, it was an insurer "of last resort" and also provided community benefits. Some older health maintenance plans, such as Kaiser Permanente, were also originally organized as charitable nonprofit institutions and expected to contribute to the community's health needs. For nonprofit health plans, community benefits take the form of subsidies for premiums, health screenings and immunization programs, or health education activities.

However, changes in the delivery of health care have reduced the level of community benefits. "Contrary to common belief, 80 percent of uninsured people are not receiving any reduced charge or free health services" (Kaiser Family Foundation, 1998). As discussed in the chapter on managed care, the current competitive market has made it more difficult for physicians and hospitals to finance uncompensated care. To compete for contracted services, health plans (which include doctors and hospitals) accept lower payment rates. This, in turn, makes it more difficult for doctors and hospitals to provide free care. According to Cunningham and associates (1999), in 1996 and 1997, physicians in the Washington, DC, area who received 85 percent or more of their income from managed care plans provided only 5.2 hours per month of charity care. In comparison, physicians who received no income from managed care plans provided 10.0 hours per month of charity care to the community.

The managed care market also affects hospitals. In the past fifteen years, many hospitals that have traditionally been organized on a nonprofit or local government basis have been purchased by private, for-profit organizations. For example, until the 1998 decision by Columbia/HCA to close many of its hospitals, Columbia/HCA owned 310 hospitals (Community Catalyst, 1998a). One study of such conversions conducted by Needleman and colleagues (1999) found that charity care declined substantially in Florida between 1981 and 1996. Public hospitals provided much less uncompensated care after their conversion to for-profit status.

Finally, the complexity of hospital structures also contributes to the confusion surrounding free care. Today's hospitals are made up of multiple subsidiaries, each with its own policies and procedures. Some services may be offered as free care, while others are not. For example, an individual patient may find that the hospital stay was free, yet is charged for diagnostic work or other medical services (Community Catalyst, 1998b).

Highlights

- The United States remains the only industrialized nation that does not have a system of health care with access to services for all of its citizens, regardless of race, ethnicity, gender, age, employment status, or income.

- In the United States, the two primary means of access to health insurance are employment-based coverage and government-sponsored programs, primarily Medicare and Medicaid. Roughly 60 percent of the population relies on employment-based health insurance, whereas 25 percent relies on government-sponsored health insurance.

- The remaining 15 percent of the population is uninsured. Historically, hospitals have provided some "free care" or "charity care" to people who lack insurance. However, in the age of managed care, community benefits have declined substantially.

■ Given the structure of our health care system, the primary reasons for lack of insurance are rising costs and declining coverage by employers. These conditions have caused more and more people to lack access to health insurance. Those affected most are working adults with moderate incomes and their dependent family members.

■ In an effort to meet the rising cost of health insurance, employers have eliminated benefits, reduced coverage for family members, or increased the employee share of insurance premiums.

■ Although retired adults benefit from the Medicare program and poor adults and their children are eligible for Medicaid, those at greatest risk for lack of health insurance are the so-called near poor with incomes between 100 percent and 300 percent of the federal poverty level.

■ Health insurance coverage also varies by employment status, income level, size of employer, and type of employment. Full-time workers are far more likely than are temporary and part-time workers to have coverage, yet not all full-time workers receive health insurance benefits. Small employers have a much harder time than large employers in providing coverage, and nonprofessional, nonunionized workers are less likely to receive health insurance benefits.

■ Age, race, and ethnicity also play a considerable role in access to coverage. Latina/os and African Americans lack health insurance more than other racial groups, whereas young adults ages 18–24 are in the age group at greatest risk for lack of coverage.

■ The lack of health insurance has an adverse effect on utilization of health care services, particularly early and preventive care. Those without insurance seek care more infrequently, are more apt to postpone or avoid care, and, as a result, are more likely to be hospitalized for conditions that could have been treated with ambulatory care. Latina/os and African Americans are more susceptible to these utilization patterns.

Websites to Obtain Updated and Additional Information

www.census.gov/population
U.S. Census Bureau
Current Population Surveys

www.kff.org
Kaiser Family Foundation
Commission on Medicaid and the Uninsured

www.ahrq.gov
Agency for Healthcare Research and Quality U.S. Department of Health
    and Human Services
Medical Expenditure Panel Survey

REFERENCES

Aiu, P. (2000, June–July). Comparing Native Hawaiians to the Nation. *Closing the Gap*. Washington, DC: U.S. Department of Health and Human Services.

Altman, S. H., Reinhardt, U. E., and Shields, A. E. (Eds.). (1998). *The Future U.S. Healthcare System: Who Will Care for the Poor and Uninsured?* Chicago: Health Administration Press.

Bennefield, R. (1995). *Dynamics of Economic Well-Being: Health Insurance 1991 to 1994*. U.S. Bureau of the Census, Current Population Report 70–43. Washington, DC: U.S. Government Printing Office.

Billings, J., Anderson, G. M., and Newman, L. S. (1996). Recent Findings on Preventable Hospitalizations. *Health Affairs, 13,* 3, 239–249.

Bovee, T. (1992, September 18). Census Finds Asian-Americans More Devoted to Education. *Concord Monitor,* p. A5.

Brooke, J. (1995, October 15). In the Budget Talk from Washington, Indians See the Cruelest Cuts of All. *New York Times,* p. 10.

Carrasquillo, O., Himmelstein, D. U., Woolhandler, S., and Bor, D. H. (1999, January 14). A Reappraisal of Private Employers' Role in Providing Health Insurance. *New England Journal of Medicine, 340,* 2.

Centers for Disease Control and Prevention. (1998, January 30). State-Specific Prevalence Estimates of Uninsured and Underinsured Pension-Behavioral Risk-Factor Surveillance System, 1995. *Mobidity and Mortality Weekly Report, 47,* 3, 51–55 (Online). Available: www.cdc.gov/mmwr.

Chen, J., Rathore, S. S., Radford, M. J., Wang, Y., and Krumholz, H. M. (2001, May 10). Racial Differences in the use of Cardiac Catheterization After Acute Myocardial Infarction. *New England Journal of Medicine, 344,* 19, 1443–1449.

Community Catalyst. (1998a, August). The Columbia/HCA Hospital Sales: An Opportunity to Re-Focus on Community Benefits. *States of Health, 8,* 4. Boston, MA.

Community Catalyst. (1998b, September). Strengthening the Free Care Safety Net. *States of Health, 8,* 5. Boston, MA.

Cooper, P. F. and Schone, B. S. (1997, November–December). More Offers, Few Takers for Employment-Based Heath Insurance 1987 and 1996. *Health Affairs, 16,* 6, 142–150.

Cunningham, P. J., Grossman, J. M., St. Peter, R. F., and Lesser, C. S. (1999). Managed Care and Physician's Provision to Charity. *JAMA, 281,* 12, 1087–1093.

Deane, D. (1998, October 7). Promised Land Yields Bitter Fruit for Some—Hmong Immigrants from Laos Wrestle with Great Difficulties Assimilating to Life, Laws in U.S. *USA Today,* p. 10A.

Donelan, K., Blendon, R. J., Hill, C. A., Hoffman, C., Rowland, D., Frankel, M., and Altman, D. (1996). Public Opinion and Health Care—Whatever Happened to the Health Insurance Crisis in the United States? Voices from a National Survey. *JAMA, 276,* 16, 1346–1350.

Doob, C. B. (1996). *Racism: An American Cauldron*. New York: HarperCollins. Employee Benefit Research Institute. (1997, May). *Trends in Health Insurance Coverage*. (No. 185). Washington, DC: Employee Benefit Research Insitute.

Families USA. (1999). *Losing Health Insurance—The Unintended Consequences of Welfare Reform.* Washington, DC: Families USA.

Gabel, J. et al. (1999, February). *Health Benefits in 1998 for Small Employers. A Report for the Kaiser Family Foundation.* Washington, DC: Kaiser Family Foundation.

Goldberg, C. (1997, January 30). Hispanic Households Struggle as Poorest of the Poor in U.S. *New York Times*, p. A1.

Hall, A., Collins, K. S., and Glied, S. (1999). *Employee-Sponsored Health Insurance: Implications for Minority Workers.* New York: The Commonwealth Fund.

Hannan, E. L., Kilburm, H., O'Donnell, J. F., Lukacic, G., and Shields, E. P. (1991). Interacial Access to Selected Cardiac Procedures for Patients Hospitalized with Coronary Artery Disease in New York State. *Med Care, 29,* 430–444.

Harvard University/NORC/Kaiser Family Foundation. (1995). *Getting Behind the Numbers on Access to Care.* Washington, DC: Kaiser Family Foundation.

Health Insurance Association of America. (1999). *HIAA Study: 1 Out of 5 Non-Elderly Americans Will Lack Health Insurance in 2007* (Online). Available at www.hiaa.org.

Himmelstein, D. U. and Woolhandler, S. (1994). *The National Health Program Book: A Source Guide for Advocates.* Monroe, ME: Common Courage.

Iglehart, J. K. (1997, May/June). Changing with the Times: The Views of Bruce C. Vladeck. *Health Affairs 16,* 3, 58–71.

Indian Health Services. (1998). *1997 Trends in Indian Health.* Washington, DC: U.S. Department of Health and Human Services.

Jang, M., Lee, E., and Woo, K. (1998, May). Income, Language, and Citizenship Status: Factors Affecting the Health Care Access and Utilization of Chinese Americans. *Health and Social Work, 23,* 2, 136–145.

Jaret, C. (1995). *Contemporary Racial and Ethnic Relations.* New York: HarperCollins.

Jiang, S. P. (2000, June–July). Correcting the Visions of Paradise. *Closing the Gap.* Washington, DC: U.S. Department of Health and Human Services.

Kaiser Commission on Future of Medicaid. (1997, December). *Legislative Summary: State Children's Health Insurance Program.* Washington, DC: Kaiser Family Foundation.

Kaiser Commission on Medicaid and the Uninsured. (2000a, May). *The Uninsured and Their Access to Health Care.* Washington, DC: Kaiser Family Foundation.

Kaiser Commission on Medicaid and the Uninsured. (2000b, June). *Health Insurance Coverage and Access to Care Among American Indians and Alaska Natives.* Washington, DC: Kaiser Family Foundation.

Kaiser Commission on Medicaid and the Uninsured (1998a, July). *Uninsured Facts: The Uninsured and their Access to Health Care.* Washington, DC: Kaiser Family Foundation.

Kaiser Commission on Medicaid and the Uninsured (1998b, September). *How Well Does the Unemployment-Based Health Insurance System Work for Low-Income Families?* Washington, DC: Kaiser Family Foundation.

Kaiser Family Foundation. (2000). *Employer Health Benefits, 2000 Summary of Annual Survey.* Washington, DC: Kaiser Family Foundation,

Kaiser Family Foundation. (1998). *Uninsured in America, Key Facts about Gaps in Health Insurance Coverage Today.* Washington, DC: Kaiser Family Foundation.

Kaiser Family Foundation. (1997, December). *Working Families at Risk: Coverage, Access, Costs, and Worries, Kaiser/Commonwealth National Survey of Health Insurance.* Washington, DC: Kaiser Family Foundation.

Kass, B. L., Weinick, R. M., and Monheit, A. C. (1996). *Racial and Ethnic Differences in Health. MEPS Chart Book No. 2* (AHCPR Pub. No. 99-0001). Rockville, MD: Agency for Health Care Policy and Research.

Kottak, C. (1994). *Cultural Anthropology*, 6th ed. New York: McGraw-Hill.

Krauss, N., Machlin, S., and Kass, B. (1999). *Use of Health Care Services, 1996. MEPS Research Findings No. 7* (AHCPR Pub. No. 99-0018). Rockville, MD: Agency for Health Care Policy and Research.

Latino Coalition for a Healthy California. (1996). *Latinos and Access to Health Care in California* (Online). Available at www.lchc.org.

Levan, R., Brown, E. R., Lara, L., and Wyn, R. (1998, December). *Nearly One-Fifth of Urban Americans Lack Health Insurance.* Los Angeles, CA: UCLA Center for Health Policy Research.

McLemore, S. D. and Romok, H. D. (1998). *Racial and Ethnic Relations in America* (5th ed.). Boston: Allyn and Bacon.

Mills, R. (1999). Health Insurance Coverage. Current Population Reports. U.S. Bureau of the Census (Online). Available at census.gov/population/socdemo/.

National Conference of State Legislators and National Governors Association. (1999). *State Children's Health Insurance Program, 1998 Annual Report.* Washington, DC: National Conference of State Legislators and National Governors Association.

National Institute of Medicine Pacific Partnerships for Health. (1998). *Charting a Course for the 21st Century.* Washington, DC: National Academy Press.

Needleman, J., Lamphere, J., and Chollet, D. (1999, July–August). Uncompensated Care and Hospital Conversions in Florida. *Health Affairs, 18,* 4, 125–133.

Newacheck, P. W., Hughes, D. C., and Cisternas, M. (1995, Spring). Data Watch: Children and Health Insurance: An Overview of Recent Trends. *Health Affairs, 14,* 1, 244–275.

O'Hare, W. P., Pollard, K. M., Mann, T. L., and Kent, M. M. (1991, July). African Americans in the 1990s. *Population Bulletin, 46,* 29–30. Washington, DC: Population Reference Bureau.

Pear, R. (1999, May 9). Many States Slow to Use Children's Insurance Fund. *New York Times,* pp. A1, A16.

Preston, J. (1996, April 14). Hospitals Look on Charity Care as Unaffordable Option of Past. *The New York Times,* p. A1.

Reschovsky, J. D. and Cunningham, P. J. (1998, August). CHIPping Away at the Problem of Uninsured Children. *Issue Brief, No. 14.* Washington, DC: Center for Health Systems Change.

Rhoades, J. and Chu, M. (2000, December). *Health Insurance Status of the Civilian Noninstitutionalized Population. MEPS Research Design Findings No. 14* (AHRQ Pub. No. 01-0011). Rockville, MD: Agency for Healthcare Research and Quality.

Rosenthal, E. (1995, June 26). Two Hospitals Charging Poor for Medicine. *The New York Times,* B1.

Ross, H. (2000, June–July). New Federal Standards Recognize Native Hawaiians and Other Pacific Islanders as Distinct Group. *Closing the Gap.* Washington, DC: U.S. Department of Health and Human Services.

Rovner, J. (1997, May). The Uninsured: An American Time Bomb. *Business and Health, Supplement, 15,* 5, 55–59.

Rowland, D. (1994, February 10). *Uninsured in America* (Testimony before Committee on Finance, U.S. Senate Hearing on Health Coverage for the Uninsured). Washington, DC: Kaiser Family Foundation.

Shearer, G. (1998, January). *Hidden from View: The Growing Burden of Health Care Costs.* Washington, DC: Consumers Union.

Stelzer, I. M. (1994, January 25). There Is No Health Care Crisis. *Wall Street Journal,* p. A12.

Thorpe, K. (1999, March–April) Why are Workers Uninsured? Employer-Sponsored Health Insurance in 1997. *Health Affairs, 18,* 2, 213–219.

Thorpe, K. (1997, October). The Rising Number of Uninsured Workers: An Approaching Crisis in Health Care Financing. Washington, DC: National Coalition on Health Care.

U.S. Census Bureau. (2000). *Race and Ethnic Classifications Used in Census 2000 and Beyond* (Online). Available at www.census.gov/population/socdemo/race.

U.S. Census Bureau. (1987–2000). March Demographic Profiles. *Current Population Surveys* (Online). Available at www.census.gov/population/socdemo/.

U.S. Census Bureau. (1996). Asian and Pacific Islander Population in the U.S.: March. *Current Population Reports* (Online). Available at www.census.gov/population/socdemo/race.

U.S. Department of Health and Human Services. (2001, August). *Mental Health: Culture, Race, and Ethnicity* (Supplement to Surgeon General's Report on Mental Health). Rockville, MD: U.S. Department of Health and Human Services, Substance Abuse and Mental Health Services Administration, Center for Mental Health Services, National Institute of Mental Health.

U.S. General Accounting Office. (1995, July). *Health Insurance for Children—Many Remain Uninsured Despite Medicaid Expansion* (GAO/HEHS-95-175). Washington, DC: U.S. Government Printing Office.

U.S. General Accounting Office. (1993, April). Indian Health Service—Basic Services Mostly Available. Substance Abuse Problems Need Attention (GAO/HRD-93-48). Washington, DC: U.S. Government Printing Office.

U.S. General Accounting Office. (1992, January). Hispanic Access to Health Care—A Significant Gap Exists (GAO/PEMD-92-6). Washington, DC: U.S. Government Printing Office.

Weinick, R. M. and Drilea, S. K. (1998). Usual Sources of Health Care and Barriers to Care. *Statistical Bulletin Metropolitan Insurance Companies, 789,* 1, 11–17.

Weissman, J. S., Gatsonis, C., and Epstein, A. M. (1992). Rates of Avoidable Hospitalization by Insurance Status in Massachusetts and Maryland. *Journal of the American Medical Association, 268,* 2388–2394.

Wenneker, M. and Epstein, A. (1989). Racial Inequalities in the Use of Procedures for Patients with Ischemic Heart Disease in Massachusetts. *Journal of the American Medical Association, 261,* 253–257.

Wiatrowski, W. J. (1995, June). Who Really Has Access to Employer-Provided Health Benefits? *Monthly Labor Review, 118,* 6, 36–44.

Wilson, W. J. (1987). *The Truly Disadvantaged: The Inner City, the Underclass, and Public Policy.* Chicago: University of Chicago Press.

Zaldivar, R. A. (1991, June 12). New Variety Seen among U.S. Asians. *The New York Times,* pp. A1, A16.

4 The Growth and Development of Managed Care

From the beginning, health care in the United States was organized on an individualistic and private basis. The original physicians were entrepreneurs who learned their craft by apprenticing with established physicians (Patel and Rushefsky, 1999). As medicine developed and became more professional, physicians remained committed to this individualistic approach and jealously guarded against encroachment from "private corporations" and "agencies of government" (Starr, 1982, p. 200). Physicians also strongly supported a fee-for-service approach, which reimburses providers for each service (Patel and Rushefsky, 1999).

The result was what Dranove (2000) calls "Marcus Welby medicine." General practitioners working in individual offices dominated the health care system. Individuals would visit the physician of their choice, who would diagnose the problem and prescribe a course of care (Dranove, 2000). The physician would bill the patient directly for this treatment, based on the number of services provided. If a patient were sick enough to require hospital care, this was available as well. Although hospitals were generally independent institutions, "physicians held the strings to the hospital purse, since they influenced the patient's choice of facility" (Robinson, 1999, p. 20).

This system was reinforced by the insurance industry, which generally offered coverage on an indemnity basis. In exchange for a premium, individuals were reimbursed specific amounts for the cost of various services (Robinson, 1999). Blue Cross offered a slightly different arrangement, reimbursing physicians directly (Robinson, 1999). Regardless of the approach, insurers did not intervene between physician and patient and reimbursed physicians retrospectively, "on the basis of their usual charges" and the prevailing fee structure "in the community" (Robinson, 1999, p. 22).

Although this Marcus Welby model was the dominant one, there were exceptions. During the 1800s, fraternal organizations, unions, and some industrialists contracted with physicians to offer services on a prepaid basis to their members or employees (Friedman, 1996). During the 1930s, Henry J. Kaiser, a leading industrialist, began offering prepaid health care to his workers (Starr, 1982). "For the first time, workers' families were given full medical coverage, wives for seven cents a day and children for twenty-five cents a week" (Kotelchuck, 1976, p. 365). A decade later, Kaiser built ships for the war effort and again established clinics for his workers (Kotelchuck, 1976).

After the war, Kaiser opened his plan to the public, calling it the Kaiser-Permanente Plan; by 1969, Kaiser-Permanente had two and a half million subscribers (Kotelchuck, 1976). Kaiser-Permanente contracted with groups of physicians to offer services to its members, and Kaiser-Permanente owned the facilities in which these physicians worked; for this reason, Kaiser became known as a group-model HMO (Davis, Collins, and Morris, 1994).

Kaiser-Permanente was not the only type of prepaid group practice. During the early postwar years, a group of Seattle farmers and workers created the Group Health Cooperative of Puget Sound (GHCPS) (Starr, 1982). By the 1980s, GHCPS had grown to 320,000 members and was "run by a community board elected by its consumer-members" (Rachlis and Kushner, 1989, p. 224). GHCPS was known as a staff-model HMO, because physicians were employees of the organization.

The AMA strongly opposed prepaid group practices and went to great lengths to suppress them (Starr, 1982). In 1938, the federal government indicted the association and its affiliates for violating antitrust laws. Although the Supreme Court upheld these charges, the AMA succeeding in convincing state legislatures to enact laws hindering the development of prepaid group practices (Starr, 1982).

The Health Maintenance Act (HMO) of 1973

As noted in Chapter 2, health care costs increased dramatically during the 1960s. Between 1960 and 1970, national health expenditures grew by 174 percent and went from 5.3 percent of gross domestic product to 7.4 percent (Levit et al., 1994). Much of this increase took place after the enactment of Medicare and Medicaid. Between 1966 and 1970, when the consumer price index increased by 19.1 percent, health care costs increased by 29.1 percent (Kotelchuck, 1976). Physicians' fees and hospital charges grew even more rapidly. In July 1969, President Richard Nixon warned that the nation faced "a breakdown in our medical system" (cited in Starr, 1982, p. 381).

What caused the increase in health care costs? Much of the problem was due to the peculiar reimbursement structure adopted by Medicare. To ensure the bill's enactment, Lyndon Johnson made extraordinary concessions to the American Hospital Association. The administration not only agreed to reimburse hospitals retroactively, for their costs, but also agreed to allow them to include in these costs expenditures for new equipment and facilities (Starr, 1982, p. 375). Hospitals were also able to choose "'fiscal intermediaries,'" in most cases Blue Cross, to oversee and regulate billing and payments (Starr, 1982). "Since the elderly are the medically neediest members of society and require the most invasive procedures, Medicare clients immediately constituted more than 75 percent of all hospitalized patients" (Garrett, 2000, p. 347). Hospital expenditures and incomes grew dramatically between 1966 and 1970 (Garrett, 2000).

Johnson also sought to placate physicians. The law itself explicitly prevented the government from exercising "'any supervision or control'" over "'compensation'" to institutions or individuals "'providing health services'" (Starr, 1986, p. 110). Instead, physicians were reimbursed on the basis of their "customary" fee structure and were even allowed to balance bill, or charge patients more than Medicare paid (Starr, 1986). In short, as Garrett (2000) notes, Medicare effectively placed "hospitals and physicians," as well as Blue Cross, "in the driver's seat of cost control" (p. 346).

The Nixon administration, in an effort to bring costs under control, turned to Paul Ellwood, a physician from Minnesota. Ellwood had long criticized the fee-for-service system, which he believed promoted inefficiency and waste by encouraging doctors to provide too much care (Starr, 1982). Ellwood argued that the government should encourage new incentives through the development of prepaid group practices, which, in exchange for an annual fee, would provide "comprehensive" health care services to their members (Ellwood et al., 1976). These prepaid group practices, or "health maintenance organizations" (HMOs), as Ellwood called them, would reward physicians for preventing illness and keeping "people healthy" (Ellwood et al., 1976, p. 348).

With encouragement from Nixon and others, support for HMOs began to grow. Rothfield (1976) noted that in 1973 *Fortune* magazine observed that "HMOs have expanded and proliferated throughout the nation at an unprecedented rate" (p. 352). He estimated that by "the mid-1980s," 50 million people might belong to HMOs and noted that "Blue Cross alone" hoped "to have 280 HMOs in operation by then" (Rothfeld, 1976, p. 353). In 1971, the Nixon administration created an office to distribute funds for the "planning and development" of HMOs (Rothfeld, 1976).

Nixon also redefined the nature of prepaid health care. In the traditional prepaid plans, physicians generally worked "exclusively" for the organization, either as salaried employees (GHCPS) or as part of a group (Kaiser) (Dranove, 2000). The term *health maintenance organization,* however, referred not only to this type of plan but also to independent practice associations, which reimbursed "independent physicians" on a fee-for-service basis (Starr, 1982). In addition, the traditional prepaid plans were nonprofits. However, the Nixon administration encouraged the involvement of "banks, Wall Street investors," and other for-profit entities in the HMO business (Rothfeld, 1976, p. 354).

Congress enacted the HMO Act of 1973 to promote the development of HMOs (Kronenfeld and Whicker, 1984). The act overturned state laws restricting prepaid group practices, subsidized "HMO start-ups," and required businesses (with twenty-five or more workers) that provide coverage to their employees to offer an HMO option along with indemnity insurance (Robinson, 1999). The act also required federally assisted HMOs to offer comprehensive benefits, allow consumer input in governance, and charge no more than "traditional forms of health insurance" (Patel and Rushefsky, 1999, p. 173). The HMO Act was the opening volley in what Fuchs (1993) calls the "revolution in health care financing," a determined effort to root out inefficiency and waste in the health care system (p. 187).

From HMOs to Managed Care

Despite the HMO Act, HMOs grew slowly, and through the 1970s they were confined largely to the West Coast and Minnesota (Dranove, 2000). Toward the end of the decade, Luft (1978) published data showing that traditional HMOs, such as Kaiser, were less expensive than fee-for-service medicine. In a review of the literature, he found that individuals belonging to HMOs had premium and out-of-pocket costs that were 10 percent to 40 percent below those for individuals with other types of coverage (Luft, 1978). Much of this difference was due to hospitalization rates, which were about a third lower for individuals in HMOs (Luft, 1978). Although other studies confirmed Luft's findings, it remained unclear whether the HMOs' advantage was due to greater efficiency, reduced quality, or healthier populations (Dranove, 2000).

The same year that Luft's study appeared, Alain Enthoven, a Stanford professor, and an official in the Carter administration, proposed a new HMO strategy, the Consumer Choice Health Plan (CCHP) (Enthoven, 1978). The CCHP was based in part on the Federal Employees Health Benefits Program (FEHBP), which covers most federal employees (Enthoven, 1993). Under the FEHBP, workers choose from a menu of "competing health plans" and the government pays a "fixed" share of the premium cost (Robinson, 1999, p. 40). An individual who selects an inexpensive plan thus pays less than does someone who selects a more expensive one. Under the CCHP, employers paid a share of the premium cost. Enthoven assumed that, given a choice, workers would prefer low-cost HMOs to more expensive indemnity coverage (Robinson, 1999). Although versions of the CCHP were introduced in Congress, they were unsuccessful (Patel and Rushefsky, 1999).

The "'competition revolution,'" and the move away from open-ended financing, accelerated during the 1980s, as health care costs continued to grow (Fuchs, 1993). In 1982, Congress enacted the Tax Equity and Fiscal Responsibility Act (TEFRA), which made changes in Medicare that resulted a year later in the introduction of the Medicare Prospective Payment System (PPS) (Patel and Rushefsky, 1999). As noted in Chapter 2, the PPS created a fee schedule, so that hospitals knew in advance precisely how much Medicare would reimburse them (Patel and Rushefsky, 1999). TEFRA also allowed HMOs to enroll Medicare beneficiaries, though a great number of older adults continued to prefer the traditional, fee-for-service Medicare.

It was also during the 1980s that preferred provider organizations, or PPOs, developed (Dranove, 2000). PPOs consist of networks of providers who remain in private practice and receive payment on a fee-for-service basis, though often at discounted rates (Dranove, 2000). A consumer obtaining care from providers within the network, that is, from preferred providers, owes only a small copayment; a consumer who obtains care outside the network must pay a higher amount. Because "preferred providers" are guaranteed a steady stream of patients, they have an incentive to reduce their fees (Dranove, 2000).

In the beginning, PPOs were hindered by state laws making it illegal for insurers to refuse to negotiate agreements with "any willing provider" (Dranove, 2000). If insurers were unable to discriminate among physicians, they would also be unable to "boost volumes" for preferred providers. Providers then would have no incentive to charge less or change their practice patterns. With California leading the way, the states began changing their laws "to permit selective contracting by insurers" (p. 70). Large employers also began self-insuring, or creating their own health care plans, which under federal law are exempt from state regulation (Dranove, 2000).

By the mid-1980s, the concept of managed care had emerged to refer to a range of efforts to control costs. Ultimately, managed care relies on three techniques: selective contracting, innovative incentives, and utilization review (UR) (Dranove, 2000). With selective contracting, insurers enter agreements with providers offering the lowest prices, forcing providers to compete among themselves, to the benefit of insurers and, in theory, consumers. By innovative incentives, Dranove (2000) means the new forms of reimbursement introduced by prepaid health care. In staff-model HMOs, providers receive a salary and have no incentive to overtreat patients. Under capitated systems, providers receive a flat sum (and no more) for each patient and there is an incentive to undertreat patients. This is a far cry from the fee-for-service system. Finally, UR refers to techniques aimed at reducing unwarranted care, such as "preadmission screening, to determine if the patient should enter the hospital or receive treatment elsewhere" and "surgical second opinion programs" (Dranove, 2000, p. 81).

From Managed Care to Managed Competition

Despite the rise of managed care, health care inflation continued to accelerate. By 1990, national health expenditures equaled 12.1 percent of GDP, up from 8.9 percent in 1980 (Levit et al., 1996). At the same time, 33.4 million people had no coverage for the year and tens of millions more had limited or inadequate coverage (Lee, Soffel, and Luft, 1994). These were clearly related. As health care costs grew, many employers stopped covering their workers or shifted the burden by increasing employees' share of the premium cost and copayments and deductibles (Roberts and Clyde, 1993). Rising health care costs also contributed to the stagnation of wages during the 1980s, as employers sought to make up ground by paying workers less (White House Domestic Policy Council, 1993). This made it even more difficult for workers to afford health care coverage.

During the early 1990s, Enthoven, Ellwood, and others began to advocate an influential plan they called "managed competition" (Iglehart, 1994). Managed competition would transform the health care system into an "array of managed care plans," which would compete for patients based on cost and quality (Enthoven and Kronick, 1994, p. 286). This new system would be regulated by "quasi-public" agencies, which would promote competition and certify plans offering a minimum benefit package (Enthoven and Kronick, 1994). Employers would contribute 80 percent of the cost of insuring their workers in an average plan, with employees contributing the other 20 percent, and the government covering individuals without jobs.

In the final analysis, the success or failure of managed competition, as the new approach was called, hinged on whether managed care actually could control costs. Enthoven (1993) believed it could, citing studies showing that "Group Health Cooperative of Puget Sound cared for its randomly assigned patients for a cost 28 percent below that for comparable patients assigned to a fee-for-service plan" (Enthoven, 1993, p. 37).

The data were not clear-cut, however. The Congressional Research Service (CRS) found that staff- and group-model HMOs were only about 15 percent cheaper than indemnity plans and suggested that this difference was largely due to one-time savings from lower hospital costs (CRS Issue Brief, 1993). The CRS also reported IPAs, PPOs, and other forms of managed care achieved "much smaller savings" than traditional prepaid plans (CRS Issue Brief, 1993, p. 11).

Critics of managed competition argued that managed care organizations (MCOs) faced the same "cost pressures as other insurers" (CRS Issue Brief, 1993, p. 11). Newhouse (1993) contended that the public was less concerned with the "level" of health care spending than with its "rate of growth" (Newhouse, 1993, p. 155). Since the 1940s, "real health spending" has risen by "roughly 4 percent per year in each decade" (except for the 1960s, when it rose by 6 percent per year) (Newhouse, 1993, p. 155). Newhouse (1993) attributed "the bulk of the cost increase" to "technological advances," which explained why HMO and fee-for-service costs were "rising at a similar rate" despite lower *levels* of spending among staff- and group-model HMOs (Newhouse, 1993, p. 162).

These concerns were generally disregarded, however, and managed competition was widely heralded as the solution to the nation's health care problems (Iglehart, 1994). President George Bush "included elements" of managed competition in his proposal for health care reform, and the Conservative Democratic Forum developed a managed competition plan, which was introduced in Congress as the Cooper bill (H.R. 5936) (CRS Issue Brief, 1993). California's insurance commissioner, John Garamendi, also developed a managed competition proposal (CRS Issue Brief, 1993).

As noted in Chapter 2, Bill Clinton incorporated elements of managed competition in his Health Security Act. However, there were crucial differences between Clinton's approach and the Enthoven/Jackson Hole version of managed competition (Starr and Zelman, 1993). To control costs, Clinton proposed competition, managed care, and, as a "backstop," a limit on the rate of growth of insurance premiums (Zelman, 1994). Enthoven was highly critical of these premium caps and believed they would doom Clinton's plan to failure (Enthoven and Singer, 1994). He characterized the Health Security Act as "a single-payer system in Jackson Hole clothing," which relied on "the heavy hand of government control," rather than the market, "to control costs" (Enthoven and Singer, 1994, p. 81).

By the mid-1990s, health care inflation seemed to have moderated (Huskamp and Newhouse, 1994). "Spending in the year 2000 will be approximately $300 billion below projections made by the Congressional Budget Office in 1993" (Dranove, 2000, p. 84). Many analysts believe that managed care played an essential role in this development (Dranove, 2000). The Congressional Budget

Office (1997) concluded that the rise of managed care, and the growth of competition, had "caused premiums for all types of health plans, including fee-for-service ones, to increase more slowly" (p. 19). Cutler and Sheiner (1997) found that as HMO enrollment in an area increased, health care inflation decreased (largely because of reduced growth in health care costs); the growth of HMOs also tended to reduce spending on new technology.

Again, however, the evidence is mixed (Sullivan, 2000). Aaron (1994) noted that inflation had declined before, particularly when health care reform seemed imminent, only to accelerate again when the threat passed. Jensen and associates (1997) suggested that the decline in the growth of insurance premiums might have had more to do with conditions within the industry than with managed care. Berk and Monheit (2001) suggest that managed care has done little to slow the diffusion of technology.

Even if MCOs do reduce costs, it is not clear why. Critics have long argued that MCOs are able to attract younger and healthier people than fee-for-service medicine (Dranove, 2000). Altman, Cutler, and Zeckhauser (2000) found that, compared with indemnity plans, HMOs' lower costs were due to healthier patients and their ability "to pay lower prices for the same treatment." Glied (1999), in a review of the literature, also concluded that MCOs tend to enroll healthier individuals than does "conventional insurance."

Managed Care Backlash

As scholars and politicians debated the merits of managed competition, managed care became the dominant force in the nation's health care system. By 1995, 73 percent of workers receiving coverage through an employer belonged to managed care plans; 38 percent of these individuals belonged to HMOs, 34 percent to PPOs, and 27 percent to point-of-service plans (Jensen et al., 1997). Physicians' participation in managed care also increased. Between 1988 and 1997, the fraction of physicians in practices with managed care contracts grew from 61 percent to 92 percent (Kaiser Family Foundation, 1998b).

The nature of managed care also changed. Although the original MCOs were nonprofits, during the 1990s, the fastest growing MCOs were for-profit companies (Gabel, 1997). By 1997, 63 percent of HMO enrollees belonged to for-profit plans, up from 46 percent in 1989 (Kaiser Family Foundation, 1998b). The Kaiser Family Foundation (1998b) noted that the "stock market" played "an increasing role in the health industry, and investors' goals to maximize shareholder value have an increased role in driving health care companies' decision-making" (p. 68).

As managed care spread, observers began to express concern about its impact on the quality of care (Eckholm, 1994; Kassirer, 1995). Kane, Turnbull, and Schoen (1996), in case studies of IPAs and network-model HMOs in Boston, Los Angeles, and Philadelphia, found little connection between a plan's "market success" and the "quality of care" it "provided" (p. ii). Similarly, Gabel (1997), in a discussion of changes in HMOs during the 1990s, observed that the "market" did not seem to penalize plans that failed to "deliver above-average quality of care" (p. 143). Feldman and Scharfstein (1998) also concluded that MCOs might offer poorer quality care than fee-for-service plans.

Miller and Luft (1997), in a survey of peer-reviewed studies of managed care published between 1993 and 1997, found that HMOs do not necessarily deliver worse care than fee-for-service plans and in some instances provided better care. However, three studies found that HMOs deliver significantly worse care to "patients with chronic conditions or diseases who need care the most" (p. 14). In a sense, these findings were not surprising, since "plans and providers face strong financial disincentives to excel in care for the sickest and most expensive patients" (Miller and Luft, 1997, p. 20). This argument, of course, lends credence to those who argue that managed care primarily reduces costs by treating only the healthiest patients.

A 1999 survey of physicians and nurses provides additional insight into the question of quality (Kaiser Family Foundation, 1999b). Eighty-seven percent of physicians had patients who were refused coverage of "some type" during the previous two years. In more than a third of these cases, according to the physicians, the denials had caused a "serious decline" in a patient's health. Forty-six percent of doctors said that, if a friend or relative were a patient, they would be "very worried" that an MCO would care more "about saving money" than providing the right treatment. Seventy-two percent of physicians and 78 percent of nurses felt managed care had lowered quality of care (Kaiser Family Foundation/ Harvard University School of Public Health, 1999).

Consumers also expressed concern about managed care (Ginsburg, 1998; Davis, Schoen, and Sandman, 1996). In a 1997 survey, Blendon and colleagues (1998) found that 45 percent of the population believed managed care had "decreased" quality of care and 52 percent supported government regulation of MCOs. This "backlash" was based not only on media coverage but also on individuals' personal experience with managed care (Blendon et al., 1998).

In response to these concerns, President Clinton appointed an Advisory Commission on Consumer Protection and Quality in the Health Care Industry in March 1997 (*Consumer Bill of Rights and Responsibilities*, 1997). After extensive hearings, the commission released a report identifying the rights and responsibilities of consumers. These included the right to an adequate choice of provider and to access to emergency care "when and where the need arises" (p. 3).

The report also asserted that patients had a right to "fully participate" in "decisions related to their health care" (*Consumer Bill of Rights and Responsibilities*, 1997, p. 39). This was aimed at financial and contractual arrangements that thwarted communication between physicians and patients. The most publicized of these arrangements were so-called "gag rules," which prevented physicians in HMOs from making patients aware of all treatment options (*Consumer Bill of Rights and Responsibilities*, 1997).

The most controversial section of the report dealt with complaints and appeals. It stated that patients had a right to "a rigorous system of internal review and an independent system of external review" (p. 57). While most health plans had internal review systems, independent, external review systems were relatively rare.

The states were also active in efforts to protect consumers. In 1998, Families USA, an advocacy group, issued a study of state managed care laws (Families USA, 1998). It concluded that there was a lack of uniformity among the states and the laws had been enacted on a "hit or miss" basis. No state had enacted all of the thirteen identified protections, while thirty-three states had enacted between only one and four (Families USA, 1998).

The study also addressed a serious limitation of state efforts, however well intentioned. This was the Employee Retirement Income Security Act (ERISA), which Congress enacted in 1974 to regulate employee pension and benefit plans (Families USA, 1998). The courts have ruled that ERISA prevents states from regulating self-insured health plans, in which an "employer assumes...financial risk for the care provided to its employees rather than simply purchasing coverage from an insurer" (Families USA, 1998, p. 27). Due to ERISA, a third of individuals with employer-based coverage were not protected by state regulations (Families USA, 1998). ERISA also prevents almost anyone with employer-based coverage from suing in state courts for "improper delays or denials of needed health care" (Families USA, 1998, p. 27). Although individuals can sue in federal court, they can seek only "provision of the denied service or the cost of the denied service;" they cannot sue for "compensatory or punitive damages" (p. 28).

During the past few years, Democrats and Republicans have introduced "patients' bill of rights legislation," often on a bipartisan basis (Patel and Rushefsky, 1999). The ultimate point of disagreement has been over the right to sue for compensatory damages, which Democrats generally support, and Republicans oppose. Bipartisan bills granting individuals the right to sue were introduced in the House and the Senate in 2001 (www.ama-assn.org/ama/pub/article/1611-5074.html). The Congressional Budget Office estimated that legislation that includes the right to sue would ultimately increase employers' insurance premiums by an average of 2.6 percent (www.cbo.gov/showdoc.cfm?index=29348&sequence=0&from=7).

Before concluding, it is worth noting that concerns have been raised about the quality of health care generally in the United States (Knox, 1999; Mullan, 2001; Singer, 2000). Berwick (1998) notes that both managed care and fee-for-service are "plagued" by "serious and significant" problems of overuse, underuse, and misuse (p. i). In 1998, more people died from "preventable medical errors" than from "breast cancer, AIDS and motor vehicle accidents *combined*" (emphasis added) (Leape, 2000, p. 2). This is clearly a serious problem, which merits immediate and widespread attention.

Managed Care and Medicare

The Tax Equity and Fiscal Responsibility Act of 1982 allowed approved HMOs to enroll Medicare beneficiaries on a capitated basis. In exchange for a monthly, per-patient payment, Medicare HMOs, or risk plans, agree to provide enrollees the same services guaranteed to traditional, or fee-for-service, beneficiaries. "If a risk plan's projected average cost of providing Medicare services is less than Medicare's payment, then the plan must offer additional benefits of equivalent value" (Medicare Payment Advisory Commission, 1998b). These additional benefits often include prescription drug coverage (in 1999, the cost of purchasing such coverage separately, through a Medigap policy, ran $200 or more a month [Iglehart, 1999]).

Medicare managed care grew slowly; by 1993, only 5 percent of the Medicare population had joined HMOs (Kaiser Family Foundation, 1999a). During the next four years, enrollment accelerated, and by 1997, 14 percent of the Medicare population belonged to HMOs (Kaiser Family Foundation, 1999). Since then, the growth in Medicare HMO enrollment has slowed, and between 1999 and 2001, the number of individuals enrolled in Medicare HMOs fell from 6.1 million to 5.6 million (Kaiser Family Foundation, 2001).

Part of the reason for this decline was a drop in the number of MCOs (Medicare HMOs and other private health plans) participating in Medicare (from 346 in 1998 to 177 in 2001) (Kaiser Family Foundation, 2001). The number of Medicare+ Choice (see next section) enrollees whose plans have stopped "serving their counties" was expected to increase from 327,000 in 2000 to 934,000 in 2001 (Gold, 2000). These withdrawals disproportionately affect vulnerable groups, and many "beneficiaries affected by the HMO withdrawals…experienced a decline in their supplemental benefits, an increase in their premiums, and some disruption in their care arrangements" (Laschober et al., 1999, p. 157).

Medicare+ Choice (Part C)

In 1997, in an effort to expand enrollment in Medicare managed care, Congress, as part of the Balanced Budget Act (BBA), created Medicare Part C, the Medicare+ Choice (M+C) program (see Figure 4.1). M+C expands the types of plans that may be offered under Medicare to include not only HMOs, and other types of coordinated care plans, but also private fee-for-service plans and medical savings accounts (Medicare Payment Advisory Commission, 1998a)

Although the purpose of M+C was to allow beneficiaries a greater choice of plans, it has been a source of controversy and confusion (Patel and Rushefsky, 1999). The private fee-for-service and medical savings account options, in particular, have generated concern (Patel and Rushefsky, 1999). According to Moon (2001), "some" M+C plans have "treated" beneficiaries poorly, "limiting access to new technology" and inappropriately denying care (p. 2). Jane Bryant Quinn, a well-known financial writer, describes M+C as "'the first step'" toward a stratified system of "strict" managed care for lower-income people and "private fee-for-service" for "'wealthier'" people (cited in Patel and Rushefsky, 1999, p. 130). Gold (2001), in an "interim" assessment of whether M+C has met its goals, such as expanding choice and improving measures of quality, concluded that the plan deserves at best a grade of "D."

FIGURE 4.1   New Options in Medicare+ Choice

Preferred Provider Organizations (PPOs)

A network of health care providers established by a health plan/insurer to provide
   services on a fee-for-service basis to a group of enrollees
Rates are negotiated and lower than for nonenrollees
Beneficiaries can receive services outside the network, but must pay for part of it

Provider-Sponsored Organizations (PSOs)

A group of providers and hospitals that establishes its own network and assumes
   financial liability for the plan
Services are provided for enrollees for a fixed cost

Private Fee-for-Service

A private indemnity health insurance policy with coverage no less than Parts A and B
No limitations on providers or hospitals
Monthly premiums paid by Medicare; no limits on monthly premiums charged to
   enrollees
Out-of-pocket costs cannot exceed "average amount" expended in traditional fee-for-
   service
Plan, not Medicare program, determines reimbursement rate for providers and hospitals

Medical Savings Accounts (MSAs): Demonstration Project 1999–2002

A high-deductible ($ thousands) catastrophic plan with monthly premiums paid by
   Medicare
Balance of monthly contributions deposited in a tax-free medical savings account
Beneficiaries draw from their account to cover expenses, including deductibles
If beneficiaries keep 60 percent of the annual deductible in the account, they can
   withdraw tax-free funds for nonhealth purposes
Providers and hospitals set fees
Enrollees may not have a Medigap plan

Source: AARP Federal Health Update, 1997.

Although many observers assume that managed care reduces Medicare costs,
thus far, the data show otherwise. Historically, Medicare payments were based on
a measure known as the adjusted average per capita cost (AAPCC), a "county-level
estimate of the average cost incurred for each beneficiary in fee-for-service" (Medicare Payment Advisory Commission, 1998a, p. 185). Because Medicare HMOs have
healthier patients than does fee-for-service medicine, risk plans receive 95 percent
of the AAPCC. However, studies during the 1990s found that Medicare HMOs
were actually able to treat enrollees for 88 percent to 92 percent of the AAPCC (Iglehart, 1997). The upshot has been that Medicare HMOs have "actually cost the
government money" (Iglehart, 1997, p. 68). Although the Balanced Budget Act of

1997 requires Medicare to develop a more accurate payment mechanism, it is not clear that Medicare will succeed in doing so.

Future Reforms

Looking to the future, Senators John Breaux (D-LA) and Bill Frist (R-TN) have introduced two Medicare reform bills that also rely heavily on managed care (www. ncpssm.org/issues/issues/viewpoints/mc_reform.html#top). Breaux-Frist I, the Medicare Preservation and Improvement Act (S. 357), would transform Medicare into a premium support program (frwebgate.access.gpo.gov/cgi-bin/getdoc. cgi?dbname=107_cong_bills&docid=f:s357is.txt.pdf). Breaux-Frist I was modeled on a proposal developed by Senator Breaux and Representative Bill Thomas (R-CA), in their capacity as chairs of National Bipartisan Commission on the Future of Medicare, which Congress created under the BBA (medicare. commission.gov/ medicare/index.html). Moon (2000)summarizes these proposals as follows:

> Medicare beneficiaries would choose from a range of insurance plans—in this case, both private plans and traditional Medicare. The government would pay part of the premium with the contribution established as a share of the national average premium price. Individuals who choose more expensive plans would pay a substantially higher price than those choosing less expensive plans. The goal would be to give beneficiaries a financial incentive to opt for less expensive plans while offering them a choice among a variety of options (pp. 1–2).

Critics have raised several concerns about these proposals. First, they rely on competition and managed care, which have not resulted in lower costs to Medicare (Families USA, 2000). Second, they would likely increase costs for fee-for-service Medicare and force many beneficiaries into low-cost HMOs, which do not have a good record in caring for older adults with "chronic illness" (Bodenheimer et al., 1999). Third, unless the value of the premium support keeps up with inflation, the proposals will increase beneficiaries' out-of-pocket costs (Bodenheimer et al., 1999).

Breaux-Frist II, the Medicare Prescription Drug and Modernization Act of 2001 (S. 358), is a scaled-down version of Breaux-Frist I (frwebgate.access.gpo.gov/ cgi-in/getdoc.cgi?dbname=107_cong_bills&docid=f:s358is.txt.pdf). Breaux-Frist II "adds a universal prescription drug benefit to Medicare" (www.house.gov/ ways_means/health/107cong/2-28-01/2-28brea.htm). This benefit "offers standard outpatient prescription drug coverage, which includes a $250 deductible, $2,100 in initial coverage and 50% cost-sharing" (www.house.gov/ways_means/ health/107cong/2-28-01/2-28brea.htm). All individuals would receive a 25 percent premium subsidy, with additional subsidies for individuals with incomes up to 150 percent of poverty; no individual would have to pay more than $6,000 (www. house.gov/ways_means/health/107cong/2-28-01/2-28brea.htm). Critics point out that this proposal relies on MCOs, many of which have dropped or increased the cost of Medicare prescription drug coverage, and provides inadequate subsidies for beneficiaries (www.citizen.org/congress/drugs/beaux-frist testimony.html).

The Breaux-Frist bills are likely to remain a focus of discussion and debate. They represent the only bipartisan (though beyond Breaux, few Democrats support them) approach to reforming Medicare, and President Bush also supports them. They also address the heated question of how to add prescription drug coverage to Medicare and offer conservative and business groups an approach to Medicare and prescription drug coverage that deemphasizes the role of the government (www.bettermedicare.org/who/). Conversely, liberal and progressive groups strongly oppose Breaux-Frist as a further step toward undermining fee-for-service Medicare and privatizing the entire system.

Managed Care and Medicaid

Medicaid managed care dates back to the Omnibus Budget Reconciliation Act of 1981, which allowed states to seek federal waivers from their obligation to provide Medicaid recipients fee-for-service coverage. Between 1988 and 1992, in an effort to reduce costs, the states actively pursued managed care and lobbied for further reforms in the waiver process (Families USA, 2001).

Throughout the 1990s, the U.S. Department of Health and Human Services promoted the expansion of Medicaid managed care by using its authority to grant waivers and establish statewide demonstration programs (Kaiser Family Foundation, 1998a; Rosenbaum and Darnell, 1998). Consequently, the number of Medicaid beneficiaries enrolled in managed care grew from 750,000 (3 percent of all Medicaid beneficiaries) in 1983 to more than 17 million in 1997 (47.8 percent) (Kaiser Family Foundation, 1998d).

Initially, the demonstration programs were small scale and "carefully" limited to only the healthiest recipients—poor or low-income pregnant women, children, and families (Families USA, 2001). However, the potential for cost savings was less than it might have been for elderly or disabled Medicaid beneficiaries (Holahan et al., 1998).

During the mid-1990s, states experimented with managed care plans for all Medicaid beneficiaries, including SSI recipients. By 1998, 25 percent of all Medicaid recipients with disabilities were enrolled in managed care plans (Kaiser Family Foundation, 1998a). The Government Accounting Office raised concerns about the impact of managed care on these (and other vulnerable) individuals, and told the states to find ways of ensuring that managed care plans provided appropriate, quality care (U.S. Government Accounting Office, 1996).

Balanced Budget Act of 1997

The Balanced Budget Act of 1997 significantly altered the Medicaid program. The act gave states the right to make managed care *mandatory* without federal waivers, except in the case of the Medicare-Medicaid (or dual eligible) population, children with special needs, and Native Americans. Dual-eligible recipients present a special challenge for managed care: In addition to being in very poor health, they are few in numbers and economically disadvantaged. Approximately a third of this population is also disabled (U.S. General Accounting Office, 1996). The Balanced Budget Act also provided protections for Medicaid recipients, though the states have often failed to abide by them (Families USA, 2001).

State Medicaid Managed Care Plans

State managed care plans have continued to develop. From 1997 to 2000, Medicaid managed care enrollment grew from 47.8 percent to 57.0 percent of beneficiaries. Sixteen states (including Hawaii) and Puerto Rico have 75 percent to 100 percent of their recipients enrolled in managed care options. Three states—Tennessee, Michigan, and Washington—have 100 percent of their Medicaid populations enrolled in managed care. Unlike Medicare, which, by comparison, has relatively few beneficiaries enrolled in managed care plans, managed care is now the primary model in Medicaid (Health Care Financing Administration, 2001).

Future Concerns

While there is some evidence that managed care may reduce the rates in spending growth, there is concern that this may be at the expense of quality. The Kaiser Family Foundation, in a twenty-year review of Medicaid managed care programs, found a decrease in referrals to specialists and emergency care, and little evidence of increased preventive care (Rowland et al., 1995). As noted by Holahan and colleagues (1998), managed care provides incentives for health care plans to undertreat enrollees. Therefore, the states must find ways to "deter poor-quality care, monitor plan performance, and provide recourse in the event of complaints" (p. 54).

Finally, a particular concern to social work and other mental health care providers is the issue of reduced access to social services. In the traditional fee-for-service Medicaid program, states often funded services for case management, substance abuse, personal care, and public health. Under Medicaid managed care plans, these services are often limited. Thus, savings generated by managed care for the states in one area of service may simply be costs that are shifted to other state programs (Holahan et al., 1998).

Managed Behavioral Health Care

Managed care has also been used in behavioral health care. Managed behavioral health care (MBHC) developed in response to the rapid growth of mental health and substance abuse services during the 1970s and 1980s (Freeman and Trabin, 1994; Boyle and Callahan, 1995). In 1999, almost four out of five (78 percent) individuals with health insurance, including those in public plans, belonged to an MBHC plan (Findlay, 1999). This industry became particularly concentrated during the 1990s. In 1999, fifteen companies cumulatively controlled almost 89 percent of the market, and the top two companies had a cumulative share of almost 50 percent, which amounted to 86.3 million individuals (Findlay, 1999).

Managed Behavioral Health Care Plans

Managed behavioral health care takes several forms. About a fifth (19 percent) of beneficiaries belong to plans with case management and utilization review services, in which MBHC companies monitor the use of services; another quarter (24 percent) belong to plans with employee assistance plans (EAPs) (Findlay, 1999). A smaller number of beneficiaries (8 percent) belong to plans that "provide an integrated behavioral health and EAP benefit" (Findlay, 1999, p. 119).

About half (49 percent) of MBHC enrollees belong to "carve-out" plans (Findlay, 1999). Carve-outs are specialized health care plans "devoted exclusively to mental health and chemical dependency issues" (Freeman and Trabin, 1994, p. 3). In exchange for a negotiated payment, carve-outs oversee the behavioral health care and treatment of a defined population. The employer determines the specific benefit package.

Twenty-eight percent of carve-out beneficiaries belong to "risk-based" plans, in which the plan assumes financial responsibility for treatment (Findlay, 1999). The remaining 21 percent of carve-out enrollees belong to "non-risk-based" (or administrative-services only) plans, whereby employers contract with MBHC companies but "retain full insurance risk" (Findlay, 1999, p. 118). In addition, 19 million enrollees belong to "carve-in" plans, which offer a range of health care services, including behavioral health care (Findlay, 1999).

Carve-out plans rely on many of the same techniques as other MCOs do to control costs, including utilization review, gatekeeping, and case management (National Association of Social Workers, 1994). Carve-outs can also limit the availability of services, impose copayments, and determine payments to providers (Frank, McGuire, and Newhouse, 1995). Capitation is another powerful means of reducing costs (Freeman and Trabin, 1994, p. 27).

Carve-out plans also have discretion over the type of providers and arrangements used for service delivery (Vandivort-Warren, 1998; Frank, McGuire, and Newhouse, 1995). Freeman and Trabin (1994) have identified three types of delivery systems used by carve-outs. One is the "network model," which consists of groups of individual practitioners from a range of disciplines, including psychiatrists, psychologists, social workers, and mental health counselors. As a condition of inclusion, providers agree to lower their prices, utilize "managed care procedures," and adhere to "cost-effective approaches to treatment" (Freeman and Trabin, 1994, p. 4). A second type is the traditional, staff model, in which clinicians serve as salaried employees; this approach, of course, raises concerns about undertreatment (Freeman and Trabin, 1994). The third type is the "hybrid model," which combines "groups and clinics" with "networks of independent providers" (p. 4).

Carve-out plans also have had to address the issue of access, a particular problem in the area of behavioral health. Surgeon General David Satcher notes that, although every year mental and behavioral disorders impact a fifth of the population, they still are "spoken of in whispers and shame" (U.S. Department of Health and Human Services, 1999, p. vi). Due to this negative connotation or stigma, many people are reluctant to seek help for behavioral health problems (Freeman and Trabin, 1994). Some individuals are also emotionally and psychologically unable to find assistance, and others may seek help from practitioners who are "unable to respond to their needs" (p. 26). To address these problems and facilitate access, carve-out plans have taken a number of steps, including offering free, twenty-four-hour phone lines to link "prospective" patients with practitioners and reducing required copayments (Freeman and Trabin, 1994). They have also introduced "telephonic warm lines for counseling and consultation" and other "innovations" aimed at integrating the "delivery system" with the lives and everyday needs of patients (p. 26).

Medicaid Behavioral Health Carve-Out Plans

In an effort to reduce costs, almost every state has introduced some form of managed care into its Medicaid program. The 1981 Omnibus Budget Reconciliation Act allowed states to seek permission from the federal government to waive the "provisions" of the law that give Medicaid recipients the right to choose their own providers (Rosenbaum and Darnell, 1998). During the 1990s, the federal government expanded the waiver process to encourage states to experiment with alternative approaches to service delivery to Medicaid populations. These Section 1115 waivers, as they are known, allow states to modify requirements related to eligibility, benefits, and administration for up to five years (Rosenbaum and Darnell, 1998). By 1997, almost half (47.8 percent) of Medicaid recipients were enrolled in managed care plans (Kaiser Family Foundation, 1998a).

States have also experimented with behavioral health carve-out plans for Medicaid beneficiaries. Massachusetts pioneered this approach by creating a mental health and substance abuse carve-out in 1992 (Callahan et al., 1995). By 1998, fifteen states had adopted Medicaid MBHC carve-outs for mental health care (U.S. Department of Health and Human Services, 1999). In some states, the carve-outs have organized provider networks, provide payments, and engage in utilization review, while in others, the state has assumed responsibility for utilization (U.S. Department of Health and Human Services, 1999).

Managed Behavioral Health Care and Cost Control

A range of evidence suggests that MBHC does control costs. Frank, McGuire, and Newhouse (1995) pointed out that DuPont, Federal Express, and other large corporations "reported cost reductions of 30–50 percent" after introducing managed behavioral health care (p. 53). A study by Callahan and associates (1995) of Massachusetts's Medicaid carve-out plan found that costs were 22 percent lower than they would have been in the absence of managed care. Later studies also found sizable reductions in mental health costs following the introduction of MBHC (Goldman, McCulloch, and Sturm, 1998; Ma and McGuire, 1998).

Not surprisingly, however, analysts have expressed concern that MBHC's success in containing costs has come at the expense of access and quality (U.S. Department of Health and Human Services, 1999; www.thenationalcoalition.org/foyer.htm). Several years ago, Freeman and Trabin (1994) suggested that capitated plans were more likely "to deny care and create access barriers" than were noncapitated ones (p. 26). Although there is some evidence to support this view, it is far from clear-cut (Burnam and Escarce, 1999; Rosenthal, 1999). The larger question of how access and quality fare under managed care, capitated or not, also remains unanswered (Goldman, McCulloch, and Sturm, 1998; Ma and McGuire, 1998; Rosenthal, 1999; Zarin et al., 1999; U.S. Department of Health and Human Services, 1999; Burnam and Escarce, 1999; Young et al., 2001).

Managed Behavioral Health Care and Parity

The spread of MBHC has also sparked debate about mental health parity. As noted elsewhere, in 1996, Congress enacted the Mental Health Parity Act, preventing employers "from imposing annual or lifetime dollar limits on mental health coverage that are more restrictive than those imposed on medical and surgical coverage" (U.S. General Accounting Office, 2000, p. 3). However, this act expired in September 2001. Although Congress passed a temporary extension until December 31, 2002, as of this writing, Congress has yet to address the future of parity. Serious questions have been raised, however, about the meaning of parity under managed care.

Mechanic and McAlpine (1999) suggest that under managed care, in which health care is essentially rationed, parity may work against individuals with serious mental illness, who often require more intense care than patients with other conditions. Others contend that parity should be seen as a necessary step toward a broader goal of *equity* (Burnam and Escarce, 1999; Hennessy and Goldman, 2001). Equity occurs if, when the costs of a treatment equal its benefits, an individual with "a mental health problem" has the same likelihood of receiving care as an individual with a nonbehavioral health problem (Burnam and Escarce, 1999). In response, Gitterman, Sturm, and Scheffler (2001) argue that efforts for equity may undermine real steps toward "full parity in benefits" (p. 73). They suggest that equity matters less to patients than to providers, who see it as a way of opposing carve-outs, which have made parity possible, while lowering psychiatrists' incomes (Gitterman, Sturm, and Scheffler, 2001).

Managed Behavioral Health Care and Social Work

MBHC has brought both challenges and opportunities to individual social workers and the profession. Vandivort-Warren (1998) points out that before managed care was introduced, clinical social workers were regularly excluded from fee-for-service reimbursement mechanisms. Behavioral health MCOs, on the other hand, have included social workers as approved providers in their networks of independent providers. At the same time, reimbursement rates for social workers and other mental health providers have declined, and the demands for record keeping and billing have increased.

MBHC has brought other challenges as well. Some provider networks exclude social workers, and even those that include them reject many practitioners because they lack requisite skills or training or the network has filled its social work positions (Jackson, 1994). MCOs have also found it more efficient to develop relationships with "group practices rather than solo practitioners" (p. 4). In addition, because referrals no longer come through colleagues or clients, social workers must develop ties with primary care physicians, case managers, and other "'gatekeepers'" (Jackson, 1994).

MBHC has also "placed in question" the "long-held" belief that, as Siskind (1998) puts it, "*[m]ore treatment is better than less treatment*" (emphasis in original) (p. 182). Managed care has shifted practitioners' focus toward "short-term therapies," which have more specific goals and require less time, and thus less expense, than "long-term therapy" (Dziegielewski, Shields, and Thyer, 1998, pp. 288–289). This is not necessarily negative. Numerous studies have demonstrated the efficacy of many types of short-term therapy. As a result:

> The use of time-limited treatment, mutually negotiated goals and objectives, empirically based treatment, and careful clinical assessments taken before and during treatment are becoming part of responsible mental health practice (Dziegielewski, Shields, and Thyer, 1998, p. 302).

Managed care also places new demands on schools of social work. Schools have had to change "existing clinical courses, models, and theoretical content" and introduce "new courses to the curriculum" (Davis, 1998, p. 417). Students need to learn a wide range of skills, including working with, and "tailoring services" to, diverse populations, client assessment from a "strengths" perspective, brief and crisis interventions, advocacy, and prevention (Veeder and Peebles-Wilkins, 1998, p. 489). Social workers also have to be able to work in interdisciplinary settings and develop "collaborative relationships" and engage in research (Veeder and Peebles-Wilkins, 1998).

Finally, MBHC raises ethical issues. The NASW (1996) Code of Ethics states that although social workers' "primary" obligation is to their clients, they are also bound by "commitments" made to their employer. This raises the question of "'divided'" loyalty (Reamer, 1998). What should practitioners do if they believe clients "require greater assistance than managed care will authorize" (p. 295)? What if their employer requires them to expose "clients to possible privacy and confidentiality invasions" (p. 295)? These and related dilemmas raise ethical questions that practitioners, and schools of social work, must address (Reamer, 1998; Corcoran and Vandiver, 1996).

The Future of Managed Care

Managed care is clearly in a state of "flux" (Lesser and Ginsburg, 2000). The ability of managed care to control costs hinges on shifting risk to providers and limiting care to consumers. These factors now seem to be unraveling. The backlash against managed care has resulted in movement "away" from capitated plans "in favor of" PPOs and point-of-service plans, which allow consumers much more choice than traditional prepaid plans (Lesser and Ginsburg, 2001). In addition, providers have regained much of the power they had lost and can now resist efforts by plans to shift risk to them.

As managed care unraveled, health care inflation, which was falling during the mid-1990s, began to increase again at the end of the decade (Heffler et al., 2001; Hogan, Ginsburg, and Gabel, 2000). This resurgence in inflation has been fueled by technology and prescription drug costs, particularly by the latter (Swartz, 2000). According to Angell and Relman (2001): "Prescription drug costs are rising at an unsustainable rate—19 percent per year—and will soon exceed payments to doctors as the largest item on the health bill after hospital costs." The ability of managed care to control technology and prescription drug costs remains in doubt (Berk and Monheit, 2001). If managed care continues to unravel, health care reform will likely again become a focus of national debate.

Highlights

■ In an effort to reduce costs, the delivery of health care in the United States has shifted from a fee-for-service model to a system of managed care. The first managed care plans, Kaiser-Permanente and Group Health Cooperative of Puget Sound, emerged soon after WWII ended. The AMA strongly opposed prepaid group practices.

■ With the dramatic increase in health care costs during the 1960s, Congress enacted the HMO Act in 1973. This legislation, which required businesses with twenty-five or more employees to provide optional HMO coverage to their employees, radically altered the health care system in the United States.

■ Initially, HMOs seemed to be less expensive than fee-for-service medicine, though it was unclear whether greater efficiency, reduced quality, or healthier populations were the cause. But health care costs continued to rise during the 1980s.

■ To reduce Medicare spending, Congress enacted the Tax Equity and Fiscal Responsibility Act in 1982. A system of prospective payments with an advance fee schedule was established.

■ Preferred provider organizations (PPOs), networks of providers that receive payment on a fee-for-service basis, also emerged during the 1980s. The concept of managed care evolved from group-model HMOs (providers employed by health plans to provide services on a prepaid basis) to a variety of techniques to control costs including selective contracting, innovative incentives, and utilization review.

■ Inflation continued to plague the health care system despite the growth of managed care. By 1990, national health expenditures reached about 12 percent of

GDP. Yet, more than 33 million people lacked health insurance coverage. As health insurance costs grew, employees shifted their costs to employees through higher cost sharing, including premiums, deductibles, and copayments.

■ Managed competition, which encouraged competition based on cost and quality, was introduced as a remedy for the nation's health care system. A number of bills were introduced and President Clinton incorporated elements of managed competition in his Health Security Act (HSA) of 1993. The HSA, which ultimately failed to be enacted, included competition but relied on federal regulation to ensure universal coverage.

■ By the mid-1990s, health care inflation seemed to moderate, though again it was not clear why. One major change was the growth of for-profit managed care health plans; critics argued that quality of care was inferior to fee-for-service plans, particularly for individuals with chronic diseases. Consumers also expressed growing dissatisfaction with managed care.

■ In 1997, the Clinton administration pursued a policy of consumer protections, known as the patients' bill of rights. The most controversial element was the introduction of *external* reviews to address consumer complaints and appeals.

■ State managed care laws were also scrutinized and attention was drawn to the ERISA policy, which prevents states from regulating *self*-insured health plans. State laws did not protect a third of individuals with employment-based insurance.

■ The Balanced Budget Act of 1997 transformed Medicare and Medicaid. Medicare+ Choice plans (new Part C) were introduced to encourage enrollment in managed care health plans. To date, however, relatively few beneficiaries (about 14 percent) have elected this option. On the other hand, states vigorously pursued Medicaid managed care in an effort to reduce costs. More than half of Medicaid recipients, including low-income pregnant women, children, elderly, and disabled recipients, are enrolled, despite concerns about the ability of managed care plans to serve this population.

■ Managed care has also transformed behavioral health care and accounts for about 80 percent of behavioral health insurance. About half of these enrollees are covered by carve-out plans, which specialize in mental health and drug abuse services. Carve-out plans rely on many of the same managed care techniques and have experienced many of the same problems. The stigma associated with mental illness has presented special concern, and health plans have experimented with ways to encourage beneficiaries and recipients to seek services.

■ Managed care was incorporated into the Medicaid program in 1981 and expanded during the 1990s with the creation of Section 1115 waivers, which allowed states to experiment with carve-out plans. Serious concerns have been raised about the success of containing behavioral health costs at the expense of access and quality, and have fueled concerns about mental health parity. In 1996, Congress passed the Mental Health Parity Act, which is scheduled for reauthorization in 2002.

■ Managed behavioral health care has created challenges and opportunities for social work. Traditional fee-for-service medicine has regularly excluded clinical social workers from reimbursement mechanisms. Behavioral managed care organizations have included social workers as approved providers. However, reimbursement rates have declined and demands for record keeping and billing have increased. Managed behavioral health care has also placed more emphasis on short-term therapies, raised ethical practice concerns, and placed new demands on social work education.

■ The future of managed care is unclear. The ability to control costs has relied on cost shifting to consumers who are increasingly dissatisfied with this system of care. The backlash against managed care has increased interest in PPOs and point-of-service plans, which give individuals more choice than traditional prepaid plans.

Websites to Obtain Updated and Additional Information

www.healthlaw.org/managedcare
National Health Law Program

www.kff.org
Kaiser Family Foundation
Commission on Medicaid and the Uninsured

www.hcfa.gov/Medicare
www.hcfa.gov/Medicaid
Health Care Financing Administration
U.S. Department of Health and Human Services

REFERENCES

Aaron, H. J. (1994). Thinking Straight About Medical Costs. *Health Affairs, 13,* 5, 8–13.

AARP Federal Health Update. (1997, August). *Medicare Provisions in the FY98 Budget Bill.* Washington, DC: AARP.

Altman, D., Cutler, D. M., and Zeckhauser, R. (2000, August). Enrollee Mix, Treatment Intensity, and Cost in Competing Indemnity and HMO Plans. NBER Working Paper No. W7832. Cambridge, MA: NBER (Online). Available at papers.nber.org/papers/W7832.

Angell, M. and Relman, A. S. (2001, June 20). Prescription for Profit. *The Washington Post,* p. A27

Berk, M. L. and Monheit, A. C. (2001, March–April). Concentration of Expenditures, Revisited. *Health Affairs,* 20, 2, 9–18.

Berwick, D. M. (1998, September). *As Good As It Gets: Making Health Care Better in the New Millennium.* Washington, DC: National Coalition on Health Care.

Blendon, R. J., Brodie, M., Benson, J. M., Altman, D. E., Levitt, L., Hoff, T., and Hugick, L. (1998, July–August). Understanding the Managed Care Backlash. *Health Affairs, 17,* 4, 80–94.

Bodenheimer, T., Grumbach, K., Livingston, B. L., McCanne, D. R., Oberlander, J., Rice, D. P., and Rosenau, P. V. (1999, February). *Rebuilding Medicare for the 21st Century.* San Francisco, CA: The National Committee to Protect, Improve, and Expand Medicare.

Boyle, P. J. and Callahan, D. (1995). Managed Care in Mental Health: The Ethical Issues. *Health Affairs, 14,* 3, 7–22.

Brodie, M., Brady, L., and Altman, D. E. (1998, January–February). Media Coverage of Managed Care: Is There a Negative Bias? *Health Affairs, 17,* 1, 9–25.

Burnam, M. A. and Escarce, J. J. (1999). Equity in Managed Care for Mental Disorders. *Health Affairs, 18,* 5, 22–31.

Callahan, J. J., Shepard, D. S., Beinecke, R. H., Larson, M. J., and Cavanaugh, D. (1995, Fall). Mental Health/Substance Abuse Treatment in Managed Care: The Massachusetts Medicaid Experience. *Health Affairs, 14,* 3, 173–184.

Congressional Budget Office. (1997, April). *Trends in Health Care Spending by the Private Sector.* Washington, DC: Author.

Consumer Bill of Rights and Responsibilities: Report to the President of the United States. (1997, November). Washington, DC: Advisory Commission on Consumer Protection and Quality in the Health Care Industry.

Corcoran, K. and Vandiver, V. (1996). *Maneuvering the Maze of Managed Care: Skills for Mental Health Practitioners.* New York: Free Press.

CRS Issue Brief. (1993, June 4). *Health Care Reform: Managed Competition.* Washington, DC: Library of Congress.

Cutler, D. M. and Sheiner, L. (1997, August). Managed Care and the Growth of Medical Expenditures. NBER Working Paper No. W6140. Cambridge, MA: NBER (Online). Available at papers.nber.org/papers/w6140.

Davis, K. (1998). Managed Health Care: Forcing Social Work to Make Choices and Changes. In G. Schamess and A. Lightburn (Eds.), *Humane Managed Care?* (pp. 409–425). Washington, DC: National Association of Social Workers.

Davis, K., Collins, K. S., and Morris, C. (1994). Managed Care: Promises and Concerns. *Health Affairs, 13,* 4, 178–185.

Davis, K., Schoen, C., and Sandman, D. R. (1996, Summer). The Culture of Managed Care: Implications for Patients. *Bulletin of the New York Academy of Medicine, 73,* 1, 173–183.

Dranove, D. (2000). *The Economic Evolution of American Health Care.* Princeton: Princeton University Press.

Dziegielewski, S. F., Shields, J., and Thyer, B. (1998). Short-term Treatment: Models, Methods, and Research. In J. Williams and K. Ell (Eds.), *Advances in Mental Health Research* (pp. 287–308). Washington, DC: National Association of Social Workers.

Eckholm, E. (1994, December 18). While Congress Remains Silent, Health Care Transforms Itself. *The New York Times,* p. A1.

Ellwood, P. M. Jr., Anderson, N. N., Billings, J. E., Carlson, R. J., Hoagberg, E. J., and McClure, W. (1976). Health Maintenance Strategy. In D. Kotelchuck (Ed.), *Prognosis Negative: Crisis in the Health Care System.* New York: Vintage Books.

Enthoven, A. C. (1993, Supplement). The History and Principles of Managed Competition. *Health Affairs, 12,* 24–48.

Enthoven, A. C. (1978, March 30). Consumer-Choice Health Plan (second of two parts). A National-Health-Insurance Proposal Based on Regulated Competition in the Private Sector. *New England Journal of Medicine, 298,* 13, 709–720.

Enthoven, A. C. and Kronick, R. (1994). Universal Health Insurance through Incentives Reform. In P. R. Lee and C. L. Estes (Eds.), *The Nation's Health* 4th ed. (pp. 284–291). Boston: Jones and Bartlett Publishers.

Enthoven, A. C. and Singer, S. J. (1994, Spring [I]). A Single-Payer System in Jackson Hole Clothing. *Health Affairs, 13,* 1, 81–95.

Families USA. (2001, May). *Medicaid Managed Care Consumer Protection Regulations: No Patients' Rights for the Poor? Special Report.* Washington, DC: Families USA.

Families USA. (2000, March). *The Future of Medicare: #1.* Washington, DC: Families USA.

Families USA. (1999, September). *Rural Neglect: Medicare HMOs Ignore Rural Communities.* Washington, DC: Families USA.

Families USA. (1998, July). *Hit and Miss: State Managed Care Laws.* Washington, DC: Families USA.

Feldman, S. and Scharfstein, D. (1998, April). Managed Care Provider Volume. NBER Working Paper No. W6523. Cambridge, MA: NBER (Online). Available at papers.nber.org/papers/W6523.

Findlay, S. (1999, September/October). Managed Behavioral Health Care in 1999: An Industry at a Crossroads, *Health Affairs, 18,* 5, 116–225.

Frank, R. G., McGuire, T. G., and Newhouse, J. P. (1995, Fall). Risk Contracts in Managed Mental Health Care. *Health Affairs, 14,* 3, 50–64.

Freeman, M. A. and Trabin, T. (1994, October 5). *Managed Behavioral Healthcare: History, Models, Key Issues, and Future Course.* Washington, DC: U.S. Department of Health and Human Services, Center for Mental Health Services.

Friedman, E. (1996, March 27). Capitation, Integration, and Managed Care: Lessons from Early Experiments. *Journal of the American Medical Association, 275,* 12, 957–963.

Fuchs, V. (1993). *The Future of Health Policy.* Cambridge, MA: Harvard University Press.

Gabel, J. (1997). Ten Ways HMOs Have Changed During the 1990s. *Health Affairs, 16,* 3, 134–145.

Garrett, L. (2000). *Betrayal of Trust: The Collapse of Global Public Health.* New York: Hyperion.

Ginsburg, P. B. (1998, July–August). Health System Change in 1997. *Health Affairs, 17,* 4, 165–169.

Gitterman, D. P., Sturm, R., and Scheffler, R. M. (2000, July/August). Toward Full Mental Health Parity and Beyond. *Health Affairs, 20,* 4, 68–76.

Glied, S. (1999, July). Managed Care. NBER Working Paper No. W7205. Cambridge, MA: NBER (Online). Available at www.nber.org.

Gold, M. (2001, July–August). Medicare+ Choice: An Interim Report Card. *Health Affairs, 20,* 4, 120–138.

Gold, M. (2000, September). *Monitoring Medicare+ Choice: Fast Facts.* No. 3. Washington, DC: Mathematica Policy Research.

Goldman, W., McCulloch, J., and Sturm, R. (1998, March–April). Costs and Use of Mental Health Services Before and After Managed Care. *Health Affairs, 17,* 2, 40–52.

Health Care Financing Administration. (2001). *Medicaid Managed Care State Enrollment December 31, 2000* (Online). Available at www.hcfa.gov/medicaid/omcproo.pdf

Heffler, S., Levit, K., Smith, S., Smith, C., Cowan, C., Lazenby, H., and Freeland, M. (2001, March–April). Health Spending Growth Up in 1999; Faster Growth Expected in the Future. *Health Affairs, 20,* 2, 193–203.

Hennessy, K. D. and Goldman, H. H. (2001, July–August). Full Parity: Steps Toward Treatment Equity for Mental and Addictive Disorders. *Health Affairs, 20,* 4, 58–67.

Hodgson, G. (1973, October). The Politics of Health Care: What Is It Costing You? *The Atlantic.* (Online). Available at www.theatlantic.com/politics/healthca/hodgson.htm.

Hogan, C., Ginsburg, P. B., and Gabel, J. R. (2000, November–December). Tracking Health Care Costs: Inflation Returns. *Health Affairs, 19,* 6, 217–223.

Holahan, J., Zuckerman, S., Evans, A., and Rangarajan, S. (1998, May/June). Medicaid Managed Care in Thirteen States. *Health Affairs, 17,* 3, 43–63.

Huskamp, H. A. and Newhouse, J. P. (1994). Is Health Spending Slowing Down? *Health Affairs, 13,* 5, 32–38.

Iglehart, J. K. (1999, January–February). Bringing Forth Medicare+ Choice: HCFA's Robert A. Berenson. *Health Affairs, 18,* 1, 144–149.

Iglehart, J. K. (1997, May/June). Changing with the Times: The Views of Bruce C. Vladeck. *Health Affairs, 16,* 3, 58–71.

Iglehart, J. K. (1994). Managed Competition. In P. R. Lee and C. L. Estes (Eds.), *The Nation's Health,* 4th ed. (pp. 224–230). Boston: Jones and Bartlett Publishers.

Jackson, V. (1994). *A Brief Look at Managed Mental Health Care.* Washington, DC: National Association of Social Workers.

Jensen, G. A., Morrisey, M. A., Gaffney, S., and Liston, D. K. (1997). The New Dominance of Managed Care: Insurance Trends in the 1990s. *Health Affairs, 16,* 1, 125–136.

Kaiser Family Foundation. (2001, June). *Medicare at a Glance. The Medicare Program, The Kaiser Medicare Policy Project.* Washington, DC: Kaiser Family Foundation.

Kaiser Family Foundation. (1999a, September). *Medicare Managed Care.* Washington, DC: Kaiser Family Foundation.

Kaiser Family Foundation. (1999b, July). *Survey of Physicians and Nurses.* Washington, DC: Kaiser Family Foundation.

Kaiser Family Foundation. (1998a, October). *Medicaid and Managed Care. Kaiser Commission on Medicaid and the Uninsured Medicaid Facts.* Washington, DC: Kaiser Family Foundation.

Kaiser Family Foundation. (1998b, August). *Trends and Indicators in the Changing Health Care Marketplace.* Washington, DC: Kaiser Family Foundation.

Kane, N. M., Turnbull, N. C., and Schoen, C. (1996, January). *Markets and Plan Performance: Summary Report on Case Studies of IPA and Network HMOs.* New York: Commonwealth Fund (Online). Available at www.cmwf.org.

Kassirer, J. P. (1995). Managed Care and the Morality of the Market Place. *New England Journal of Medicine, 333,* 50–52.

Knox, R. A. (1999, May 2). HMOs Creator Urges Reform in Quality of Care. *Boston Globe,* pp. 1, 34.

Kotelchuck, D., ed. (1976). *Prognosis Negative: Crisis in the Health Care System.* New York: Vintage Books.

Kronenfeld, J. J. and Whicker, M. L. (1984). *U.S. National Health Policy: An Analysis of the Federal Role.* New York: Praeger Special Studies.

Laschober, M. A., Neuman, P., Kitchman, M. S., Meyer, L., and Langwell, K. M. (1999, November–December). Medicare HMO Withdrawals: What Happens to Beneficiaries? *Health Affairs, 18,* 6, 150–157.

Leape, L. L. (2000). Can We Make Health Care Safe? In S. Findlay, ed. *Reducing Medical Errors and Improving Patient Safety.* Washington, DC: The National Coalition on Health Care and The Institute for Healthcare Improvement, pp. 2–3.

Lee, P. R., Soffel, D., and Luft, H. S. (1994). Costs and Coverage: Pressures toward Health Care Reform. In P. R. Lee and C. L. Estes (Eds.), *The Nation's Health,* 4th ed. (pp. 204–313). Boston: Jones and Bartlett Publishers.

Lesser, C. S. and Ginsburg, P. B. (2001, February). Back to the Future? New Cost and Access Challenges Emerge. Issue Brief 35. Center for Studying Health System Change (Online). Available at www.hschange.org/CONTENT/296/?topic=topic07.

Lesser, C. S. and Ginsburg, P. B. (2000, November–December). Update on the Nation's Health Care System: 1997–1999. *Health Affairs, 19,* no. 6, 206–216.

Levit, K. R., Cowan, C. A., Lazenby, H. C., McDonnell, P. A., Sensenig, A. L., Stiller, J. M., and Won, D. K. (1994, Winter). National Health Spending Trends, 1960–1993. *Health Affairs, 13,* 5, 14–31.

Levit, K. R., Lazenby, H. C., and Sivarajan, L. (1996, Summer). Health Care Spending in 1994: Slowest in Decades. *Health Affairs, 15,* 2, 130–144.

Luft, H. S. (1978, June 15). How Do Health-Maintenance Organizations Achieve Their "Savings"? *New England Journal of Medicine, 298,* 24, 1336–1343.

Ma, C. A. and McGuire, T. G. (1998, March–April). Costs and Incentives in a Behavioral Health Carve-Out. *Health Affairs, 17,* 2, 53–69.

Mechanic, D. and McAlpine, D. D. (1999). Mission Unfulfilled: Potholes on the Road to Mental Health Parity. *Health Affairs, 18,* 5, 7–21.

Medicare Payment Advisory Commission. (1998a, June). *Report to the Congress: Context for a Changing Medicare Program.* Author.

Medicare Payment Advisory Commission. (1998b, July). *Health Care Spending and the Medicare Program: A Data Book.* Author.

Miller, R. H. and Luft, H. S. (1997, September–October). Does Managed Care Lead to Better or Worse Quality of Care? *Health Affairs, 16,* 5, 7–25.

Mizrahi, T. (1995). Health Care: Reform Initiatives. In R. L. Edwards (Ed.-in-Chief), *Encyclopedia of Social Work,* 19th ed. (pp. 1185–1198). Washington, DC: National Association of Social Workers.

Moon, M. (2001, May 1). Beneficiary Issues and Medicare+ Choice. Testimony before the United States' House of Representatives, Committee on Ways and Means, Subcommittee on Health. Urban Institute. Author.

Moon, M. (2000, February). *Competition with Constraints Challenges Facing Medicare Reform.* Washington, DC: Urban Institute. (Online). Available at www.urban.org/retirement/reports/cwc.pdf.

Mullan, F. (2001, January–February). A Founder of Quality Assessment Encounters a Troubled System Firsthand. *Health Affairs, 20,* 1, 137–141.

National Association of Social Workers. (1996). *NASW Code of Ethics.* Washington, DC: Author.

National Association of Social Workers. (1994, May). *A Brief Look at Managed Mental Health Care.* Washington, DC: Author.

Newhouse, J. P. (1993, Supplement). An Iconoclastic View of Health Cost Containment. *Health Affairs, 12,* 152–171.

Patel, K. and Rushefsky, M. E. (1999). *Health Care Politics and Policy in America.* Armonk, NY: M. E. Sharpe.

Rachlis, M. and Kusher, C. (1989). *Second Opinion: What's Wrong with Canada's Health Care System and How to Fix It.* Toronto: Collins.

Reamer, F. G. (1998). Managed Care: Ethical Considerations. In G. Schamess and A. Lightburn (Eds.), *Humane Managed Care?* (pp. 293–298.) Washington, DC: National Association of Social Workers.

Roberts, M. J. and Clyde, A. (1993). *Your Money or Your Life: The Health Care Crisis Explained.* New York: Doubleday.

Robinson, J. C. (1999). *The Corporate Practice of Medicine: Competition and Innovation in Health Care.* Los Angeles: University of California Press.

Rosenbaum, S. and Darnell, J. (1998, November). *Medicaid Managed Care: An Analysis of the Health Care Financing Administration's Notice of Proposed Rulemaking.* Washington, DC: The George Washington University Medical Center, Center for Health Policy Research.

Rosenthal, M. B. (1999, September–October). Risk Sharing in Managed Behavioral Health Care. *Health Affairs, 18,* 5, 204–213.

Rothfeld, M. (1976). Sensible Surgery for Swelling Medical Costs. In D. Kotelchuck (Ed.), *Prognosis Negative: Crisis in the Health Care System* (pp. 352–363). New York: Vintage Books.

Rowland, D., Rosenbaum, S., Simon, L., and Chait, E. (1995). *Medicaid and Managed Care: Lessons from the Literature*. Kaiser Commission on Medicaid and the Uninsured Update. Washington, DC: Kaiser Family Foundation.

Singer, S. J. (2000, July–August). What's Not to Like About HMOs. *Health Affairs, 19,* 4, 206–209.

Siskind, A. B. (1998). Agency Mission, Social Work Practice, and Professional Training in a Managed Care environment. In G. Schamess and A. Lightburn (Eds.), *Humane Managed Care?* (pp. 180–186.) Washington, DC: National Association of Social Workers.

Starr, P. (1994). *The Logic of Health Care Reform*. New York: Penguin Books.

Starr, P. (1986). Health Care for the Poor: The Past Twenty Years. In S. H. Danziger and D. H. Weinberg (Eds.), *Fighting Poverty: What Works and What Doesn't* (pp. 106–132). Cambridge, MA: Harvard University Press.

Starr, P. (1982). *The Social Transformation of American Medicine*. New York: Basic Books.

Starr, P. and Zelman, W. A. (1993, Supplement). Bridge to Compromise: Competition under a Budget. *Health Affairs,* 7–23.

Sullivan, K. (2000, July/August). On the "Efficiency" of Managed Care Plans. *Health Affairs, 19,* 4, 139–148.

Swartz, K. (2000, Fall). Health Insurance Problems Are Not Going Away. *Inquiry, 37,* 3 (Online). Available at www.inquiryjournal.org/newfall2000.html.

U.S. Department of Health and Human Services. (1999, December). *Mental Health: A Report of the Surgeon General*. Rockville, MD: U.S. Department of Health and Human Services, Substance Abuse and Mental Health Services Administration, Center for Mental Health Services, National Institute of Mental Health.

U.S. General Accounting Office. (2000, May). *Mental Health Parity Act: Despite New Federal Standards, Mental Health Benefits Remain Limited*. Washington, DC: Author.

U.S. General Accounting Office. (1996). *Medicaid Managed Care: Serving the Disabled Challenges State Programs* (GAO/HEHS-96-136). Washington, DC: U.S. Government Printing Office.

Vandivort-Warren, R. (1998). How Social Workers Can Manage Managed Care. In G. Schamess and A. Lightburn (Eds.) *Humane Managed Care?* (pp. 255–267). Washington, DC: National Association of Social Workers.

Veeder, N. W. and Peebles-Wilkins, W. (1998). Research Needs in Managed Behavioral Health Care. In G. Schamess and A. Lightburn (Eds.), *Humane Managed Care?* (pp. 483–504). Washington, DC: National Association of Social Workers.

Ware, J. E., Bayliss, M. S., Rogers, W. H., Kosinski, M., and Tarlov, A. R. (1996, October, 12). Differences in 4-Year Health Outcomes for Elderly and Poor, Chronically Ill Patients Treated in HMO and Fee-for-Service Systems: Results From the Medical Outcomes Study. *JAMA, 276,* 13, 1039–1047.

White House Domestic Policy Council (1993). *Health Security: The President's Report to the American People*. Washington, DC: U.S. Government Printing Office.

Young, A. S., Klap, R., Sherbourne, C. D., and Wells, K. B. (2001, January). The Quality of Care for Depressive and Anxiety Disorders in the United States. *Archives of General Psychiatry, 58,* 1, 55–61.

Zarin, D. A., West, J. C., Pincus, H. A., and Tanielian, T. L. (1999, September–October). Characteristics of Health Plans That Treat Psychiatric Patients. *Health Affairs, 18,* 5, 226–236.

Zelman, W. A. (1994, Spring [1]). The Rationale Behind the Clinton Health Care Reform Plan. *Health Affairs, 13,* 1, 9–29.

CHAPTER

5

Medicare and Medicaid

After decades of political reform efforts to achieve national health insurance, Congress enacted Medicare and Medicaid in 1965 as Titles XVIII and XIX of the Social Security Act. Medicare is a social insurance program; Medicaid is a means-tested public assistance program (to be eligible, recipients must demonstrate their need for assistance by meeting established income and asset eligibility criteria).

Robert Ball, one of the architects of Medicare and commissioner of Social Security under Presidents Kennedy, Johnson, and Nixon, has argued persistently that Medicare's original designers viewed Medicare as a first step toward universal coverage (Ball, 1995). They reluctantly crafted a program that was politically viable by focusing on the elderly and building on a Social Security pension system that already provided income support for adult retirees.

Before Medicare, half the nation's older adults lacked health care coverage, and millions more had inadequate coverage. Private insurance rates for older adults were very expensive and the idea of pooling risks for this population was appealing. The final element of the compromise was to establish a separate program for low-income families. With the spotlight on economically disadvantaged groups during President Johnson's War on Poverty, Congress enacted Medicaid to address the needs of this population.

Medicare and Medicaid have enabled millions of adults and children to access health care and have contributed significantly to the social and economic welfare of individuals and the nation as a whole. Medicare has reduced poverty among older adults and people with disabilities measurably. Medicare provided health care coverage to 39.9 million people in 1999, while Medicaid provided health and long-term care coverage to 41.1 million people (Health Care Financing Administration, 2000a, 2000b).

When the programs were enacted, the federal government did not place any limits or restrictions on hospital and physician fees. Within a few years, however, the nation's health care costs skyrocketed. As discussed in Chapter 2, during the 1970s, HMOs emerged, and during the 1980s, the Reagan administration, despite its opposition to regulation, established a prospective payment system. Today, the costs associated with the Medicare and Medicaid programs continue to draw attention. In 1996, Medicare expenditures totaled $200 billion, while those for Medicaid came to more than $155 billion (Kaiser Family Foundation, 1998a, 1998c).

This chapter will provide an overview of the provisions of Medicare and Medicaid, recent proposals for reform, and future issues of concern to social work. In the absence of a universal system for health insurance, Medicare and Medicaid remain the two most important health care programs in the United States. Medicare finances approximately one-fifth of all physician services and one-third of all hospital services (Kaiser Family Foundation, 2001b). Medicaid is the primary payer for long-term care (Kaiser Family Foundation, 1999a).

Medicare

Benefits and Financing

Medicare is one of a group of social insurance programs legislated by the Social Security Act referred to as OASDHI—Old Age (OA), Survivors (S), Disability (D), and Health Insurance (HI or Medicare). The original Social Security Act of 1935 provided old age pensions for retired workers. In 1939, retirement benefits were extended to workers' dependents and survivors. Congress amended the act again in 1956 to add disability insurance for employed workers who were unable to continue working due to physical or mental impairments. Medicare was added in 1965.

Medicare has two essential components: Hospital Insurance (Part A) and Medical Insurance (Part B). Hospital Insurance Part A is mandatory (employers and employees must participate), provides coverage primarily for hospital expenses, and is financed by a payroll tax on employers and employees (1.45 percent each). Self-employed workers contribute both taxes (2.9 percent). The revenue from the taxes is held in the Hospital Insurance Trust Fund.

Hospital Insurance (Part A).   Medicare Part A provides coverage for the first 60 days of hospitalization (semiprivate rooms, meals, general nursing, supplies, and other services) subject to a deductible per benefit period ($812 in 2002). It requires beneficiaries to pay a daily coinsurance ($203 in 2002) for hospital stays between days 61 and 90. For stays longer than 90 days, beneficiaries must tap into their lifetime reserve days and pay an even higher daily coinsurance ($406 in 2002).

Part A also provides 20 days of *skilled*-nursing facility benefits (semiprivate rooms, meals, nursing and rehabilitative care, supplies, and other services) subject to a 3-day prior hospitalization requirement. Beneficiaries must pay a daily coinsurance (up to $101.50 for 2002) for days 21 to 100 and for all costs after day 100. Part A covers home health care (part-time *skilled* nursing, physical therapy, occupational therapy, speech–language therapy, home health aides, supplies, durable medical equipment, and other services). Coinsurance payments are not required for home health care, but beneficiaries must pay 20 percent of the approved cost of durable medical equipment. Most nursing home care is custodial and is *not* covered by Medicare. Finally, Part A covers hospice care from a Medicare-approved hospice (medical and support services, drugs, short-term respite care, and other services). Beneficiaries pay a small copayment for prescription drugs and respite care.

Most retired workers receive Medicare benefits at age 65 because they or their spouses have worked the forty quarters of employment required by the Social Security system. Retired workers with less than thirty employment quarters can receive Medicare benefits if they pay a monthly premium ($319 in 2002); employers with thirty to thirty-nine employment quarters pay a lower monthly premium ($175 in 2002) (Health Care Financing Administration, 2002).

Medical Insurance (Part B).   Medicare Part B is voluntary (beneficiaries are not required to enroll) and is financed primarily with general revenues. Approximately 95 percent of beneficiaries take advantage of this option. Beneficiaries must contribute by paying a monthly premium ($54 in 2002). Federal revenues and individual premiums are held in the Medical Insurance Trust Fund. Part B provides coverage for medical services (physician services, outpatient medical and hospital services and supplies, diagnostic tests, approved ambulatory surgery, and durable medical equipment). Mammograms and other cancer screening tests were added in 1997. Part B covers outpatient therapy, occupational therapy, speech–language therapy, and outpatient mental health care. Beneficiaries are subject to an annual deductible ($100 in 2002) and must pay a 20 percent coinsurance for most services.

Part B also provides coverage for approved clinical laboratory tests at no cost to the beneficiary. Home health visits not covered by Part A and other outpatient hospital services are covered. The beneficiary is responsible for 20 percent of the approved cost of durable medical equipment and a predetermined copayment for outpatient services (Health Care Financing Administration, 2002; see www. medicare. gov for new amounts for Part A and Part B premiums, deductibles, and copayments).

Gaps in Coverage and Cost Sharing.   A major concern with Medicare is its gaps in coverage. Medicare does not provide payment for outpatient prescription drugs, routine dental and eye examinations, hearing aids, routine or yearly physical examinations, and immunizations (except annual flu shots and shots for pneumonia and hepatitis B, which are covered). Medicare does not cover long-term custodial care, home health visits not covered by Part A, and other outpatient services (Health Care Financing Administration, 2001).

A second concern is out-of-pocket costs and cost-sharing requirements. Most physicians who treat Medicare patients accept the program's approved fees as full payment for their services, but others exercise their right to charge beneficiaries an additional restricted fee. The cost of physician fees, omissions in coverage, premiums, deductibles, and copayments add up to significant costs that must be paid either out-of-pocket or with supplemental insurance. The three largest out-of-pocket costs for older adults are (1) long-term care, (2) physician payments, and (3) prescription drugs (Health Care Financing Administration, 2000b).

According to the 1997 Medicare Current Beneficiary Survey, about one-fourth of beneficiaries purchased private Medigap, or Medicare Supplement Insurance, to provide coverage for the gaps in Medicare. A third received supplemental coverage through employee retirement benefits. Fourteen percent had Medicaid coverage through the Medicare buy-in program, and 14 percent participated in Medicare HMOs (Kaiser Family Foundation, 2001b).

The Medicare buy-in program was originally introduced in the 1988 Medicare Catastrophic Coverage Act (see Chapter 2). Although the 1988 legislation was repealed, the provisions of the buy-in program were adopted and expanded through legislative reforms passed in 1990, 1993, 1995, and again in 1997 with a block grant program. The Medicare buy-in program allows Medicaid to cover premiums, deductibles, and coinsurance payments for beneficiaries whose incomes are below or near the federal poverty level (FPL) (see Figure 5.1) (Families USA, 1998).

Even with supplemental coverage, about a quarter of beneficiaries lack prescription drug benefits, which is a major concern given the high cost of prescription drugs (Kaiser Family Foundation, 2001b), and very few beneficiaries can afford long-term-care insurance. Despite Medicare, the elderly spend a higher percentage of their income on medical care than does the general population. They have higher medical costs and lower incomes than the general population (Health Care Financing Administration, 2000b).

The Medicare buy-in program was established to prevent individual financial hardship, yet, in 1997, between 3.3 million and 3.9 million eligible beneficiaries were not enrolled (Families USA, 1998). A number of studies show that the group with the lowest enrollment is Specified Low-Income Medicare Beneficiaries (SLMB) (see Figure 5.1); only about 16 percent of these beneficiaries participate (Kaiser Family Foundation, 1999a). Insufficient outreach efforts, poor enrollment processes, and delays in activating eligibility are contributing factors. Staff and beneficiaries seem insufficiently aware of the program. Beneficiaries often need to apply at local public

FIGURE 5.1   **Medicaid Benefits Available to Medicare Beneficiaries**

	Part B Premium	**Copayments**	**Deductibles**
Qualified Medicare Beneficiaries (QMB) ≤ 100 % FPL	X	X	X
Specified Low-Income Medicare Beneficiaries 100–120 % FPL	X		
Qualified Individual Beneficiaries (1) 120–135 % FPL	X		
Qualified Individual Beneficiaries (2) 135–175 % FPL	Partial coverage		

Source: Schneider et al., Kaiser Commission on Medicaid and the Uninsured, 1999.

assistance offices, rather than Social Security offices, which may deter them from enrolling (Families USA, 1998; Kaiser Family Foundation, 1999a).

Prescription Drug Coverage.   In recent years, support has grown for adding prescription drug coverage to Medicare (Gorin, 2001). Through the 1970s, this was not a major issue, as pharmaceuticals played a relatively minor role in health care for older adults (Steinberg et al., 2000). However, this began to change during the 1980s, and by 1998, Medicare recipients spent 4.1 percent of their incomes on prescription drugs (versus 1.9 percent in 1978) (Medicare Payment Advisory Commission [MedPAC], 2000). In 1997, Medicare enrollees represented only 14 percent of the population; however, they were responsible for 40 percent of the nation's prescription drug expenditures (U.S. House of Representatives, 2001). The Congressional Budget Office (CBO) estimates that older adults will spend almost $1.5 billion on prescription drugs between 2002 and 2011 (U.S. House of Representatives, 2001).

The Kaiser Family Foundation (2000a) identified several factors contributing to the growth of prescription drug expenditures between 1993 and 1998. Eighteen percent of the growth was attributable to higher prices, as the cost of many drugs, particularly those for older adults, rose more rapidly than the overall rate of inflation. Between 1999 and 2000, of the top fifty drugs used by older adults, half had price increases that were double the rate of inflation (Families USA, 2000b).

Forty-three percent of the growth was due to increased use, as the average number of prescriptions per older adult grew from 19.6 in 1992 to 28.5 in 2000 (Kaiser Family Foundation, 2000b; Families USA, 2000b). Thirty-nine percent was due to the replacement of less expensive drugs with more expensive ones (Kaiser Family Foundation, 2000b). Because many new drugs are simply older ones with minor variations, it is unclear whether the newer medications are superior to the ones they replaced (Pryor, 1990). In addition, the use and replacement of drugs is influenced by direct advertising to consumers, which has also grown in recent years (Wilkes, Bell, and Kravitz, 2000). Although the clinical effect of direct-to-consumer advertising is unclear, it seems certain to increase in the future (Berndt, 2001b).

How do Medicare beneficiaries pay for prescription drugs? According to the CBO, in 1997, 28.1 percent of beneficiaries had employment-based coverage (U.S. House of Representatives, 2001). However, this source of coverage seems relatively unstable. Between 1995 and 1996, 11.3 percent of beneficiaries with employment-based insurance lost their coverage, a figure that will likely increase in the future (Stuart, Shea, and Briesacher, 2001; Kaiser Family Foundation, 2001b).

Almost 14 percent had coverage through Medicaid (U.S. House of Representatives, 2001). These individuals are, of course, among the poorest older adults. In 1996, more than one-half of Medicare beneficiaries with incomes below the federal poverty line were not enrolled in Medicaid, and many beneficiaries with low incomes were ineligible for the program (Kaiser Family Foundation, 2000a).

Approximately 12 percent of beneficiaries had coverage through HMOs (a figure that fell to around 10 percent in 2001) (U.S. House of Representatives, 2001; Kaiser Family Foundation, 2001). According to the director of the CBO, most Medicare HMOs have limits on prescription drug benefits and many impose charges for prescription drugs (U.S. House of Representatives, 2001). About 11 percent of beneficiaries had Medigap coverage, the cost of which has increased dramatically, largely due to increases in prescription drug costs (U.S. House of Representatives, 2001; Kaiser Family Foundation, 2001c; Freudenheim, 2001). According to Diane Archer of the Medicare Rights Center, it has become "increasingly clear that private health insurers cannot offer affordable prescription drug coverage even to middle-income older and disabled Americans" (quoted in Freudenheim, 2001, p. C15).

Around 31 percent of beneficiaries had no prescription drug coverage (U.S. House of Representatives, 2001). This figure may underestimate the scope of the problem, however, because it does not take into account that many beneficiaries have intermittent coverage. In 1996, 20 percent of beneficiaries with coverage "had it for only part of the year" (Stuart et al., 2001, p. 86). Individuals who lacked coverage were predominantly residents of rural areas, nearly poor, and over age 85 (Poisal and Murray, 2001). They also filled fewer prescriptions than beneficiaries with coverage (twenty-four versus sixteen) and paid more in out-of-pocket costs (Kaiser Family Foundation, 2001c).

Legislative Proposals. President George W. Bush has proposed the "Immediate Helping Hand Plan," which would give states funds to subsidize drug coverage to beneficiaries with incomes up to 175 percent of the federal poverty line (Congressional Progressive Caucus, 2001; Pear, 2001). Critics argue that this plan fails to include millions of people whose incomes are above 175 percent of poverty, including 8.2 million individuals with no prescription drug coverage (AARP Public Policy Institute, 2000). The plan also imposes no standards on the states and would likely result in skewed and uneven coverage (Pear, 2001).

How much would a more comprehensive plan cost? The CBO has developed estimates for a benefit that would cover outpatient prescription drug costs for all beneficiaries (U.S. House of Representatives, 2001). The government would pay half the premium cost, and beneficiaries would contribute the other half at a rate of $55 per month. Enrollees would also be responsible for half their prescription drug costs, with no individual responsible for more than $4,000 in out-of-pocket costs. Individuals with incomes up to 150 percent of poverty would receive subsidies. In 2004, this plan would cost the government $31.6 billion (U.S. House of Representatives, 2001).

Finally, Democrats have introduced two bills—the Prescription Drug Fairness for Seniors Act (H.R. 664) and the International Prescription Drug Parity Act (H.R. 1885)—that address the cost of prescription drugs and could complement a Medicare benefit. H.R. 664 would require pharmaceutical companies to charge pharmacies the same discounted prices the companies charge federal agencies, such as the Veterans Administration (U.S. House of Representatives, 1999a). These discounts could then be passed on to Medicare beneficiaries (U.S. House of Representatives, 1999a). H.R. 1885 would allow pharmacists to import back into the United States those drugs approved by the Federal Drug Administration that were previously exported by U.S. manufacturers to other countries (U.S. House of Representatives, 1999b). Because the United States, unlike many other countries, does not regulate drug prices, consumers here generally pay higher prices than do consumers in other countries. For example, between 1992 and 1997 older adults in the United States spent roughly 1.5 times as much on prescription drugs as their counterparts in Canada, the United Kingdom, and Germany (U.S. House of Representatives, 1999b). Wholesalers in the United States currently are prohibited from importing prescription drugs, even those that were originally manufactured in the United States. H.R. 1885 would change this.

The pharmaceutical companies argue that these measures would hinder their research and development efforts (U.S. House of Representatives, 1999b). However, this argument is debatable. The pharmaceutical industry is the most profitable in the nation, with profits of $26.2 billion in 1998 (U.S. House of Representatives, 1999b). Although the industry spent $17 billion on research and development, it spent $11 billion on marketing and advertising (U.S. House of Representatives, 1999b). "To cite a typical example, last year Glaxo Smith Kline spent 37 percent of its revenues on marketing and administration and only 14 percent on R&D, while making a 28 percent profit" (Angell and Relman, 2001).

Medicare Benefit Payments. From 1987 to 1997, Medicare spending increased at an average rate of 10 percent each year. The 1997 Medicare reforms (discussed in a later section) mandated $115 billion in savings by 2002; from 1997 to 2000, the average rate of growth in spending declined to 1.4 percent annually. Medicare benefits in 2001 are projected to reach $237 billion, or about 12 percent of the federal budget. In 1999, Medicare financed almost a third of the nation's hospital care and a fourth of physician services (Kaiser Family Foundation, 2001b). Medicare is the second-largest social insurance program in the nation; the largest is the Social Security retirement system.

In 1997, 75 percent of Medicare expenditures were spent on only 15 percent of the program's beneficiaries. These beneficiaries had much higher than average individual medical needs and costs; the average cost per enrollee was over $10,000. In comparison, the average cost per beneficiary in 1999 was $5,410 (Health Care Financing Administration, 2000b).

Beneficiaries

In 1999, Medicare insured 34 million older adults over age 65 and 5.9 million individuals with disabilities and end-stage kidney disease; Medicare was amended in 1972 to include the latter group. The Medicare program serves the medical needs of a diverse population with variations in age, race, ethnicity, gender, income, and health status. However, Medicare serves more elderly women (7 percent) than elderly men, and more disabled men (9 percent) than disabled women. Only 7 percent of the Medicare population in 1999 was African American and only 6 percent was Latina/o. These disparities reflect the racial disparities in health discussed in Chapter 6. Thirty percent of Medicare's beneficiaries live alone; 72 percent of these beneficiaries are women and the vast majority is very poor (Health Care Financing Administration, 2000b).

Older Adults.   The overwhelming majority of Medicare beneficiaries are over age 65. Demographic projections for the United States suggest that the elderly population is likely to continue to grow as a percentage of the population. In the late 1990s, older adults made up 13 percent of the U.S. population; by 2030, this group is expected to grow to 20 percent. Moreover, within the elderly population, those over age 85 are the fastest-growing group of older adults and by 2050 could represent 23 percent of the Medicare population. Older people tend to be sicker than do those who are younger and to spend more on health care. Thus, the changing demographics of Medicare fuel concerns about financing the program's costs (Fronstin and Copeland, 1997).

Adults with Disabilities.   In the United States, the majority of working-age adults with disabilities (about 29 million) are employed. However, approximately half have severe disabilities and only one of every four in this group is employed. Most of the 5.9 million Medicare beneficiaries who are disabled have disabilities that are classified as severe. Disability (see Terminology Box for a discussion of this term) is a broad concept for conditions that can result from a number of different physical, developmental, or mental conditions ranging from spinal cord injury to AIDS to Alzheimer's disease.

One of the primary issues regarding disability and Medicare is the definition that is used. The definition used by the Medicare program to determine eligibility is not a medical definition; it is a socially defined, functional term. To qualify, recipients must be unable to work. Thus, beneficiaries who can return to work are at risk for losing their health insurance.

Women.   Women make up more than half of Medicare's beneficiaries and 70 percent of beneficiaries with incomes below the federal poverty line. Half the female beneficiaries who live in poverty have incomes that are below twice the poverty level. In addition, 70 percent of Medicare beneficiaries over age 85 are women. Almost two-thirds of these women have incomes that are under double the poverty level (Kaiser Family Foundation, 1999b). Two-thirds of Medicare beneficiaries who need assistance with one or more activities of daily living, such as eating, are women. Two-thirds of Medicare beneficiaries who receive home health services are women. Women represent three-quarters of nursing home patients (Kaiser Family Foundation, 1999b).

Clearly, the Medicare program is vitally important to women. Women are more likely to live in poverty than men are and many outlive their husbands. As discussed in Chapter 7, women have experienced economic inequity through occupational segregation, job discrimination, and pay inequity. Consequently, older women in particular are often dependent on their spouses for financial support; widowhood or divorce compounds this problem.

Women are also more likely to live alone than are men due to increased longevity, a tendency to marry slightly older men, and higher remarriage rates for widowed men than for widowed women (Health Care Financing Administration, 2000b). Because of their longevity, women are more susceptible to multiple chronic

TERMINOLOGY BOX
Disability

Disability is defined as *inability to function*. To be included in the U.S. Bureau of the Census as disabled, individuals must meet one of the following criteria:

Disabled	Severely Disabled
Difficulty with functional activities, including sight, hearing, walking	Use of wheelchair for mobility or long-term use of canes, crutches, walkers
Difficulty with activities of daily living, including bathing, dressing, eating	Completely unable to perform activities of daily living
Difficulty with instrumental activities of daily living, such as taking prescribed medication or keeping track of money	
Specific conditions such as learning disability, Alzheimer's disease, Down syndrome, mental retardation, or other developmental or mental conditions	Alzheimer's disease Developmental disabilities
Limited in ability to do housework	Completely unable to do housework
Limited in ability to work	Completely unable to work
Receiving federal benefits based on inability to work	Receiving federal disability benefits

Source: Alliance for Health Reform, 1997b.

conditions, such as hypertension, arthritis, and osteoporosis, and have a greater need for long-term care. These concerns are addressed in greater depth in Chapter 7.

Managed Care and Medicare

Chapter 4 describes the introduction of managed care into the Medicare program in the early 1980s, its growth and development through the 1990s, and the problems encountered in efforts to enroll beneficiaries and attract health plans. In 1997, after bitter legislative struggles between the Republican-controlled Congress and the Clinton administration, Congress passed the Balanced Budget Act. The legislation established a new Medicare Part C, known as Medicare+ Choice (described in Chapter 4). The act also expanded prevention services (mammography and other cancer screening) and created incentives for managed care plans to enter underserved rural areas.

To expand the role of managed care in Medicare, beneficiaries were encouraged to enroll in HMOs, and a demonstration project was established to allow 390,000 beneficiaries to create medical savings accounts (MSAs). The new plans were required to include quality assurance programs that emphasized health outcomes and provided data to monitor, evaluate, and measure quality, effectiveness, consumer satisfaction, and continuity and coordination of care (AARP, 1997).

The new Medicare+ Choice option received strong criticism from consumer protection groups. Consumer Union's year-long investigation found a "system in turmoil"; insurance companies were charging more for Medigap plans, HMOs were reducing benefits and raising costs, and enrollees were faced with a confusing array of choices. Average families could not afford preferred provider organizations (PPOs) and private fee-for-service plans. Medical savings accounts were described as a "gamble against an insurance company that you will stay healthy" (Lieberman, 1998, p. 33)

In 1998, the *Washington Post* reported that HMOs were "abandoning older adults in droves" by leaving the Medicare managed care business altogether or dropping the unlimited drug benefit that attracted older adults to HMOs in the first place (Kuttner, 1998). In late 1998, almost 100 health plans withdrew from Medicare+ Choice, followed by an additional withdrawal of 100 plans in 1999 (U.S. General Accounting Office, 2000b).

Serious doubts were raised about the private sector's desire and ability to expand Medicare health plans, the ability of beneficiaries to comprehend the complexities of these options, and the government's ability to regulate their quality. Concern was also raised about using the HMO model for the most vulnerable beneficiaries of Medicare, low-income older adults and individuals with serious, chronic health problems (Neuman and Langwell, 1999). Today, the vast majority of Medicare beneficiaries remain enrolled in the traditional fee-for-service plan (82 percent) (U.S. General Accounting Office, 2000b).

Medicaid

Benefits and Financing

Medicaid was also enacted in 1965 as part of the compromise reform effort to expand health insurance coverage in the United States. Today, millions of low-income children, adults, older adults, and individuals with disabilities depend on Medicaid for access to health care. Medicaid is a jointly funded federal–state program administered by the states. It provides a broad range of basic health and long-term-care services.

When Medicaid was first enacted, it was designed to provide insurance to older adults, disabled individuals, and dependent children and mothers. The program has undergone reforms in recent years to extend coverage to low-income children and pregnant women, and some Medicare beneficiaries who would not have met earlier guidelines for Medicaid eligibility. The duration of certain benefits has been extended. More money has been spent on nursing facilities and home health care as the population has continued to age and live longer. In an effort to reduce cost, the most significant change has been the rapid growth in managed care as a means of delivering Medicaid services.

Mandatory and Optional Benefits.   States participate in the Medicaid program on a voluntary basis; however, all states participate. To receive federal funding, states must provide coverage for the following services:

Inpatient and outpatient hospital care

Physician, medical, and surgical dental services

Pediatric and family nurse practitioner services

Nurse midwife services (authorized by the state)

Laboratory and X-ray services

Nursing facility care for adults over age 21

Home health care

Early and periodic screening, diagnosis, and treatment (EPSDT) for children and youth under age 21

Family planning services and supplies

Rural health clinic services and federally qualified health center services (Health Care Financing Administration, 2000a)

Each state receives between 50 percent and 80 percent of the cost of these mandated services based on a formula that incorporates per capita income (Schneider, Fennel, and Long, 1998).

States also have the option to provide other health care services. The most common services covered by the states are prescription drugs, dental care, optometrist services and eyeglasses, prosthetic devices, hearing aids, TB-related services, nursing facility care for individuals under age 21, and intermediate care facilities services for mentally retarded persons. With the enactment of the Breast and Cervical Cancer Prevention and Treatment Act of 2000, states also have the option to cover services for some women with breast and cervical cancer (Health Care Financing Administration, 2001b; www.hcfa.gov/medicaid). More than 50 percent of Medicaid spending funds optional populations or optional services (Schneider, Fennel, and Long, 1998).

Mandatory and Optional Eligibility.   The federal government provides matching funds (on an open-ended basis) to the states to finance the cost of benefits covered by Medicaid. Benefits must be provided to five specific categories of *poor or low-income individuals* (see Figure 5.2): (1) pregnant women, (2) children, (3) older adult Medicare recipients (called dual eligibles because they are eligible for both

FIGURE 5.2   *Mandatory* **Medicaid Categories**

Primary Categories	Other Categories
Pregnant Women	
Pregnant women < 133% FPL	
Low-Income Children	
Infants < age 1 < 133% FPL	
Children age 1 to 6 < 133% FPL	
Children age 6 to 15 < 100% FPL	
Section 1931 children: States must cover families who meet the income and resource eligibility criteria in effect prior to the repeal of AFDC (7/16/1996), and have the option to use less restrictive guidelines	
Children in TANF families	
Title IV-E foster care children	
Title IV-E adoption assistance children	
Children provided transitional coverage following family loss of TANF eligibility, or Section 1931 AFDC eligibility	
Low-Income Adults	
Section 1931 adults (see above)	
Dual eligibles (Medicare and Medicaid)	
Adults provided transitional coverage following family loss of TANF eligibility, or Section 1931 AFDC eligibility	
Children with Disabilities	
Supplemental Security Income (SSI)	SSI Recipients as of 8/22/1996
Adults with Disabilities	
Supplemental Security Income (SSI)	"Pickle Amendment" recipients: individuals who lose SSI eligibility due to employment earnings or increased Social Security benefits
	Widows/widowers with disabilities ineligible for SSI due to increased income benefits

Sources: Schneider et al.; Kaiser Commission on Medicaid and the Uninsured, 1998, 1999.

Medicare and Medicaid), (4) adults under age 65 with dependent children (historically AFDC recipients; currently Temporary Assistance to Needy Children [TANF] recipients), and (5) children and adults with disabilities (Supplemental Security Income (SSI) recipients).

There are, however, millions of poor and low-income individuals who do not meet the criteria for these defined categories, including adults without dependent children and those who are not disabled. Without federal support, states are not likely to extend coverage to these individuals because the states would need to bear the full cost of coverage. In addition, federal matching funds may be available for *some* individuals within an eligible category, yet not available for others; these options are discussed next (Schneider, Fennel, and Long, 1998).

States must comply with five broad eligibility policies, two that are based on financial criteria (income limits and resource limits) and three that are based on social status and residency criteria (categorical eligibility, immigration status, and residency) (Schneider, Fennel, and Long, 1998). The requirements for each are as follows.

1. *Categorical eligibility:* Eligibility is limited to the five broad groups just specified; however, there are many different eligibility categories (see Figures 5.2 and 5.3). In many cases, categories overlap and individuals may qualify for Medicaid under more than one category. For example, a child with disabilities may qualify under SSI or as a member of a low-income family with dependent children (Schneider, Fennel, and Long, 1998).

2. *Income eligibility:* Eligibility is limited to individuals with financial need and is determined with income tests that vary by category and state. For example, for children, pregnant women, and Medicare dual eligibles, the eligibility standard used is a percentage of the FPL, such as 133 percent of poverty. For older adult recipients and recipients with disabilities, the standard used is a specific dollar amount or a multiple of a dollar amount (SSI payments). Thus, different standards are used to determine eligibility for different groups. In addition, different methodologies are used to calculate income eligibility. In some cases, all income, both earned and unearned, from any source is counted. In other cases, certain kinds of income, such as earned income, are disregarded. Some eligibility categories, particularly the medically needy category (discussed later), allow recipients to reduce (spend down) their incomes to a level that meets state eligibility criteria by deducting incurred health care expenses from their incomes (Schneider, Fennel, and Long, 1998).

3. *Resource eligibility:* Eligibility is restricted to individuals who have limited assets in most of the eligibility categories. In most states, the most common assets considered to determine eligibility are automobiles and savings. Like income eligibility, different standards and methodologies are employed. For adults with dependent children, elderly adults, or individuals with disabilities, different dollar amounts are used as the standard; in addition, these standards are not indexed to inflation and are not adjusted on a regular basis. In some cases, the full value of a resource (assets) is counted, in others a specific portion of the value is disregarded. Since 1986, states have had the option to exclude resource tests for low-income pregnant women and children. Since 1998, most states have exercised this option, primarily because of the high cost of identifying and determining the value of resources (Schneider, Fennel, and Long, 1998).

FIGURE 5.3 *Optional* **Medicaid Categories**

Primary Categories	Other Categories
Women	
Pregnant women < 185% FPL Low-income women diagnosed with breast or cervical cancer	Medically needy: Individual/family incomes adjusted by deducting catastrophic medical bills
Low-Income Children	
Infants < age 1 < 185% FPL Children age 1 to 6 < 185% FPL Children age 6 to 15 <133% or 185% FPL S-CHIP children up to 300% FPL Non Title IV-E foster care children Non Title IV-E adoption assistance children Low-income TB-infected children	Medically needy Ribicoff children: "Street kids" < age 21 who meet income and resource eligibility criteria, but are not dependents
Low-Income Adults	
Adults in two-parent households with dependent children Low-income TB-infected adults	Medically needy COBRA continuation beneficiaries: Benefits extended to adults treated by hospitals participating in Medicare regardless of income level or insurance
Children with Disabilities	
Katie Beckett children: Certain children with disabilities < age 18 living at home who would be eligible if placed in a hospital or nursing home Certain children in home or community care	Medically needy
Adults with Disabilities	
Medically needy Medically needy in nursing facilities	Certain adults in home or nursing care

Sources: Schneider et al., Kaiser Commission on Medicaid and the Uninsured, 1998, 1999; HCFA, 2000a.

   4. *Immigration status:* Two categories of legal immigrants were created by the Personal Responsibility and Work Opportunity Reconciliation Act of 1996 for determining Medicaid eligibility. Medicaid benefits are denied to legal immigrants who entered the United States after August 22, 1996, for a period of five years, except in the case of emergency care. At the end of the five-year period, states have the option to offer Medicaid services or continue to deny services until these immigrants become citizens. The Congressional Budget Office estimates that 260,000 elderly, 65,000 people with disabilities, 140,000 children, and 175,000 other adults will be denied coverage by 2002 under the new regulations (National Association of Social Workers, 1996). States have the option to provide benefits to legal immigrants who were living in the United States prior to August 22, 1996; essentially, all states have elected this option (Schneider, Fennel, and Long, 1998).

5. *Residency:* To be eligible for Medicaid, an individual must be a resident of the state that is offering the health insurance benefits. However, a state cannot deny benefits to a resident because he or she has not lived in the state for a specified minimum period. For nursing facility care, the state where the nursing facility is located is responsible for determining eligibility and financing services, not the state where the family or spouse lives (Schneider, Fennel, and Long, 1998).

Medicaid Benefit Payments. From 1990 to 1992, Medicaid spending grew 27 percent, primarily due to increases in hospital payments for disproportionate share reimbursements. These are payments made to hospitals that serve a disproportionate share (DSH) of poor or low-income patients, and are supplemental to the regular payments hospitals receive from Medicaid. However, between 1992 and 1995, growth in spending declined significantly to approximately 10 percent annually. This occurred for several reasons, including low rates of inflation and new federal limits on DSH payments (Kaiser Family Foundation, 1999d).

From 1995 to 1997, growth in spending declined to an historic low of approximately 3 percent annually. The reasons for this decline are rooted in the welfare reforms discussed earlier and a reduction in DSH payments. With TANF and Medicaid delinked, one of the major unintended consequences of welfare reform was the decline in the number of Medicaid beneficiaries. In addition, payments to disproportionate share hospitals declined overall during this period due to legislation passed in 1993 (Kaiser Family Foundation, 1999d).

From 1997 to 1998, enrollments remained steady, but spending increased significantly ($8.7 billion). There are multiple reasons for the increase, including the rising cost of prescription drugs, the increase in home and community-based care, and the increase in the size of the disabled population. Projections indicate that both enrollments and the rate of growth in spending will increase (Kaiser Family Foundation, 2001a).

Recipients

In 1998, the Medicaid program provided health insurance coverage for 41.1 million people to three primary groups of recipients: children and their parents, senior citizens, and people with disabilities. The program served 18.9 million children, 7.9 million adults in families with dependent children, 6.6 million individuals with disabilities, and 3.9 million older adults (Health Care Financing Administration, 2000a). Although the vast majority of recipients are children and adults living in poor families, approximately two-thirds of the cost of Medicaid is spent on the elderly and people with disabilities (Kaiser Family Foundation, 1999c).

During the early 1990s, the number of Medicaid recipients increased significantly when the program expanded to include pregnant women, infants, and young children up to 133 percent of the FPL. The states were also given the option to expand coverage to pregnant women and infants up to 185 percent of the FPL. Court decisions also mandated coverage to learning-disabled children. However, enrollments have declined steadily since 1995 due to state and federal reforms in AFDC that culminated in the Personal Responsibility and Work Opportunity Reconciliation Act of 1996 (Kaiser Family Foundation, 1999c). Enrollment projections show modest growth (1 percent annually) until 2010 (Health Care Financing Administration, 2000a).

Poor and Low-Income Pregnant Women, Children, and Families.   Until   the mid-1980s, Medicaid was essentially limited to recipients of public assistance (AFDC and SSI). Some states provided Medicaid to people defined as medically needy. *Medically needy* is a term used to describe individuals who meet the *categorical* requirements of Medicaid and have catastrophic *medical expenses*, but whose incomes are too high to meet the *income* requirements of the program. In these cases, states have the option to allow these individuals to spend down, or offset their excess income by deducting their medical expenses from their income during a specified period of time. This process allows them to qualify for Medicaid (U.S. General Accounting Office, 1995).

In 1986, Congress expanded access to Medicaid by giving states the *option* to cover pregnant women, infants, and children (up to age 8) with family incomes up to 185 percent of the FPL. Beginning in 1989, states were *required* to cover individuals with incomes at or below 75 percent of the FPL. They were also required to cover pregnant women and children up to age 6 with family incomes up to 133 percent of the FPL by 1990. In 1990, states were also given the *option* to gradually phase in children born before September 30, 1983 (aged 6 to 10), with family incomes up to 100 percent of the FPL. The purpose of the phase-in expansion was to encourage states to cover all poor children through age 18 by 2002 (U.S. General Accounting Office, 1995).

After almost a decade of federal–state efforts to expand coverage to children, Medicaid "helped cushion the effect of [the] declining employment-based health insurance" discussed in Chapter 3, but many children remained uninsured (U.S. General Accounting Office, 1995, p. 20). In 1995, only twenty-seven states had expanded coverage in their Medicaid programs to 185 percent of the FPL. Only twelve states had increased coverage to children to the upper age limit of 19 (U.S. General Accounting Office, 1995).

By 1997, only two more states (Wisconsin and Arkansas) had expanded coverage to 185 percent of the FPL. A number of states increased the upper age limit from 12 to 14, 16, 17, or even age 18, but no additional states had expanded coverage to the age of 19. Even among children eligible for Medicaid, more than a third had not been enrolled (U.S. General Accounting Office, 1995; National Governors Association and National Conference of State Legislatures, 1998). Studies found that families seemed to be unaware of their children's eligibility or avoided enrollment because they perceived stigma attached to Medicaid (U.S. General Accounting Office, 1995).

State Children's Health Insurance Program (S-CHIP). In 1997, as part of the Balanced Budget Act, Congress enacted Title XXI of the Social Security Act, the State Children's Health Insurance Program (S-CHIP). The purpose of S-CHIP, which became effective January 1, 1999, was to increase health insurance coverage to children in low-income working families. Matching funds were provided to the states to expand coverage to children in families with incomes up to 200 percent of the FPL. States were given three broad options to increase coverage:

1. States could expand Medicaid by increasing the age of eligibility, the income level for eligibility, or both. The program had to be offered statewide.
2. States could establish new state programs or expand the state-run health insurance programs already available to children.
3. States could provide some combination of both options by changing the state Medicaid program and establishing or expanding a state-run program (Edelman, 1999).

States that had already made provisions for families at 200 percent of the FPL were allowed to expand coverage to 300 percent. Medicaid, health maintenance plans (HMOs), the state employees' plan, or the federal employees' Blue Cross Blue Shield plan could administer the benefit plans; in most states, the Medicaid plan was already the most comprehensive. Premiums or copayments could be charged only if the state decided to establish a new plan. Children eligible for traditional Medicaid coverage (family incomes less than 133 percent of poverty) would not be eligible for the new S-CHIP program (Edelman, 1999).

The primary targets of the S-CHIP program were children with parents who were unemployed, in transition between jobs, or employed in jobs that did not provide health insurance benefits. The states had to identify and reach families through outreach, and provide flexible approaches to coverage to expand coverage to children in these families. Private insurance mechanisms, such as waiting periods for new employees, premiums, copayments, and deductibles, were known to be barriers to coverage for families with moderate incomes. The S-CHIP program allowed states to coordinate benefits coverage with private employers; subsidize employer-based insurance; pay for private insurance copayments and deductibles; and simplify the application, enrollment, and eligibility determination process. The stigma associated with Medicaid was also addressed by giving the states the option to give the program its own name (Reschovsky and Cunningham, 1998).

Initially, states moved quickly to receive the program's matching federal funds. By September 1998, fifty states had submitted plans for their state programs. Four states raised eligibility to 300 percent of the FPL, and four others established eligibility requirements higher than 200 but lower than 300 percent of the FPL. Nineteen more states determined eligibility as 200 percent of FPL, but the remaining states were still at 185 percent or less (National Governors Association and National Conference of State Legislatures, 1998).

By 1999, there was concern about the failure of states to reach out to uninsured children; in May 1999, less than 20 percent of available funds were being spent (Pear, 1999). In addition, a Families USA (1999d) study of the twelve states with the largest number of uninsured children (totaling two-thirds of all uninsured children in the United States) showed that from 1996 to 1999 almost 1 million children had lost Medicaid. Although the S-CHIP program had expanded coverage to children in low-income working families, AFDC reforms enacted in 1996 (Personal Responsibility and Work Opportunity Reconciliation Act) had reduced the number of enrollees. The combined effect was a decline in coverage for children.

Personal Responsibility and Work Opportunity Reconciliation Act of 1996.   The Personal Responsibility and Work Opportunity Reconciliation Act (PRWOPA) of 1996 ended Aid to Families with Dependent Children (AFDC), the federal income assistance program that originated with the Social Security Act of 1935. The bill replaced AFDC with Temporary Assistance for Needy Families (TANF), a block grant program that provides state funds for income assistance for low-income families. PRWOPA eliminated the federal entitlement to public assistance and gave each state a block grant to administer its own program.

The legislation delinked Medicaid and TANF; prior to these reforms, most AFDC recipients were *automatically* eligible for Medicaid. This changed with the creation of TANF; eligibility for TANF and Medicaid became separate determinations. However, states are required under Section 1931 of the Social Security Act to provide coverage for families with dependent children who meet the income and resource eligibility criteria in effect prior to the repeal of AFDC on July 16, 1996 (Greenberg, 1998). However, income eligibility standards (percent of FPL) for AFDC had been set so low by the states that many working parents were ineligible for coverage (Families USA, 2000a). Congress gave states the option to use less restrictive guidelines and, as of August 1998, to provide coverage to two-parent low-income families (Health Care Financing Administration, 2000a). Thus, even if families were no longer eligible for TANF because of time limits, they were still likely to be eligible for Medicaid.

In 1997, as an "unintended consequence" of the new legislation, "an estimated 675,000 low-income people became uninsured...more than three out of five (62 percent) were children" (Families USA, 1999d, p. 2). The Families USA study found that most of the children should not have lost coverage because they were still eligible for Medicaid. Coverage was lost in three primary ways. First, when recipients were terminated from income assistance, they were not informed of their eligibility for Medicaid. TANF recipients are terminated after two years if the recipient does not find employment, or if he or she reaches the lifetime maximum of five years. As families reached these time limits, administrative errors led to loss of Medicaid.

Second, recipients lost coverage when they moved from "welfare to work," as prescribed by the PRWOPA. Adult recipients typically found employment in jobs that did not offer health insurance benefits and were eligible for Medicaid only if they earned very little money (less than the FPL). Their children, on the other hand, were eligible at higher (family) income eligibility standards; yet, they too were terminated at this point. Third, some states discouraged enrollment in the TANF program. They diverted families from the application process toward job-seeking activity, lump-sum cash payments, and other options. If families were unaware of their right to Medicaid independent of the TANF program, they were at risk of losing coverage.

Studies conducted by the Urban Institute (Ellwood, 1999; Garrett and Holahan, 2000) confirmed these findings. A follow-up study by Families USA (2000a) showed that Medicaid enrollments declined from 1996 to 1999 not only for children but also for low-income parents. In the fifteen states with the highest enrollments of low-income adults, almost a million parents lost Medicaid coverage. In addition to the causes cited in the earlier study, this study found that few states had taken advantage of the options to expand coverage to low-income parents. A report prepared for the government suggested "an urgent need for welfare workers to be given assistance in understanding complex eligibility rules, and for automated eligibility systems to be brought up to date" (Dion and Pavetti, 2000, p. 32).

As of fiscal year 2000, seventeen states had not reached the expanded income eligibility standard of 200 percent FPL, while ten states exceeded the standard with 200 to 300 percent FPL criterion. S-CHIP had reached and enrolled over 3 million children, but more than 6 million were eligible and still not enrolled (Health Care Financing Administration, 2000c; Children's Defense Fund, 2000; see www.hcfa.gov/init/fy200_.pdf for new state enrollment statistics). In an effort to reach these children, Congress passed the Medicare, Medicaid, and S-CHIP Benefits Improvement and Protection Act in December 2000. This legislation adjusts the formula for reallocation of the unspent funds. The bill allows states that have spent their allocation to apply for up to 40 percent of the unspent funding, whereas states that have not used their full allocation can receive up to 60 percent. All states can use 10 percent of the funds for outreach activities (Children's Defense Fund, 2000).

Poor and Low-Income Children and Adults with Disabilities. Most Medicaid recipients with disabilities qualify for the program because they are eligible for Supplemental Security Income (SSI) program. SSI was established under President Nixon in 1972 as a federal income-assistance program for poor elderly, blind, and disabled persons. Age is not a factor; SSI provides income assistance to children, youth, and adults. In January 2000, SSI served 6.3 million individuals (Social Security Administration, 2000); approximately 70 percent were adults. However, the number of children with disabilities served by SSI has grown since the *Sullivan v. Zebley* case (discussed next). SSI recipients are eligible for assistance due to a wide range of disabling conditions, including mental retardation, mental illness, drug addiction and alcoholism, blindness, and diseases of the central nervous system.

SSI and Children. Before 1983, SSI used a different definition of disability for adults than children. For adults, disability was defined as physical or mental health problems that interfered with the ability to work. For children, specific medical criteria, such as mental retardation or deafness were used. In 1983, a class action suit, *Sullivan v. Zebley*, was brought against the federal government by the Legal Services office in Philadelphia on behalf of all children with disabilities who had been denied benefits. The Supreme Court ruled in favor of the children in 1990 and expanded the program's listing of eligible medical conditions to include learning disabilities, such as attention deficit disorder (ADD), and other functional impairments of activities of daily living, including speaking, walking, and bathing. In addition, because of the court's decision, two new standards for determination of eligibility were established: individualized functional assessments (IFA) and functional equivalence. In essence, children who could not function at a level appropriate for their age became eligible for SSI (U.S. General Accounting Office, 1998).

As a result of these changes, between 1983 and 1990, the federal government reevaluated 288,000 denied cases at a cost of $3 billion in back payments (Pear, 1990). From 1989 to 1996, the number of children eligible for SSI tripled to almost 1 million because of the Supreme Court decisions (U.S. General Accounting Office, 1998). In 1995, as part of its focus on welfare reform, Congress considered elimination of the IFA and revision of the medical listings. With the program's growth and the increase in the number of children eligible for SSI and Medicaid, the Republican-controlled Congress questioned the objectivity and consistency involved in determining need. It also believed that some families were guilty of fraud and abuse because of coaching their children to misbehave or fake disabilities (Pear, 1997b).

The Personal Responsibility and Work Opportunity Reconciliation Act of 1996 changed the SSI eligibility criteria for children by eliminating the IFA and restricting the medical listings, thus making it more difficult for children to qualify. Under the new law, effective July 1, 1997, children with medically proven physical or mental conditions that resulted in *marked* and *severe* functional limitations would be eligible, whereas children with more moderate, maladaptive conditions would not. The Social Security Administration projected that children with mood disorders would be affected most. However, they also found that children with pulmonary tuberculosis, mental retardation, burns, intercranial injuries, schizophrenia, and arthritis would be denied benefits. The Congressional Budget Office estimated that 48,000 children would lose coverage between 1997 and 2003 and that 315,000 children who would have qualified under the previous law would be denied coverage (National Association of Social Workers, 1996).

In fact, in 1997 disability benefits were terminated for 95,180 children; most had mental health disorders (Pear, 1997a). However, in appeals and reviews of these cases, it was determined that many children were wrongly terminated and the decisions were reversed (Pear, 1997b). More importantly, the Balanced Budget Reconciliation Act of 1997 *restored* Medicaid eligibility for children with disabilities who lost their SSI benefits due to the new restrictions (National Association of Social Workers, 1997). In 1998, the Social Security Administration issued a new plan for quality reviews of children's disabilities to improve the accuracy and consistency of determinations across the states (U.S. General Accounting Office, 1998).

SSI and Adults. The Personal Responsibility and Work Opportunity Reconciliation Act of 1996 also had a significant impact on adults with disabilities. Under the new policy, SSI benefits were denied to *legal* immigrants (for exceptions, see Figure 5.4)

FIGURE 5.4   **Legal Immigrants with *Mandatory* Medicaid Eligibility (no restrictions)**

Veterans and their dependents
Active-duty military personnel and their dependents
Refugees, asylees, and Cuban and Haitian immigrants for seven years after entering
   country
Amerasian immigrants for five years after entering country
Permanent residents with Social Security (40 credited quarters)
Canadian-born immigrants with 50% or more North American Native heritage

Source: Families USA, 1999c.

until they became U.S. citizens, and Medicaid was denied to *legal* immigrants for a period of five years after entering the country. *Legal immigrants with disabilities* would be denied SSI and Medicaid until they could meet these new requirements.

However, the Balanced Budget Reconciliation Act of 1997 restored Medicaid benefits to some immigrants by giving states the option to provide coverage to legal immigrants who entered the country prior to August 22, 1996, if they became disabled after this date. Legal immigrants who entered the country after this date can receive emergency medical services only. S-CHIP, however, must be made available to legal immigrant children who entered after August 22, 1996. In 1998, new regulations restored SSI-Medicaid-linked benefits to legal immigrants who were denied coverage based on the 1996 reforms, if they were receiving benefits on August 22, 1996.

Other changes in SSI have had a significant impact on the Medicaid program and coverage for adults with disabilities. In 1988, the U.S. Justice Department included Acquired Immune Deficiency Syndrome (AIDS) in the list of approved medical conditions. Today, Medicaid serves over 50 percent of all individuals living with AIDS; most of theses recipients are SSI recipients. Medicaid is the single largest payer of services for people with AIDS. The Health Care Financing Administration (2001a) estimated that over $4 billion in federal and state Medicaid dollars would be spent providing coverage to 116,000 individuals in fiscal year 2001.

One of the most dramatic changes in the SSI program was the elimination of drug and alcohol addiction as the sole reason for eligibility for SSI and Medicaid. In 1994, Congress passed the Social Security Independence and Program Improvements Act, which restricted SSI benefits to thirty-six months and required recipients to be in treatment. SSI recipients dropped from SSI could continue to receive Medicaid, as long as they remained in treatment for twelve successive months. In 1999, *all* benefits (SSI and Medicaid) for *all* individuals solely disabled by alcohol or drug addiction were terminated from the program, effective January 1, 1997. Over 200,000 recipients were notified and after reviewing their disability status, 50,000 were terminated. This group was given a second look in 1998, and a few hundred additional enrollees were terminated (Nibal, 2000).

The most significant change for disabled individuals who want to work is the Ticket to Work and Work Incentives Improvement Act of 1999. Beginning on

October 1, 2000, states had the option to expand Medicaid to (1) individuals with disabilities who want to work by increasing the amount they can earn and to (2) employed individuals with medically improved disabilities who lost their Medicaid coverage because they no longer met SSI's adult definition of disability. States can establish their own income and resource eligibility standards and impose premiums on a sliding scale basis (Health Care Financing Administration, 2001c).

Medically Needy.   Children and adults with disabilities can qualify for Medicaid if they are "medically needy" and "spend down" to the state's standard. Although states have the option to set standards for income that should be protected from high medical expenses, the federal government limits the standard to 133 percent of the state's 1996 AFDC payment level. Thus, the medically needy standard is usually set well below SSI payment levels.

In addition, because there is significant variation in the 1996 AFDC payment levels among the states, there are significant disparities in access based on medical need. For example, in 1999 in Vermont elderly recipients had to spend down to a monthly income of $683, whereas elderly recipients in Louisiana were required to spend down to $100 monthly income. These guidelines also create inequities among older adults within states. For example, in Louisiana, an elderly SSI beneficiary with disabilities would receive full Medicaid coverage and $500 monthly income, whereas someone who is medically needy would receive only $100 monthly income. To make matters worse, nearly a third of the states have no programs or coverage for the medically needy at all (Families USA, 1999a).

Poor and Low-Income Elderly (Medicare and Medicaid Dual Eligibles).   Without question, the largest health insurance program in the United States for older adults is Medicare. However, Medicaid is also a vital source of health insurance for poor and low-income older adults. Approximately 16 million (45 percent) of Medicare's beneficiaries have incomes either below FPL (5 million or 14 percent) or near poverty level between 100 and 200 percent FPL (11 million or 31 percent). Medicare beneficiaries with incomes *below* the FPL are eligible for Medicaid services not covered by Medicare (prescription drugs, long-term care) and assistance with the cost of Medicare Part B premiums and cost sharing. Medicare beneficiaries with incomes near poverty are eligible for Medicaid assistance with the cost of Medicare Part B premiums and cost sharing (see Figure 5.5) (Kaiser Family Foundation, 1999a).

Although Social Security and Medicare play a major role in reducing poverty among the elderly, many older adults still struggle to get by. In 1996, 43 percent of the elderly had incomes below 200 percent of the FPL; of these, 12 percent were living on incomes *below* the FPL (Schneider et al., 1999). As discussed earlier, average out-of-pocket expenses and cost-sharing requirements are very high; for this population of poor and low-income recipients, these expenses can be financially devastating.

Medicare-Medicaid dual eligibles tend to be over age 85, female, and people of color. They are also likely to live alone and have a mental or cognitive disorder

FIGURE 5.5   **Medicare/Medicaid Dual Eligibles**

Category	Eligibility Criteria	Benefits
Full Medicaid Benefits:	**Mandatory Coverage** SSI Eligibility * (73% of FPL) or 209(b) State rules "Pickle Amendment" Widows/widowers who lose SSI due to higher Social Security benefits **Optional Coverage** Medically Needy Institutionalized ** State Supplementation Payment recipients Certain home and community-based individuals***	Prescription drugs Long-term care Medicare Part B premiums and cost sharing (deductibles, copayments) Wrap around benefits
Qualified Medicare Beneficiary (QMB)	< 100 % of poverty	Medicare Part B premium and cost sharing
Specified Low-Income Beneficiary (SLMB)	100–200 % of poverty	Medicare Part B premium
Qualifying Individuals 1 (QI1)	120–135% of poverty****	Medicare Part B premiums
Qualifying Individuals 2 (QI2)	135–175% of poverty****	Medicare Part B premiums

*States have the option to expand coverage to 100% of poverty.
**Income must be no higher than 300% of SSI standard.
***Individuals who would be eligible if institutionalized.
****QI programs are block grants and are available only on a first-come, first-served basis.

Source: Schneider et al., 1999, Kaiser Commission on Medicaid and the Uninsured, 1999.

or a chronic illness, such as diabetes (Alliance for Health Reform, 1997b). Yet, Medicaid does not cover nearly half of all poor and low-income Medicare beneficiaries eligible for coverage (Schneider et al., 1999). There are many reasons for the low-enrollment including the complexity of the program, inadequate outreach efforts, and the stigma associated with public assistance programs (Nemore, 1997).

As shown in Figure 5.5, states have the option to expand Medicaid coverage to poor and low-income Medicare beneficiaries through a number of options. In addition, the Balanced Budget Act of 1997 expanded these options by creating block grants for the states (which expire in 2002). These funds are available to qualifying individuals to cover all or a portion of the cost of the Medicare Part B premium. The block grants are a fixed amount of federal dollars provided each year to the states with no requirement for state matching funds. When the funds run out, states will have no funds available for qualifying individuals.

Prior to the Balanced Budget Act of 1997, states met the 20 percent cost-sharing requirement for dual eligibles who received full Medicaid benefits. However, because state Medicaid payments are often set lower than Medicare rates, states are now required to pay cost sharing only up to the Medicaid rate. Finally, the Balanced Budget Act of 1997 prohibited physicians and other Medicare providers from billing dual eligibles for copayments and deductibles not covered by the state.

Managed Care and Medicaid

Chapter 4 provides an overview of the origins and development of Medicaid and managed care. In 1981, states were given the option to seek federal waivers to establish mandatory managed care plans. From 1983 to 1997, states experimented with managed care plans primarily for AFDC recipients; enrollment in these plans grew from 3 million to 17 million recipients (Kaiser Family Foundation, 1998d).

In 1997, Congress passed the Balanced Budget Act, which allowed states to mandate managed care plans without pursuing federal waivers, except for Medicaid-Medicare dual eligibles, children with special needs, and Native Americans (U.S. General Accounting Office, 1996). It also allowed states to create managed care plans with 100 percent Medicaid enrollment. By 1998, 25 percent of all *disabled* Medicaid recipients were enrolled in managed care plans due to state initiatives to experiment with plans for the disabled (Kaiser Family Foundation, 1998d). By 2000, the majority (57 percent) of Medicaid managed care recipients were enrolled in managed care plans (Health Care Financing Administration, 2001b).

A few states have sought federal waivers to establish managed care plans for dual eligibles, but very few are enrolled (U.S. General Accounting Office, 2000c). However, many states have experimented with mandatory managed care plans for children with special needs (see Figure 5.2 and 5.3 for eligible groups of low-income and disabled children) through the waiver process. Children eligible for SSI are most often enrolled; the number of children enrolled in both SSI and Medicaid managed care has increased from 32 percent in 1990 to 71 percent in 1998 (National Academy of State Health Plans, 1999). The GAO's report of safeguards to ensure access to specialists shows that states vary tremendously in these efforts (U.S. General Accounting Office, 2000a).

The initial growth of managed care in the Medicaid program was driven by state efforts to reduce rising costs, particularly during the late 1980s and early 1990s (Families USA, 2001). However, doubts have been raised about the ability of managed care to adequately serve low-income recipients, older adults, and individuals with greater health needs than the rest of the population (see Chapter 4). Studies raise concern about inadequate access to medical specialists and social services, and cost shifting rather than cost savings (Rowland et al., 1995; Holahan et al., 1998). Studies also identify problems with inadequate consumer information about plans, interruptions in treatment, barriers to filing grievances, and insufficient assurance of quality of care (Families USA, 2001).

Highlights

■ Medicare and Medicaid were established in 1965 as Titles XIII and XIX of the Social Security Act.

■ Medicare, a social insurance program, provides health insurance to almost 40 million adult retirees, employed individuals with disabilities who have difficulty continuing their employment, and individuals with end-stage kidney disease.

■ Medicaid, a means-tested program, provides health insurance to more than 41 million individuals of all ages who are poor and low-income pregnant women, children, and families; elderly adults; and people with disabilities. Although the vast majority of recipients are children and adults living in poor families, approximately two-thirds of the cost of Medicaid is spent on the elderly and people with disabilities.

■ Medicare has two parts: (Part A) Hospital Insurance and (Part B) Medical Insurance. Medicare is financed by a payroll tax on employers and employees; self-employed workers pay both taxes. Recipients incur substantial out-of-pocket expenses for additional physician fees, copayments, deductibles, and services not covered by Medicare. The most costly services that are not covered are prescription drugs, long-term care, and physician payments.

■ About two-thirds of Medicare beneficiaries purchase Medigap insurance or have supplemental insurance through their employers that provides additional coverage; the remaining third have reduced some of their expenses by joining managed care plans or participating in the Medicare buy-in program. However, many eligible enrollees do not participate in the buy-in program as dual eligible beneficiaries.

■ Medicaid, which is administered by the states, has mandatory and optional benefits. Mandatory benefits include hospital and health care provider services, and nursing facility and home health care. Optional benefits, which many states provide, include prescription drugs, dental care, hearing devices, and intermediate care for mentally retarded individuals. General revenues finance the program; the federal government provides matching funds to the states. States must comply with a number of eligibility policies that limit coverage to specific groups of poor and low-income persons who meet income and assets criteria, immigration status, and residency requirements.

■ The most significant expansion of the Medicaid program occurred in 1997 with the creation of the State Children's Health Insurance Program (S-CHIP). Starting in 1999, states had the option to expand coverage to children in working families with incomes between 200 and 300 percent of the FPL. However, by 2000, only one third of eligible children had been enrolled by state expansions of Medicaid.

■ In an effort to encourage states to make use of their S-CHIP allocations, Congress enacted legislation that allowed states that had exhausted their funding to apply for additional funds. However, with a decrease of about 1 million children from Medicaid between 1996 and 1999 due to welfare reforms enacted in 1996, coverage for children declined further.

■ The most significant reform in both Medicare and Medicaid was the introduction of managed care in the early 1980s and its expansion during the 1990s. Today about 14 percent of Medicare beneficiaries are enrolled in managed care plans, while approximately 57 percent of Medicaid recipients participate in managed care plans.

■ The introduction of managed care to the Medicaid program represents a dramatic change in the way services are delivered to this population. The impact of this change is not yet clear. However, many concerns have been raised about the inability of managed care to reduce costs with low-income families with few resources, and disabled and poor elderly individuals with significant health and medical needs. Studies have shown that state Medicaid managed care plans have had difficulty ensuring adequate access to specialists and raise doubts about cost saving with this population.

Websites to Obtain Updated and Additional Information

www.hcfa.gov/Medicare
www.hcfa.gov/Medicaid
Health Care Financing Administration
U.S. Department of Health and Human Services

www.kff.org
Kaiser Family Foundation

REFERENCES

AARP. (1997, August). AARP Wins in Budget Debate. *AARP Federal Health Update.* Washington, DC: AARP.

AARP Public Policy Institute. (2000 October). *The Cost of Prescription Drugs: Who Needs Help?* Washington, DC: AARP.

Alliance for Health Reform. (1997a, March). Medicare and Medicaid Dual Eligibles. *Managed Care and Vulnerable Populations.* Washington, DC: Alliance for Health Reform.

Alliance for Health Reform. (1997b, November). Adults with Disabilities. *Managed Care and Vulnerable Populations.* Washington, DC: Alliance for Health Reform.

Angell, M. and Perman, A. S. (2001, June 20). Prescription for Profit. *The Washington Post,* p. A27.

Ball, R. (1995, Winter). Perspectives on Medicare: What Medicare's Architects Had in Mind. *Health Affairs, 14,* 4, 62–100.

Berndt, E. R. (2001, March/April). The U.S. Pharmaceutical Industry: Why the Major Growth in Times of Cost Containment. *Health Affairs, 19,* 2, 100–114.

Chapman, T. (1999, October–November). Closing the Gap for the Nation's Most Vulnerable Population. *Closing the Gap.* Washington, DC: Office of Minority Affairs, U.S. Department of of Health and Human Services.

Children's Defense Fund. (2000, Spring). Unspent Funds Mean Uninsured Children. *Sign Them Up!* Washington, DC: Children's Defense Fund.

Congressional Progressive Caucus. (2001). Medicare Extension of Drugs to Seniors (MEDS) Plan. (Online) Available: www.bernie.house.gov/pc

DiNitto, D. (1995). *Social Welfare: Politics and Public Policy,* 4th ed. Boston: Allyn & Bacon.

Dion, M. R. and Pavetti, L. (2000, March). *Access to and Participation in Medicaid and the Food Stamp Program.* Washington, DC: Mathematica Policy Research.

Edelman, M. W. (1999). *The State of America's Children, Children's Defense Fund Yearbook 1999.* Boston: Beacon Press.

Ellwood, M. (1999). *The Medicaid Eligibility Maze, Coverage Expands, but Enrollment Problems Persist: Findings from a Five-State Study.* Occasional Paper No. 30. Washington, DC: Urban Institute.

Families USA. (2001a, May). *Medicaid Managed Care Consumer Protection Regulations: No Patients' Rights for the Poor? Special Report.* Washington, DC: Families USA.

Families USA. (2000a). *Go Directly to Work, Do Not Collect Health Insurance: Low-Income Parents Lose Medicaid.* Washington, DC: Families USA.

Families USA. (2000b). Cost Overdose: Growth in Drug Spending for the Elderly, 1992–2000. Washington, DC: Families USA.

Families USA. (1999a). *Expanding Medicaid State Options.* Washington, DC: Families USA.

Families USA. (1999b). *Hard to Swallow, Rising Drug Prices for America's Seniors.* Washington, DC: Families USA.

Families USA. (1999c). *Immigrant Eligibility and Medicaid and CHIP Programs.* Washington, DC: Families USA.

Families USA. (1999d). *Losing Health Insurance, the Unintended Consequences of Welfare Reform.* Washington, DC: Families USA.

Families USA. (1999e). *One Step Forward, One Step Back, Children's Health Coverage After CHIP and Welfare Reform.* Washington, DC: Families USA.

Families USA. (1998). *Shortchanged: Billions Withheld from Medicare Beneficiaries.* Washington, DC: Families USA.

Freudenteim, M. (2001, February 8). Insurers Push Rates High for Medigap. *The New York Times,* pp. C1, C15.

Fronstin, P. and Copeland, C. (1997, September). Medicare on Life Support: Will It Survive? *Employee Benefits Research Institute Issue Brief, 189.* Washington, DC: Employee Benefits Research Institute.

Garrett, B. and Holahan, J. (2000, March). Welfare Leavers, Medicaid Coverage, and Private Health Insurance. *Assessing the New Federalism, Series B,* No. B-13. Washington, DC: The Urban Institute.

Gorin, S. H. (2001, May). Medicare and Prescription Drugs: Prospects for Reform. *Health and Social Work, 26,* 2, 115–118.

Greenberg, M. (1998, September). Participation in Welfare and Medicaid Enrollment. *Kaiser Commission on Medicaid and the Uninsured Issue Paper.* Washington, DC: Kaiser Family Foundation.

Health Care Financing Administration. (2002). *Medicare and You, 2002* (Online). Available at www.medicare.gov

Health Care Financing Administration. (2001a, February). *Medicaid and AIDS and HIV Infection, Fact Sheet.* Baltimore, MD: U.S. Department of Health and Human Services.

Health Care Financing Administration. (2001b). *Medicaid Managed Care State Enrollment December 31, 2000* (Online). Available at www.hcfa.gov/Medicaid/omcpr00.pdf

Health Care Financing Administration. (2001c). *Ticket to Work and Work Incentives Improvement Act Fact Sheet*. Baltimore, MD: U.S. Department of Health and Human Services.

Health Care Financing Administration. (2000a, September). *A Profile of Medicaid, Chartbook 2000*. Baltimore, MD: U.S. Department of Health and Human Services.

Health Care Financing Administration. (2000b, July). *Medicare 2000, 35 Years of Improving America's Health and Security*. Baltimore, MD: U.S. Department of Health and Human Services.

Health Care Financing Administration. (2000c). *S-CHIP Aggregate Enrollment Statistics for FY2000* (Online). Available at www.hcfa.gov/init/fy2000.pdf

Holahan, J., Zuckerman, S., Evans, A., and Rangarajan, S. (1998, May–June). Medicaid Managed Care in Thirteen States. *Health Affairs, 17,* 3, 43–63.

Kaiser Family Foundation. (2001a, February). Medicaid Enrollment and Spending Trends. *Kaiser Commission on Medicaid and the Uninsured Medicaid Facts*. Washington, DC: Kaiser Family Foundation.

Kaiser Family Foundation. (2001b, June). Medicare at a Glance. *The Medicare Program, The Kaiser Medicare Policy Project*. Washington, DC: Kaiser Family Foundation.

Kaiser Family Foundation. (2000a, March). *Medicare and Prescription Drugs*. Washington, DC: Kaiser Family Foundation.

Kaiser Family Foundation. (2000b, July). *Prescription Drug Trends: A Chartbook*. Washington, DC: Kaiser Family Foundation.

Kaiser Family Foundation. (2000c, January). *Post-Election Survey Finds Health Issues Rank High for Voters*. Washington, DC: Kaiser Family Foundation.

Kaiser Family Foundation. (1999a, May). Medicare and Medicaid for the Elderly and Disabled Poor. *Kaiser Commission on Medicaid and the Uninsured Key Facts*. Washington, DC: Kaiser Family Foundation.

Kaiser Family Foundation. (1999b, May). Women and Medicare. *The Medicare Program, The Kaiser Medicare Policy Project*. Washington, DC: Kaiser Family Foundation.

Kaiser Family Foundation. (1999c, July). *The Medicaid Program at a Glance. Kaiser Commission on Medicaid and the Uninsured Key Facts*. Washington, DC: Kaiser Family Foundation.

Kaiser Family Foundation. (1999d, September). Medicaid Enrollment and Spending Trends. *Kaiser Commission on Medicaid and the Uninsured Medicaid Facts*. Washington, DC: Kaiser Family Foundation.

Kaiser Family Foundation. (1998a, July). Medicare at a Glance. *The Medicare Program, The Kaiser Medicare Policy Project*. Washington, DC: Kaiser Family Foundation.

Kaiser Family Foundation. (1998b, July). Medicare Managed Care. *The Medicare Program, The Kaiser Medicare Policy Project*. Washington, DC: Kaiser Family Foundation.

Kaiser Family Foundation. (1998c, October). The Medicaid Program at a Glance. *Kaiser Commission on Medicaid and the Uninsured Medicaid Facts*. Washington, DC: Kaiser Family Foundation.

Kaiser Family Foundation. (1998d, October). Medicaid and Managed Care. *Kaiser Commission on Medicaid and the Uninsured Medicaid Facts*. Washington, DC: Kaiser Family Foundation.

Kuttner, R. (1998, November 23). Bad Medicine for the Elderly. *The Washington Post*, p. A23.

Lieberman, T. (1998, September). Medicare: New Choices, New Worries. *Consumer Reports*, pp. 27–38.

Medicare Payment Advisory Commission. (2000). *Report to the Congress: Selected Medicare Issues*. (Online) Available: www.ppvc.gov

National Academy of State Health Plans. (1999, March). *Medicaid Managed Care: A Guide for States*, Vol. I, 4th ed. Washington, DC: National Academy of State Health Policy.

National Association of Social Workers. (1997, August). Balanced Budget Act of 1997: Significant Changes Made in Children's Health, Welfare, Medicaid, and Medicare. *Government Relations Update.* Washington, DC: Author.

National Association of Social Workers. (1996, August 27). Personal Responsibility and Work Opportunity Reconciliation Act of 1996, Summary of Provisions. *Government Relations Update.* Washington, DC: Author.

National Governors Association and National Conference of State Legislatures. (1998). *State Children's Health Insurance Program.* Washington, DC: National governor's…

Nemore, P. B. (1997). *Variations in State Medicaid Buy-in Practices for Low-Income Medicare Beneficiaries.* Washington, DC: Kaiser Family Foundation.

Neuman, P. and Langwell, K. (1999, January–February). Medicare's Choice Explosion? Implications for Beneficiaries. *Health Affairs, 18,* 1, 150–161.

Nibal, K. (2000, September 12). Testimony to the House Committee on the Budget, Task Force on Welfare on Implementation of the Drug and Alcohol Provisions of P.L. 104-121. (Online). Available at www.ssa.gov/cgi-bin/cqcgi

Pear, R. (2001, January 30). Bush Proposes Drug Cost Aid for Medicare. *The New York Times,* pp. A1, A18.

Pear, R. (1999, May 9). Many States Slow to Use Children's Insurance Fund. *The New York Times,* pp. A1, A16.

Pear, R. (1997a, August 15). After a Review, 95,180 Children Will Lose Cash Disability Benefits. *The New York Times,* p. A1.

Pear, R. (1997b, November 16). U.S. Mistakenly Cuts Benefits For Many Disabled Children. *The New York Times,* p. A1.

Pear, R. (1990, November 19). Despite Order, U.S. Stalls Aid to Poor Children. *The New York Times,* p. A1.

Poisal, J. A. and Murray, L. (2001, March/April). Growing Differences between Medicare Beneficiaries with and without Drug Coverage. *Health Affairs, 20,* 2, 74–85.

Pryor, D. (1990). A Prescription for High Drug Prices. *Health Affairs, 9,* 101–109.

Reschovsky, J. D. and Cunningham, P. J. (1998, October). *Chipping Away at the Problem of Uninsured Children.* Washington, DC: Center for Studying Health System Change.

Rowland, D., Rosenbaum, S., Simon, L., and Chait, E. (1995). Medicaid and Managed Care: Lessons from the Literature. *Kaiser Commission on the Future of Medicaid.* Washington, DC: Kaiser Family Foundation.

Schneider, A., Fennel, K., and Keenan, P. (1999, May). Medicaid Eligibility for the Elderly. *Kaiser Commission on Medicaid and the Uninsured Issue Update.* Washington, DC: Kaiser Family Foundation.

Schneider, A., Fennel, K., and Long, P. (1998, September). Medicaid Eligibility for Families and Children. *Kaiser Commission on Medicaid and the Uninsured Issue Update.* Washington, DC: Kaiser Family Foundation.

Steinberg, E. P., Guiterrez, B., Momani A. Boscarino, J. A. Newman, P., and Deverka, P. (2000, March/April). Beyond Survey Data: A Claims-Based Analysis of Drug Use and Spending by the Elderly. *Health Affairs, 19,* 2, 198–211.

Stuart, B., Shea, D., and Briesacher, B. (2001, January/February). Dynamics in Drug Coverage of Medicare: Finders, Losers, Switchers. *Health Affairs, 20,* 1, 86–99.

Social Security Administration. (2000). *2000 SSI Annual Report.* Washington, DC: Social Security Administration.

U.S. General Accounting Office. (2000a, September). *Medicaid Managed Care, States' Safeguards for Children with Special Needs Vary Significantly.* (GAO/HEHS-00-169). Washington, DC: U.S. Government Printing Office.

U.S. General Accounting Office. (2000b, August). *Medicare and Medicaid, Implementing State Demonstrations for Dual Eligibles Has Proven Challenging* (GAO/HEHS-00-94). Washington, DC: U.S. Government Printing Office.

U.S. General Accounting Office. (2000c, September). *Medicare+ Choice, Plan Withdrawals Indicate Difficulty of Providing Choice while Achieving Savings* (GAO/HEHS-00-183). Washington, DC: U.S. Government Printing Office.

U.S. General Accounting Office. (1998, May). *Supplemental Security Income: SSA Needs a Uniform Standard for Assessing Childhood Disability* (GAO/HEHS-98-123). Washington, DC: U.S. Government Printing Office.

U.S. General Accounting Office. (1996). *Medicaid Managed Care: Serving the Disabled Challenges State Programs* (GAO/HEHS-96-136). Washington, DC: U.S. Government Printing Office.

U.S. General Accounting Office. (1995). *Health Insurance for Children: Many Remain Uninsured Despite Medicaid Expansion* (GAO/HEHS-95-175). Washington, DC: U.S. Government Printing Office.

U.S. House of Representatives, Prescription Drug Task Force. (1999a). Prescription Drug Fairness for Seniors Act. (Online). Available: www.house.gov/berry/prescription drugs/studies.htm

U.S. House of Representatives, Prescription Drug Task Force. (1999b). Seniors Beware: The Need for Prescription Drug Coverage, How Drug Pricing Has Harmed Seniors and Debunking the Myths of Drug Makers. (Online). Available: www.house.gov/berry/prescription drugs/studies.htm

U.S. House of Representatives, Committee on Energy and Commerce, Subcommittee on Health. (2001, May 16). Medicare Reform: Providing Prescription Drug Coverage for Seniors, Testimony of Dan L. Crippen, Director, Congressional Budget Office. (Online). Available: www.energycommerce.house.gov

Wikes, M. S., Bell, R. A., and Kravitz, R. L. (2000, March/April). Direct-to-Consumer Prescription Drug Advertising Trends, Impact, and Implications. *Health Affairs, 19,* 2, 110–128.

6 Disparities in Health: People of Color

In Chapters 6 and 7, we examine disparities in health in the United States by focusing on at-risk or underserved populations. At-risk or underserved groups are those at greater risk for poor health than the population as a whole. They are "vulnerable to, or likely to be harmed by, a specific medical, social, political, or environmental circumstance" (Barker, 1999, p. 34). Aday (1993) provides the following definition of risk:

> The concept of risk assumes that there is always a chance that an adverse health-related outcome will occur. Correspondingly, we are all potentially at risk of poor physical, psychological, and/or social health. People may, however, be more at risk of poor health at different times in their lives, **while some individuals and groups are apt to be more at risk than others at any given point in time** [emphasis added] (p. 5).

The concept of "any given point in time" illustrates the difference in risk factors. Like everyone else, people of color, women, children, youth, and elderly adults are susceptible to poor health at "different times" in their individual lives. They experience a variety of health risks associated with biological and genetic factors, developmental stages of the life cycle, and the aging process itself. However, these groups are also "*more* at risk [emphasis added] than others at *any* [emphasis added] given point in time" due to political and socioeconomic conditions that put them in greater jeopardy than other members of our society.

As shown in Chapter 3, people of color are disproportionately poor and employed in low-income jobs, have higher rates of unemployment, and are at greater risk for lack or loss of employment-based insurance. Racial and ethnic disparities in health are so embedded in our social and political life that, unlike other countries, the United States documents health status based on race rather than social class (Navarro, 1990).

The National Center for Health Statistics (U.S. Public Health Service) collects data annually for its national report, *Health, United States,* on mortality, disparities in mortality, birth rates, morbidity, and health behaviors (these terms are discussed next) and presents the data primarily by race, not social class. Most public health databases in the United States are collected in this way. For example, state health departments do not normally collect socioeconomic data regarding health status (Krieger, Chen, and Ebel, 1997a; Krieger, Williams, and Moss, 1997b).

Measuring Health Disparities

Public health scholars and officials rely on a body of concepts and methods that have been developed to measure the health of individuals and population groups. This section provides a brief introduction to the basic demographic and epidemiological terms and measures used to describe health status and health disparities. Some terms, such as *mortality* and *morbidity,* which are used throughout Chapters 6 and 7, are discussed in greater detail. It is interesting to note that the most commonly used measures of health status do not focus on health; instead, they are measures of disease or death.

Demography

Demography is the study of population characteristics, especially population size, fertility, mortality, growth, age distribution, migration, and vital statistics. Primary vital statistics include births (fertility) and deaths (mortality), and population characteristics by age, race and ethnicity, gender, marital status, socioeconomic status (SES), residence, and migration. Mandatory reporting laws provide demographers with birth data; mandatory death certificates provide mortality data. Other data are collected by government agencies through population registries, census data, and special household surveys.

Demography is also the study of population trends—changes in population characteristics over time. Demographic transitions occur when the age distribution of a population changes significantly; this occurs primarily as a result of significant changes in birth and death rates. Natural disasters, war, famine, migration, disease patterns, and political strife also lead to substantial changes in populations.

Morbidity.   Morbidity is a public health term used to define poor health. It usually refers to the incidence or prevalence of a disease, although it can refer to severity or duration. Incidence refers to the number of *new* cases of a disease or condition in a population group during a given *period* of time; prevalence refers to the number of *new and old* cases of a disease or condition in a population group at a given *point* in time or during a *specified period* of time. Morbidity can be measured in a variety of ways including the number of individuals who are ill, the length of an illness, or periods of an illness.

Mortality.   Mortality (death) statistics are fundamental to the study of populations. Mortality statistics are based on mandatory reporting laws that rely on federal standards and classifications of death. U.S. death certificates provide a wide range of information including age, gender, race, ethnicity, marital status, occupation, residence, and cause of death. Immediate cause of death, underlying cause, and other significant health conditions are reported. This information allows demographers to study patterns of mortality at a given point in time or over a period of time. For example, a cohort from 2000 could be compared to a cohort from 1950 at the time of birth, or over a period of time. (A cohort is usually a group of individuals born in a given year. It may, however, be any other defined group.)

Patterns of mortality include differences or changes in age-specific mortality rates, such as infant or maternal mortality, or cause-specific mortality rates. For example, in 1999, heart disease, cancer, and HIV/AIDS mortality declined, while mortality for Alzheimer's disease, a newly classified cause of death, increased significantly (National Center for Health Statistics, 2001). The National Center for Health Statistics reports mortality statistics annually for leading causes of death (see Figures 6.1 and 6.2).

Life Expectancy.   Life expectancy refers to the average number of years a person (at a given age) is expected to live given the current mortality rates of a population. Life expectancy is traditionally measured at birth, but can be measured from any age. In the United States, life expectancy at birth has risen dramatically from 47.3 years in 1900 to 76.7 years in 1998 (National Center for Vital Health Statistics, 2000), as shown in Figure 6.3.

FIGURE 6.1   **Top Ten Leading Causes of Death in the United States, 1998**

Cause of death	**Number of Deaths All Persons**	**Number of Deaths Males**	**Number of Deaths Females**
1. Heart disease	724,859	353,897	370,962
2. Cancer	541,532	282,065	259,467
3. Stroke	158,448	63,042	97,303
4. Lung disease	112,584	61,145	55,566
5. Accidents	97,835	57,018	50,892
6. Pneumonia/influenza	91,871	40,979	35,167
7. Diabetes	64,751	29,584	34,793
8. Suicide	30,575	24,538	15,671
9. Kidney disease	26,182	16,343	13,621
10. Liver disease	25,192	14,023	13,506
ALL CAUSES	2,337,256	1,157,260	1,179,996

Source: National Center for Health Statistics, 2000.

FIGURE 6.2   **Leading Causes of Death by Race and Ethnic Group, 1998**

	Rank	White	African American	Latina/os	Asian/Pacific	Native American
Cause of Death	1	Heart disease	Heart disease	Heart disease	Heart disease	Heart disease
	2	Cancer	Cancer	Cancer	Cancer	Cancer
	3	Stroke	Stroke	Accidents	Stroke	Accidents
	4	Lung disease	Accidents	Stroke	Accidents	Diabetes
	5	Accidents	Diabetes	Diabetes	Pneumonia/influenza	Stroke

Source: National Center for Health Statistics, 2000.

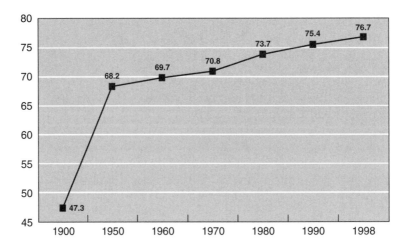

FIGURE 6.3   Life Expectancy at Birth in the United States

Source: National Center for Health Statistics (2000).

Epidemiology

Epidemiology is the study of the distribution and extent of disease (or risk factor) in a population, the causes of disease, and the identification of potential interventions to prevent, control, and treat disease. The biopsychosocial risk factors that most directly influence health outcomes are referred to as *determinants* of health. Epidemiologists study populations at risk and identify determinants of health in an effort to reduce or eliminate health problems. Although health policy is usually shaped by political factors, scientific epidemiological findings play an important role. Demographic trends have a significant impact on our health care system, and our knowledge of risk factors and causes of disease should inform policy decisions.

Health Targets.   National health insurance or universal access to health care has not been achieved in the United States. However, there has been a strong history of public health initiatives (see Chapters 1 and 2). In the late 1970s, the U.S. Department of Health and Human Services initiated a new public health initiative when it developed specific health targets for the nation. In 1979, the Surgeon General's Report on Health Promotion and Disease Prevention launched *Healthy People,* which established 5 life-stage health targets (for example, reduced mortality rates) and 226 specific health objectives to be achieved over a 10-year period (by 1990). This initiative created a precedent for establishing national objectives for health outcomes and monitoring their progress.

For the year 2000, new health targets were established in three areas: to increase healthy life spans, to reduce disparities in health, and to achieve universal access to preventive health care. The program established 297 specific health objectives in four major areas: health promotion, health protection, prevention, and surveillance systems. The current initiative of *Healthy People 2010,* has two overarching health goals: (1) to increase the number of years of healthy life and (2) to eliminate disparities in health among different segments of the population, including women, youth, the elderly, people of low income and education, and people with disabilities. Twenty-six priority areas have been established with targets set for each objective within each targeted group.

A second health promotion effort launched by the U.S. Department of Health and Human Services was the 1998 Initiative to Eliminate Racial and Ethnic Disparities in Health, which grew out of President Clinton's 1997 Initiative on Race (U.S. Department of Health and Human Services, 1998). This health promotion initiative relied on epidemiological studies of people of color to target improved health outcomes in six major areas—infant mortality, cancer, cardiovascular disease, diabetes, HIV/AIDS, and infectious diseases. Although many people in the United States are affected by these health problems (see Figure 6.1), leading causes of death vary for the racial and ethnic groups discussed in this chapter (see Figure 6.2) and the six target areas disproportionately affect racial and ethnic groups. These health risks are responsible for much of the morbidity and mortality in racial and ethnic communities in the United States.

African Americans

Life Expectancy and Infant Mortality

From the mid-1980s to the early 1990s, the gap in life expectancy between African Americans and whites actually widened. In 1988 and 1989, life expectancy for African Americans was 69.2 years, while life expectancy for whites rose from 75.6 years in 1988 to 76.0 years in 1989. The primary reason for this widening gap was the health risk of AIDS and neighborhood violence, particularly among young African American males ages 25–34 (Associated Press, 1992). From 1993 to 1998, life expectancy for African American males increased to a high of 67.6, primarily because of the decline in mortality from HIV/AIDS and homicide. However, life expectancy for whites in 1998 was still 6.0 years greater than for African Americans (see Figure 6.4).

Life expectancy for poor African Americans who live in inner cities is of even greater concern. A University of Michigan School of Public Health study found that premature death was "excessive" in all poverty-ridden areas, but reached alarming proportions in inner cities. For example, *two-thirds* of boys living in Harlem were likely to die prematurely before the age of 65 (Herbert, 1996). An often-cited study by McCord and Freeman (1990) provides similar findings. This study compared living in Bangladesh, one of the world's poorest countries, to living in Harlem and found that poor inner-city African Americans living in Harlem had less chance of surviving to age 65 than did people living in Bangladesh.

Since the early 1980s, infant mortality in the U.S. general population has declined substantially from about 11 to 7 deaths per 1,000 live births. During this period, the infant mortality rate among African Americans also declined. However, the gap between infant mortality rates for African Americans and whites is wider

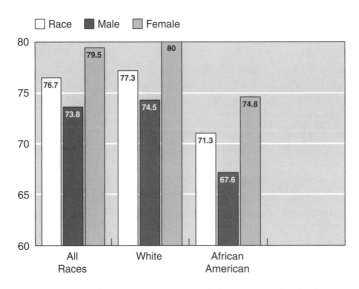

FIGURE 6.4   Life Expectancy at Birth by Race and Ethnicity, 1998

Source: National Center for Health Statistics, 2000.

than the gap between whites and any other racial or ethnic group; in fact, the mortality rate for African American infants is more than twice the rate for white infants (see Figure 6.5). Schoendorf and associates (1992) found that premature births and low-birth-weight babies among women increased the risk for infant mortality. Sudden infant death syndrome is also about twice the rate found among whites (Associated Press, 1999; *Healthy People 2000,* 1998).

HIV/AIDS

The number of deaths from AIDS has declined dramatically in the United States as a result of new treatments and advances in AIDS research and medicine. However, African Americans still account for more AIDS-related deaths than does any other racial or ethnic group in the United States and are a growing proportion of persons living with the HIV virus. In the early 1990s, AIDS affected African Americans at more than twice the rate of whites. Cases of *heterosexual* AIDS were eight times higher, and African American women ages 16 to 21 were *fifteen times* as likely as white women to get the HIV virus. As a result, African American infants were at much higher risk for developing AIDS than were white infants (Kaiser Family Foundation, 2000a).

Today, AIDS remains a health crisis in the African American community. African Americans over age 13 are *nine times* as likely as whites, and *twice* as likely as Latina/os, to have AIDS. In the first half of 1999, African Americans represented 12 percent of the nation's population, but accounted for *48 percent* of new AIDS

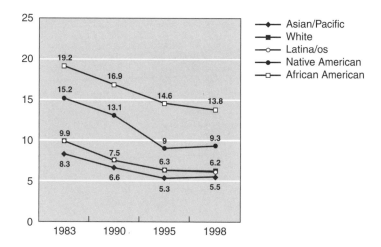

FIGURE 6.5   Infant Mortality by Race and Ethnicity, 1983–1998

Note: Number of deaths per 1,000 live births.

Source: National Center for Health Statistics, 2000.

cases (National Center for Health Statistics, 2000; Kaiser Family Foundation, 2000a). Moreover, while the rate of AIDS cases for whites steadily declined from 1990 to 1999, the rate for African Americans increased (see Figure 6.6).

AIDS is not ranked as one of the top ten causes of death for any racial or ethnic group in the United States, but according to the Centers for Disease Control, AIDS is the primary killer of African American men between the ages of 25 and 44 (Brooks, 1999) (see Figure 6.7). In 1998, the rate of AIDS among African American males over age 13 was 7 *times* the rate found among white men (see Figure 6.7), and almost 2.5 *times* as many African American men as white men were infected through intravenous drug use (Kaiser Family Foundation, 2000a).

For women in the same age group between 25 and 44 years of age, AIDS is the second leading cause of death (Brooks, 1999). However, the risk of AIDS for African American women seems to be growing. In 1998, the majority (62 percent) of new AIDS cases among *all women* in the United States were African Americans (compared to 57 percent in 1994). Female African Americans over age 13 are *twenty times* more likely than white women to have AIDS (Kaiser Family Foundation, 2000a), and *twenty times* more likely than white women to die from AIDS (see Figure 6.7).

The Office of HIV/AIDS Policy at the U.S. Department of Health and Human Services has identified several contributing risk factors. First, young people are more predisposed to engage in high-risk drug behavior, as discussed in the section that follows on children and adolescents, and African American youth are even more vulnerable to these risks. Second, the AIDS virus itself is now more widespread in the African American and Hispanic populations, which increases the risk of exposure. Third, the perceived stigma associated with the disease prevents some African Americans from seeking treatment (Brooks, 1999).

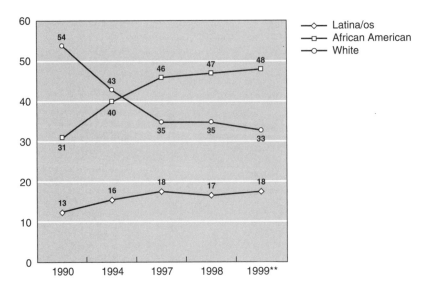

FIGURE 6.6   AIDS Cases* by Race and Ethnicity, as Percent of All Cases (all races)

*Persons 13 years of age or older at diagnosis.

**January–June 1999.

Source: National Center for Health Statistics, 2000.

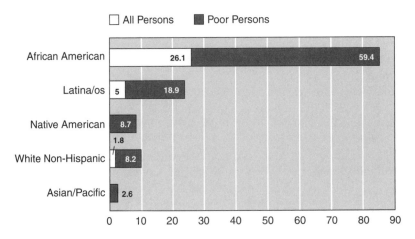

FIGURE 6.7   Death Rates* for HIV Infection by Race and Ethnicity for Women and Men Ages 25–44, 1998

*Number of deaths per 100,000.

Note: Native American and Asian/Pacific female rates based on fewer than twenty deaths.

Source: National Center for Health Statistics, 2000.

In fact, a study conducted by the Centers for Disease Control and Prevention from 1998 through 2000 among young (ages 23–29) *gay* African American males living in six major cities found that that the rate of infection is *increasing*. The Center described the findings as "alarming," because the number of new cases of AIDS has been declining for the past decade. The stigma attached to homosexuality and the reluctance of gay African American men to identify themselves as gay may be keeping test rates low (Altman, 2001).

The lack of access to health care discussed in Chapter 3 serves only to compound the problem of HIV/AIDS. African Americans are less likely to obtain drug therapy and treatment, and many who need care for HIV are not getting any care at all (Brooks, 1999). As a result, African Americans are increasingly more likely to live with the disease of AIDS than are other racial and ethnic groups.

Cancer and Cardiovascular Disease

Cardiovascular diseases and cancer are leading causes of death in the United States and all other industrialized nations. Heart disease has declined significantly since 1950, while cancer rates have been increasing. Lung cancer is the leading death-related cancer and the most common worldwide. From a public health perspective, this is a disturbing trend because lung cancer is directly linked with smoking, which is a social behavior that can be altered through health promotion and education. Smoking is also a risk factor for cardiovascular disease and many other diseases and health problems.

Cancer. Lung cancer is of particular concern among African American males who have a mortality rate that is twice the rate for the general population. Since 1990, the mortality rate for African Americans has declined significantly from 86.1 per 100,000 to 73.4 in 1996. Although cigarette-smoking habits are now about the same among African American adults as among white adults, smoking among African American *teens* has increased sharply in recent years. If this trend continues, smoking could have a negative long-term effect on the rate of lung disease.

Breast and prostate cancer are two additional cancer risks for African Americans. African American males are 38 percent more likely to get prostate cancer than are white males. More importantly, they are twice as likely to die from this disease than are whites (Associated Press, 1999; *Healthy People 2000*, 1998). Similarly, more white women than African American women get breast cancer, but African American women are still more likely to die from it (AHCPR, 1999; Meadows, 2000). In 1998, death rates from breast cancer were higher among African American women (25.3 per 100,000) than any other racial or ethnic group (see Figure 6.8). In the past decade, death rates from breast cancer have declined both in the general population and among African American women. However, the decline has not been as significant as it has been for white women; in fact, the decline for white women is twice the rate of decline experienced by African American women (see Figure 6.8).

Until 1994, lower rates of breast cancer screening among African American women over age 50 played a significant role in this health disparity. Since then,

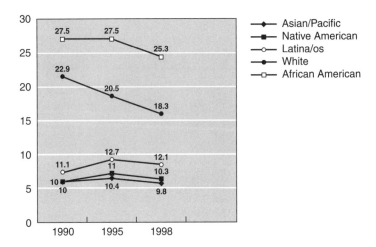

FIGURE 6.8   Age-Adjusted* Death Rates** for Breast Cancer by Race and Ethnicity

*Age-adjusted rates are more sensitive to the age distribution patterns of different populations and provide more meaningful comparisons between populations.

**Number of deaths per 100,000.

Source: National Center for Health Statistics, 2000.

however, women of all races have been equally likely to receive mammograms (*Healthy People 2000,* 1998). This dramatic change in preventive care should have a positive effect on future breast cancer rates for older African American women. The rate of breast cancer for African American women under age 35 is still of concern, however, because it is 50 percent higher than the rate for white women in this age group. Other health risks, such as lack of access to care, lack of insurance, and late diagnosis, may explain the early onset of the disease. New guidelines for mammogram screenings may be necessary for African American women (Meadows, 2000).

Cardiovascular Disease.   Cardiovascular disease refers to a group of heart-related diseases, including coronary heart disease (blocked arteries), cerebrovascular disease (stroke), and hypertension (high blood pressure). The mortality rate for cardiovascular disease has declined dramatically for both the general population and African Americans since 1950 (National Center for Health Statistics, 2000). However, African Americans, especially those living in inner cities (*Healthy People 2000,* 1998), are at greater risk for this disease than are all other racial and ethnic groups in the United States (see Figure 6.9), including whites who are still at much greater risk than others.

In addition to higher death rates, African Americans are two to four times more likely than whites to have an initial stroke before age 65 (American Heart

FIGURE 6.9   Age-Adjusted Death Rates* for Heart Disease by Race and Ethnicity and Gender

	1990 Female/Male	1995 Female/Male	1998 Female/Male
African American	168.1/275.9	156.3/255.9	146.8/231.8
White	103.1/202.0	94.9/179.7	88.1/162.3
Native American	76.6/144.6	77.3/136.7	70.0/128.7
Latina/os	76.0/136.3	68.1/121.9	63.4/109.3
Asian/Pacific Islander	58.3/102.6	57.7/106.2	47.7/92.3

*Number of deaths per 100,000.

Source: National Center for Health Statistics, 2000.

Association, 1998). Several studies (Chen et al., 2001; Schulman et al., 1999) have found that African Americans are less likely to be referred for cardiac tests than are whites.

Diabetes

Diabetes is one of the most serious chronic diseases in the United States. The incidence of diabetes has increased steadily since the 1950s (National Center for Health Statistics, 2000). Today, it is the seventh leading cause of death and affects almost 16 million people, 5.4 million of whom are undiagnosed. The prevalence of diabetes increased 33 percent among adults between 1990 and 1998; the largest increase occurred among young adults ages 30–39 (Centers for Disease Control and Prevention, 2001).

Diabetes is a condition that results from the body's insufficient or impaired production of insulin, which leads to increased glucose (from digested food) in the bloodstream. If not carefully managed, high levels of blood glucose (sugar) can damage the body's vital organs. Diabetes is related to both genetic factors and diets that are high in fats. Type 1, or insulin-dependent diabetes mellitus (IDDM), has been called juvenile diabetes because it usually affects children and adolescents. Type 2, or non-insulin-dependent diabetes (NIDDM), which is linked to obesity and physical inactivity, affects 90 percent to 95 percent of adults (usually over age 40) diagnosed with diabetes. However, type 2 is being diagnosed with greater frequency among children (Centers for Disease Control and Prevention, 2001).

Diabetes is a major risk factor for heart disease and stroke, which can lead to many complications including blindness, kidney disease (end-stage renal disease), and lower limb amputations. African Americans and Native Americans are at far greater risk for diabetes than are whites (see Figure 6.10). Diabetes-induced kidney disease kills African Americans 2.5 times more often than whites, and complications from diabetes increases the risk of other related health problems for this group. End-stage renal disease affects African Americans four times as often

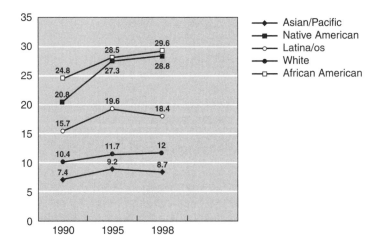

FIGURE 6.10   Death Rates for Diabetes by Race and Ethnicity

Note: *Number of deaths per 100,000.

Source: National Center for Health Statistics, 2000.

as whites (Oxendine, 1999). With diabetes triple the rate it was thirty years ago, Surgeon General Satcher called it a devastating "epidemic" in the African American community (West, 1999).

Unintentional Injuries: Neighborhood Violence

African Americans, particularly young males, are at greater risk for mortality and morbidity related to neighborhood violence (see Figure 6.11) than any other racial or ethnic group. In the early 1990s,

> more teenage boys die[d] from gunshots than from all natural causes combined, and a black male teenager [was] 11 times more likely to be murdered with a gun than a white counterpart.... In 1988, a black male age 15 to 19 was nearly three times more likely to die from a bullet than a disease (Taylor, 1991).

In 1998, the homicide rate for African American males ages 15–34 was *eight* times the rate for young white males, and more than twice the rate for young Latinos. Although the rate of violent crime, including assault, rape, robbery, and homicide, among youth generally declined from 1990 to 1998, the rate of drinking and drug use among adolescents and young adults has increased (National Center for Health Statistics, 2000).

Drugs are often linked with gang violence and street homicide. As noted by Regulus (1995), contemporary gangs are more violent, in part, due to increased drug use among gang members, and older adolescents remain connected to gangs as a source of "illicit employment in gang-controlled drug and organized criminal activities" (p. 1045).

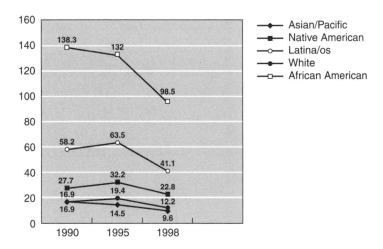

FIGURE 6.11   Death Rates for Homicide for Young* Males by Race and Ethnicity

*Number of deaths per 100,000 ages 15–24.

Source: National Center for Health Statistics, 2000.

Latinas/os (Hispanics)

Life Expectancy and Infant Mortality

Life expectancy for Latina/os (who are not white) is about the same as whites, but the causes of death tend to be different (U.S. General Accounting Office, 1992; Sorlie et al., 1993; Vega and Amaro, 1994). Latina/os have a lower rate of death from cardiovascular disease (see Figure 6.9) and cancer than whites, but they have a higher rate of death from homicide (see Figure 6.11), AIDS (see Figure 6.7), perinatal conditions, accidents, diabetes (see Figure 6.10), and cirrhosis and other liver diseases.

The infant mortality rate is about the same as the white infant mortality rates (see Figure 6.5). However, variation exists within the Hispanic population; the highest rate is found among persons of Puerto Rican descent. In 1998, the infant mortality rate was 7.8 per 100,000 live births compared to 3.6 per 100,000 live births among Cuban Americans (see Figure 6.12). In addition, from 1995 to 1998, the infant mortality rate for Central and South American and Mexican Americans declined slightly, while the rate for Cuban Americans declined significantly. These trends reflect the variable rates of poverty found within the Hispanic population (see Figure 6.13); Puerto Ricans are the poorest Hispanic group. For these reasons, the federal Initiative on Racial and Ethnic Disparities has set health goals to lower the infant mortality rate for Puerto Rican Americans (*Healthy People 2000*, 1997a).

Diabetes

Like African Americans, Latina/os are twice as likely as whites to develop diabetes and death rates from diabetes are much higher (see Figure 6.10) than that of

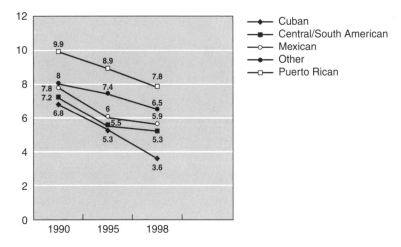

FIGURE 6.12   Infant Mortality Rates by Hispanic Ethnic Group

Note: *Number of deaths per 1,000 live births.

Source: National Center for Health Statistics, 2000.

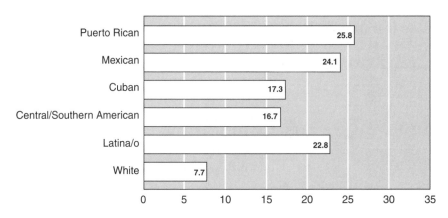

FIGURE 6.13   People Living in Poverty, As Percent of Latina/o Group, 1999

Sources: Therrien and Ramirez (2001); March Demographic Profiles, Current Population Reports (2000).

whites. However, the mortality rate for Latina/os is not as high as the rate found among Native Americans and African Americans (Oxendine, 1999; West, 1999). Latina/os are at greater risk for complications from diabetes than are whites and need to be educated about the risks of diabetes and ways to help prevent its onset. The rate of early diagnosis needs to be improved, and Latina/os need assistance with disease management. Each of these concerns is especially challenging with this population because Latina/os have the lowest rate of health insurance and the greatest difficulty accessing health care. In some cases, language barriers are also an issue. The Centers for Disease Control and Prevention, in collaboration with community groups such as the National Council of La Raza, have made a concerted effort to publish Spanish-language publications, such as the National Diabetes Fact Sheet, to do outreach to this population (Brooks, 1998).

HIV/AIDS

Latina/os are not nearly as at risk for AIDS as African Americans are, but they are far more vulnerable to this disease than are whites (see Figures 6.6 and 6.7). AIDS is the third leading cause of death among Latina/os ages 25–44 (Kaiser Family Foundation, 1999). In 1994, Latina/os were 1.7 times more likely than the general population to have AIDS (*Healthy People 2000*, 1997a). In 1998, Hispanics represented only 11 percent of the population, but they accounted for nearly 17 percent of new AIDS cases (see Figure 6.6). This was more than *three times* the rate of new AIDS cases for non-Hispanic whites (Kaiser Family Foundation, 1999).

The greatest disparity exists for Hispanic women. In 1998, Hispanic males over age 13 were more than *three times* as likely as non-Hispanic white males to have AIDS, and *three times* as likely to have contracted the disease through intravenous drug use. Hispanic females, however, were even more vulnerable. In 1997, Latinas represented 20 percent of *all female* reported cases of AIDS (*Healthy People 2000*, 1997a). In 1998, the number of new AIDS cases among Latinas over age 13 was almost *seven times* the rate found among non-Hispanic white women (see Figure 6.14). HIV/AIDS among women is especially troubling because of the risk of neonatal transmission. In 1998, the number of new AIDS cases among Hispanic infants was *five times* the rate for non-Hispanic white infants (Kaiser Family Foundation, 1999).

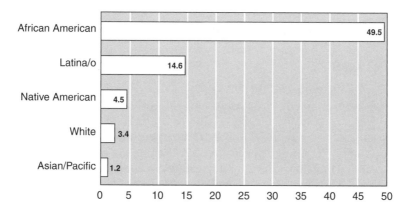

FIGURE 6.14   Female AIDS Cases* by Race and Ethnicity, July 1998–June 1999

*Number of cases per 100,000 in population.

Source: National Center for Health Statistics, 2000.

Latinas, like African American women, are disproportionately poor and face discrimination based on both race and gender. All women of color are at risk for poor health for socioeconomic reasons. However, some studies suggest that Latinas may also be at risk for AIDS for sociocultural reasons. For example, in 1998, Latinas were more likely than African American women and white women to be infected through heterosexual contact (Kaiser Family Foundation, 1999).

One concern is that Latinas who hold traditional cultural values regarding gender roles and religious attitudes toward sexual practices may be at greater risk than other women. A study conducted in 1993 by the Center for AIDS Prevention Studies at the University of California (Marin and Gomez, 1998) found that protection against infectious diseases (by using condoms) occurred less frequently among those Latina/os who held traditional views toward sexual intimacy. In addition, the opposition of the Catholic Church to contraception seemed to function as a cultural reinforcement of these practices. A second study of migrant workers, discussed by Horwitz (1998), found that the rate of AIDS among seasonal migrant workers was as much as ten times higher than the rate found in the general population. Migrant Latinas surveyed by the study said they overlooked their partners' sexual relationships because of the transient nature of their work. They were afraid to cause trouble for themselves or their spouses/partners, or risk losing their jobs, by complaining about their partners' and coworkers' behavior.

Until more research is done it is difficult to discern the significance of these studies. Few studies have been done on disparities in health between women of color and white women (Lillie-Blanton et al., 1999), and even fewer have been done on disparities in HIV/AIDS among women. It is a significant problem, however, with serious health consequences for women, children, and families. Prevention strategies that are culturally appropriate for Latina/os are still being studied (Horwitz, 1998).

Asian Americans and Pacific Islanders

Life Expectancy

Overall, Asian Americans are among the healthiest groups in the United States. In 1996, the life expectancy of Asian Americans and Pacific Islanders was 80.3 years, which is higher than the life expectancy for the total population and better than the mortality rate for whites. However, life expectancy varies significantly within this population. Japanese Americans have the highest life expectancy (82.1 years), while Native Hawaiians have the lowest (68.3 years) (*Healthy People 2000*, 1997b). Little data are available for newer Asian immigrant groups from Southeast Asia, but other socioeconomic factors indicate that life expectancy may be lower.

Cancer and Cardiovascular Disease

Cancer and heart disease play a significant role in the relatively short life spans of Native Hawaiians. According to Lin-Fu (1993), Native Hawaiians have the highest rates of cancer among Asian Americans and Pacific Islanders. Native Hawaiians also have higher rates of death from heart disease than any group in the United States (Chen, 1993).

For other Asian American groups, cancer is also of special concern. It is the leading cause of death among Chinese Americans and Vietnamese Americans. Korean Americans are five times as likely to get stomach cancer as the general population; rates of stomach cancer are also very high among Japanese Americans. Vietnamese Americans have the highest rates of liver cancer among Asian Americans, and Chinese Americans are also at much greater risk for liver cancer than are other Asian American groups. The rate of cervical cancer among Vietnamese women is five times the rate for white, non-Hispanic women (Chen, 1993; *Healthy People 2000*, 1997b).

Diabetes

The Office of Minority Health reports that very little data are available about diabetes among Asian Americans. However, data available from 1988 to 1995 indicate that Native Hawaiians are twice as likely as white Hawaiians to have diabetes (Oxendine, 1999). The Papa Ola Lokahi Native Hawaiian health care system is coordinating an effort throughout the Pacific islands to help each community address diabetes (Oxendine, 2000). One concern is nutrition and obesity and their impact on diabetes. Half of all U.S. citizens and 30 percent of the nation's children are obese; Native Hawaiians also fit this profile and are the most obese of all ethnic groups in Hawaii (Pua'ala'okalani, 2000).

Crews (1994) found that Asian Indian Americans, Japanese Americans, and Korean Americans are also at greater risk for diabetes. Rates of diabetes for these groups are closer to the rate for African Americans than for whites.

Native Americans

Chronic Diseases and Infant Mortality

The Pine Ridge reservation with a population of about 250,000 spread over more than 3,100 square miles, is the United States' own third world.... The second largest reservation...has institutionalized squalor, with rampant alcoholism, diabetes, suicide and a male life expectancy rate of 56.5 years (Kilborn, 1999).

Conditions such as these, found on the Pine Ridge reservation, are often cited to describe the extreme disparity in health experienced by Native Americans. An Indian Health Service (1998) study of Native Americans in the IHS service area (or about 60 percent of the entire Native American population) found that (age-adjusted) death rates between 1992 and 1994 were much higher than among the general population for a number of diseases and health problems:

Alcoholism—579 percent higher
Tuberculosis—475 percent higher
Diabetes—231 percent higher

Accidents—212 percent higher
Suicide—70 percent higher
Pneumonia and influenza—61 percent higher
Homicide—61 percent higher

Infant mortality statistics offer a more positive perspective. Each decade since 1950, infant mortality has declined dramatically (National Center for Health Statistics, 2000). In 1999, the infant mortality rate was significantly lower than the rate for African Americans; however, it was still much higher than the rate for non-Hispanic whites (see Figure 6.5).

Alcoholism and Alcohol-Related Health Problems.   Although heart disease is the leading cause of death (National Center for Health Statistics, 2000; Rhoades et al., 1988) among Native Americans, a government study conducted in the early 1990s (U.S. General Accounting Office, 1993) showed that alcohol and substance abuse was the leading cause of death among Native Americans ages 15–44. The mortality rate for this group was about 6.5 times higher than for the general population. In addition, other leading causes of death, including accidents (see Figure 6.15), suicide (see Figure 6.16), and homicide (see Figure 6.11), were often related to substance abuse.

According to the Indian Health Service, 75 percent of accidents and 80 percent of suicides among young adults (ages 15–24) were alcohol related. Congress passed the Indian Alcohol and Substance Abuse Prevention and Treatment Act (P.L. 99-570) in 1986 to address the severity of this problem. In 1988, the National Center for Health Statistics reported that the suicide rate was 1.3 times higher among Native Americans than among the general population (U.S. General Accounting Office, 1993). Native American teenagers were four times as likely to commit suicide as were white teenagers (Brasher, 1992). An earlier study (Snipp, 1989) found that Native Americans were twice as likely to be murdered.

Native Americans are also vulnerable to diabetes and cirrhosis of the liver. Although diabetes is related to a number of risk factors, including genetics and diet, both diseases are related to long-term patterns of heavy drinking that often begin at an early age. The mortality rate for Native Americans for diabetes in 1998 (29.6 per 100,000) was the highest rate for any racial/ethnic group, and was 2.4 times higher than the rate for whites (see Figure 6.10). The highest prevalence of diabetes in the world is found among the Pima Indians of Arizona (Kaiser Family Foundation, 2000b). Deaths from cirrhosis of the liver were also far greater (see Figure 6.17); the rate for Native Americans was more than 2.5 times the rate for the general population (*Healthy People 2000,* 1995).

Environmental Health Risks

Finally, Native Americans still suffer disproportionately from diseases such as tuberculosis, meningitis, and hepatitis, which are related to inadequate housing, poor sanitation, and lack of clean water. Rates of tuberculosis for the general population

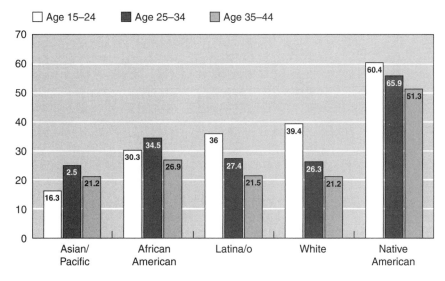

FIGURE 6.15 Death Rates* for Motor-Vehicle Injuries by Race and Ethnicity, 1998

*Number of death per 100,000 in population.

Source: National Center for Health Statistics, 2000.

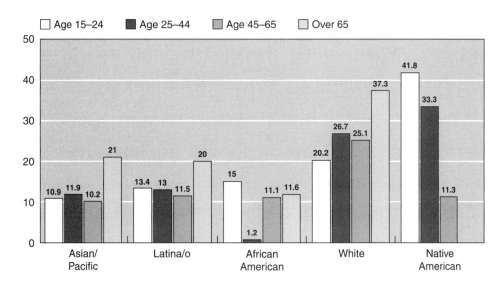

FIGURE 6.16 Male Suicide Rates** by Race and Ethnicity, 1998

*Number of deaths per 100,000 in population.

Note: Native American over 65 based on fewer than twenty deaths.

Source: National Center for Health Statistics, 2000.

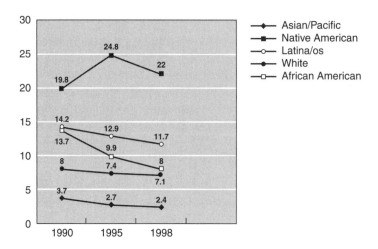

**FIGURE 6.17   Death Rates* for Chronic Liver Disease
and Cirrhosis**

*Number of cases per 100,000 in population.

Source: National Center for Health Statistics, 2000.

rose significantly between 1985 and 1992 due to the rise in HIV, which increases susceptibility to tuberculosis, and as a result of ineffective measures to control the disease in some sectors of the country. With federal public health initiatives, the rate of tuberculosis was lowered to 6.8 per 100,000 in 1998 (Kaiser Family Foundation, 2000b).

The HIV rates among Native Americans recorded by the National Center for Health Statistics are relatively low (see Figure 6.7). This may be related to the historic problem of alcohol abuse discussed earlier and a relatively low incidence of intravenous drug use (*Healthy People 2000*, 1995). However, the National Native American AIDS Prevention Center finds that HIV infection rates have been underestimated due to inadequate reporting and racial misclassification (Oropeza, 2001), and is working on a national campaign to reduce the stigma of HIV/AIDS in Native American communities. Nonetheless, the problem of tuberculosis for Native Americans is related to extreme conditions of poverty.

Racial Differences in the Delivery of Medical Care

"The consistent and repeated finding that black Americans receive less health care than white Americans...is an indictment of American health care" (Bhopal, 1998, p. 4). For at least fifteen years, studies have shown that differences exist in the treatment of African Americans and whites as patients. For example, a number of studies (Goldberg et al., 1992; Wenneker and Epstein, 1989; Whittle et al., 1993; Carlisle et al., 1997) have shown that African American patients receive less coronary surgery and fewer cardiac procedures than white patients. A Sloan-Kettering Cancer Center study (Bach et al., 1999) found that African Americans are 13 percent less likely to receive surgery for lung cancer than are whites.

As noted by Bhopal (1998), however, these studies do not provide conclusive evidence about the differences in treatment. Although many suspect that racism explains the difference, other reasons—including inadequate health care, patients' preferences for treatment; financial, organizational, and cultural barriers to treatment; and physicians' differences in treatment—all seem to play a role. The "first large-scale study" (Kamat, 1999) to show racial bias in physician decision making conducted by Schulman and colleagues (1999) found that physicians were more likely to recommend sophisticated cardiac tests for whites who complained of chest pains than for African Americans with the same symptoms. The study controlled for other explanatory factors, such as insurance and patient willingness to accept referrals. In doing so, the "study…exclusively investigate[d] the effect of race/gender bias on the resulting physician treatment recommendations" (Kamat, 1999, p. 6).

Although many studies show disparities in health care based on race, most, unlike the study of Schulman and colleagues (1999), have not focused on the role of racism. Yet, few social researchers would deny the importance of race. Disparities in socioeconomic conditions for people of color and whites, including housing, food and nutrition, environment, and safety, are precursors for poor health and increase the risk of death for African Americans and other people of color. A study conducted by the British researcher George Davey Smith, with researchers from the United States (Smith et al., 1998), concluded that racism was the underlying factor in the difference in mortality rates between whites and African Americans and needed further investigation. The study examined deaths related to heart and renal disease, stroke, lung and prostate cancer, and homicide during the 1970s and showed that the greatest mortality risks were income and socioeconomic status: The researchers found that racism had a direct impact on both.

The U.S. Department of Health and Human Services first began to study the health status of people of color, their access to care, and their utilization of services in 1985 in an effort to document continual disparities in health between whites and African Americans, Hispanics, Native Americans, some Asian Americans, and Pacific Islanders. The initial report of the Secretary's Task Force on Black and Minority Health (U.S. Department of Health and Human Services, 1986) focused on differences in health status by race and ethnicity. Since then more research has focused on access to care, patterns of utilization, and health outcomes for different racial and ethnic groups.

In 1999, the Kaiser Family Foundation published a synthesis of studies conducted between 1985 and 1998 on racial and ethnic differences in access to medical care (Mayberry et al., 1999). These studies show that racial and ethnic disparities in access to care clearly exist, but the reasons still need clarification. Further study is necessary to demonstrate to what extent racial and ethnic disparities result from "systemic and financial barriers as opposed to cultural preferences and attitudes"

(p. 3). The sections that follow summarize their findings to date on infant health, heart disease and stroke, cancer, diabetes, and HIV/AIDS.

Infant and Child Health

African American infants are placed in neonatal intensive care units (NICU) at twice the rate of white infants, but this disparity is not explained by higher rates of low birth weight. Therefore, Langkampf and associates (1990) concluded that access to NICU does not explain higher African American infant mortality rates.

Immunization rates for African American children have been lower than rates for Latina/o children, but the gap is narrowing. In 1998, the vaccination rate for white children for a full series of vaccines was 81 percent. For Hispanic children the rate was 75 percent; the rate for African American children was 74 percent (Federal Interagency Forum on Child and Family Statistics, 2001). Immunization rates are a significant measure of child protection against many communicable diseases.

In general, children of color have experienced poor access to health care services when compared to white children. Much of this problem is linked to poverty and socioeconomic status, but some differences may be due to other reasons. For example, poor children of color are more likely to visit an emergency room for care and less likely to visit a medical office or clinic (see Figure 6.18). However, one study found that African American and Hispanic children were less likely to be prescribed medications than were white children, even when socioeconomic and other factors were considered. This seems to raise questions about differences in cultural practices (Hahn, 1995).

Heart Disease and Stroke

As mentioned earlier, many studies show that whites are more likely to be treated with diagnostic and surgical procedures, including coronary angioplasty, bypass surgery, and heart transplantation, than are African Americans for heart disease and stroke. Mayberry and associates (1999) report that disparities in treatment rates ranging from 13 percent to 70 percent have been documented for both African Americans and Hispanics, though most studies have focused on disparities for African Americans. One study found that African Americans and Latinos were less likely to be screened for high cholesterol, even after controlling for socioeconomic and other factors (Naumburg et al., 1993).

African Americans who are uninsured are half as likely as whites to receive angiography and one-third as likely to receive bypass surgery (Carlisle et al., 1997). African American veterans within the Veterans Affairs medical system are a third less likely than white veterans in the system to receive cardiac catheterization and two-thirds less likely to receive recatheterization, even after controlling for socioeconomic and other factors (Oddone et al., 1993). Some studies have shown that these variations may be due to overuse of cardiac procedures by whites and greater aversion to these procedures among African Americans (Philibin and Di Salvo, 1998; Oddone et al., 1998).

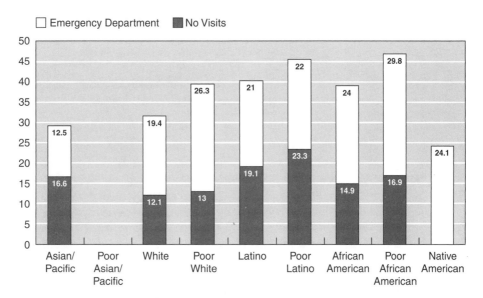

FIGURE 6.18 No Visits to Office/Clinic* and Emergency Department Visits** for Children (under age 18) by Race and Ethnicity, 1998

*Percent with NO visits during past twelve months.

**Percent with 1 or more visits during past twelve months.

Note: Statistics not available for poor Asian/Pacific Islanders and Native Americans.

Source: National Center for Health Statistics, 2000.

Cancer

Mayberry and associates (1999) report that the initial Task Force on Black and Minority Health found that people of color, particularly African Americans, had higher mortality rates from cancer as a result of delayed detection and differences in treatment, but the data available at the time of the report were limited. Since then, researchers have tried to document the role of race and ethnicity in diagnostic and treatment patterns, but have not yet provided a clear picture.

As discussed earlier, the gap in rates of mammography for African American and white women has narrowed to the point that similar rates exist today for both groups. Similarly, disparities in screening for cervical cancer for African American women and Latinas do not exist. In fact, African American women are 2.7 times more likely to have a Pap test than are white women, whereas Latinas are just as likely as white women to be tested, even after controlling for socioeconomic and other factors (Martin et al., 1996; Harlan et al., 1991).

However, other studies of both diagnostics and treatments for cancer provide conflicting data. Some studies show that African Americans and Latina/os are at greater risk for late detection (Bentley et al., 1998; Mettlin and Murphy, 1994; Mettlin et al., 1997), whereas other studies (Mitchell and McCormack, 1997;

Optenberg et al., 1995) show no difference in the stage of diagnosis for these two groups than for whites, especially after controlling for socioeconomic and other factors. Some studies find racial disparities in the use of specific interventions for ovarian cancer (Parham et al., 1997), prostate cancer (Mettlin and Murphy, 1994; Mettlin et al., 1997), and other cancers; whereas other studies find no difference in cancer treatments for African Americans, Hispanics, and/or whites (Optenberg et al., 1995; Dominitz et al., 1998).

Diabetes

Racial differences in the treatment of diabetes have not been documented consistently or clearly, but studies have shown that methods of control (disease management) and patient education have differed (Mayberry et al., 1999). One study (Cowie and Harris, 1997) showed that African Americans received more insulin treatment than did whites, but were less likely to receive injections daily or to monitor their own glucose levels. Another study (Wang and Javitt, 1996) found that elderly African American diabetics were less likely than elderly white diabetics to have an eye care visit.

HIV/AIDS

The most apparent racial disparities in medical treatment exist for people of color infected with HIV and diagnosed with AIDS. Moore and colleagues (1994) found that race was the most significant predictor for differences in drug treatment; African Americans were 41 percent to 73 percent less likely to receive specific drug therapies, even after controlling for income and other factors. Bennett and associates (1995) found that African American and Hispanic non–Veterans Administration patients were less likely to receive a diagnostic bronchoscopy than were whites, and more likely to die. These differences were not significant, however, when adjusted for health insurance status and other factors. A more recent *JAMA* study (Shapiro et al., 1999) showed more clearly, however, that race was a factor in the receipt of care. Other studies have provided evidence of underrepresentation of people of color in clinical trials for experimental drug therapies (Svensson, 1989; Diaz et al., 1995).

Highlights

■ Disparities in health exist in the United States based on race and ethnicity. African Americans, Latinas/os, Native Americans, and Alaska Natives have shorter life expectancies and worse health than do whites. Asian Americans and Pacific Islanders are among the healthiest groups in the United States, but significant variations in health status exist within this group. For example, the rate of cervical cancer among Vietnamese women is five times the rate for white, non-Hispanic women.

- The infant mortality rate in the United States has decreased significantly, yet the infant mortality rate for African Americans is still twice the rate for whites.

- Rates of heart disease, mortality from all cancers, and HIV/AIDS are all significantly higher for African Americans than for whites. Latinas/os are twice as likely to die from diabetes than whites and have higher rates of high blood pressure and AIDS. Cases of tuberculosis are rising among Asian Americans.

- Although the Indian Health Service was established to serve Native Americans, not all Native Americans live on reservations, and access and quality of care are serious problems. The mortality rate for Native Americans ages 15–44 is extraordinarily high, and diabetes, alcoholism, suicide, homicide, and accident-related deaths are disproportionately high.

- What we currently know about biological and genetic differences among people of color does not explain the health disparities experienced by these groups. These health disparities seem to be the result of a complex interaction of biopsychosocial factors.

Websites to Obtain Updated and Additional Information:

www.health.gov/healthypeople/
Healthy People 2010
Office of Minority Health
Public Health Service
U.S. Department of Health and Human Services

www.raceandhealth.hhs.gov/
Initiative to Eliminate Racial and Ethnic Disparities in Health
U.S. Department of Health and Human Services

www.kaisernetwork.org
Health Policy as it Happens
Kaiser Family Foundation

REFERENCES

Aday, L. A. (1993). *At Risk in America: The Health and Health Care Needs of Vulnerable Populations in the United States.* San Francisco: Jossey-Bass.

Agency for Health Care Policy + Research (AHCPR). (1999, April). *AHCPR Women's Health Highlights.* Fact sheet, AHCPR Pub. No. 99-P017. (Online). Available at www.ahrg. gov/research/womenl.htm.

Altman, L. K. (2001, June 1). Swift Rise Seen in HIV Cases for Gay Blacks. *The New York Times*, p. A1.

American Heart Association. (1998, February). *Stroke: A Journal of the American Heart Association.*

Associated Press. (1999, May 15). Report Details Racial Disparities in Health, Access to Care, Insurance. *Dallas Morning News*, p. A8.

Associated Press. (1992, January 8). Black–White Gap in U.S. Life Expectancies Widens, Decade-Long Trend Continues. *Concord Monitor*, p. A7.

Bach, P. B., Cramer, L. D., Warren, J. L., and Begg, C. B. (1999). Racial Difference in the Treatment of Early-Stage Lung Cancer. *New England Journal of Medicine, 341*, 16, 1198–1205.

Barker, R. L., ed. (1999). *The Social Work Dictionary.* Washington. DC: NASW Press.

Bennett, C. I., Horner, R. D., Weinstein, R. A., et al. (1995). Racial Differences in Care among Hospitalized Patients with *Pneumocystis carinii pneumonia* in Chicago, New York, Los Angeles, Miami, and Raleigh-Durham. *Archives Internal Medicine, 155*, 1586–1592.

Bentley, J. R., Delfinoa, R. J., Taylor, T. H., Stowe, S., and Anton-Culver, H. (1998). Differences in Breast Cancer Stage at Diagnosis Between Non-Hispanic White and Hispanic Populations. *Breast Cancer Research and Treatment, 50*, 1–9.

Bhopal, R. (1998, June 27). Spectre of Racism in Health and Health Care: Lessons from History and the United States. *British Medical Journal, 316*, 1970–1973.

Brasher, P. (1992, March 25). High Risk of Suicide Found in Native American Youths. *Austin American-Statesman*, p. A4.

Brooks, J. (1999). The Minority AIDS Crisis. *Closing the Gap.* Washington DC: Office of Minority Health, U.S. Department of Health and Human Services.

Brooks, J. (1998). Diabetes Fact Sheet Now Available in Spanish. *Closing the Gap.* Washington DC: Office of Minority Health, U.S. Department of Health and Human Services.

Brooks, J. (1995, October 15). In the Budget Talk from Washington, Indians See the Cruelest Cuts of All. *The New York Times*, p. 10.

Browne, A. (1993). Violence Against Women by Male Partners: Prevalence, Outcomes, and Policy Implications. *American Psychologist, 48*, 10, 1077–1087.

Carlisle, D. M., Leake, B. D., and Sahapiro, M. F. (1997). Racial and Ethnic Disparities in the Use of Cardiovascular Procedures: Associations with Type of Health Insurance. *American Journal of Public Health, 87*, 263–267.

Centers for Disease Control and Prevention. (2001). *Diabetes: A Serious Public Health Problem* (CDC Publication No. PDF-699K). Washington, DC: U.S. Government Printing Office.

Chen, J., Rathore, S. S., Radford, M. J., Wang, Y., and Krumholz, H. M. (2001, May 10). Racial Differences in the Use of Cardiac Catheterization After Acute Myocardial Infarction. *New England Journal of Medicine, 344*, 19, 1443–1449.

Chen, M. S. (1993). A 1993 Status Report on the Health Status of Asian Pacific Islander Americans: Comparisons with Healthy People 2000 Objectives. *Asian American Pacific Islander Journal of Health, 1*, 37–55.

Cowie, C. C. and Harris, M. I. (1997). Ambulatory Medical Care for non-Hispanic Whites, African Americans, and Mexican Americans with NIDDM in the U.S. *Diabetes Care, 20*, 142–147.

Crews, D. E. (1994). Obesity and diabetes. In N. W. S. Zane, D. T. Takeuchi, K. N. J. Young (Eds.), *Confronting Critical Health Issues of Asian and Pacific Islanders.* Thousand Oaks, CA: Sage.

Diaz, T., Chu, S. Y., Sorvillo, F., et al. (1995). Differences in Participation in Experimental Drug Trials among Persons with AIDS. *Journal of Acquired Immune Deficiency Syndrome Human Retrovirology, 10*, 562–568.

Dibble, U. and Straus, M. E. (1990). Some social structure determinants of inconsistency between attitudes and behaviors: The case of family violence. In M. A. Straus and R. J. Gelles (Eds.), *Physical Violence in American Families* (pp. 167–180). New Brunswick, NJ: Transaction.

DiNitto, D. M. (1995). Hunger, Nutrition, and Food Programs. In R. L. Edwards (Ed.-in-Chief), *Encyclopedia of Social Work,* 19th ed. (pp. 1428–1437). Washington, DC: National Association of Social Workers.

Dominitz, J. A., Samsa, G. P., Landsman, P., and Provenzale, D. (1998). Race, Treatment, and Survival among Colorectal Carcinoma Patients in an Equal-Access Medical System. *Cancer, 82,* 2312–2320.

Federal Interagency Forum on Child and Family Statistics. (2001). *America's Children: Key National Indicators of Well-Being 2001.* ChildStats.gov.

Goldberg, K. C., Hartz, A. J., Jacobsen, S. J., Krakauer, H., and Rimm, A. A. (1992). Racial and Community Factors Influencing Coronary Artery Bypass Graft Surgery Rates for All 1986 Medicare Patients. *Journal of the American Medical Association, 18,* 1473–1477.

Hahn, B. A. (1995). Children's Health: Racial and Ethnic Differences in the Use of Prescription Medications. *Pediatrics, 95,* 727–732.

Harlan, L. C., Bernstein, A. B., and Kessler, L. G. (1991). *American Journal of Public Health, 81,* 885–890.

Healthy People 2000. (1998, October 26). *Progress Review. Black Americans.* Washington, DC: Public Health Service, U.S. Department of Health and Human Services.

Healthy People 2000. (1997a, April 29). *Progress Review. Hispanic Americans.* Washington, DC: Public Health Service, U.S. Department of Health and Human Services.

Healthy People 2000. (1997b, September 13). *Progress Review. Asian Americans and Pacific Islanders.* Washington, DC: Public Health Service, U.S. Department of Health and Human Services.

Healthy People 2000. (1995, February 15). *Progress Report for American Indians and Alaska Natives.* Washington, DC: Public Health Service, U.S. Department of Health and Human Services.

Herbert, B. (1996, December 2). Death at an Early Age. *The New York Times,* p. A15.

Horwitz, S. R. (1998, June–July). Impact of Domestic Abuse on HIV Prevention in Hispanic Women. *Closing the Gap.* Washington, DC: Office of Minority Health, U.S. Department of Health and Human Services.

Indian Health Service, U.S. Department of Health and Human Services. (1998). *1997 Trends in Indian Health.* Washington DC: Government Printing Office.

Kaiser Family Foundation. (2000a, January). *Key Facts on Medicaid and Uninsured: HIV/AIDS and African-Americans.* Washington, DC: Kaiser Family Foundation.

Kaiser Family Foundation. (2000b, June). *Key Facts on Medicaid and Uninsured: Health Insurance Coverage and Access to Care Among American Indians and Alaska Natives.* Washington, DC: Kaiser Family Foundation.

Kaiser Family Foundation. (1999, September). *Fact Sheet: Latinos and HIV/AIDS.* Washington, DC: Kaiser Family Foundation.

Kamat, M. (1999, May–June). Blacks, Women Less Likely to Be Referred for High-Tech Cardiac Tests, According to Study. *Closing the Gap.* Washington, DC: Office of Minority Health, U.S. Department of Health and Human Services.

Kilborn, P. T. (1999, July 8). Clinton, Amid the Despair on a Reservation, Again Pledges Help. *The New York Times,* p. A1.

Krieger, N., Chen, J. T., and Ebel, G. (1997a). Can We Monitor Socioeconomic Inequalities in Health? A Survey of U.S. Health Departments' Data Collection and Reporting Practices. *Public Health Reports, 112,* 481–491.

Krieger, N., Williams, D., and Moss, N. (1997b). Measuring Social Class in U.S. Public Health Research: Concepts, Methodologies, and Guidelines. *Annual Review Public Health, 18,* 341–378.

Langkampf, D. L., Foye, H. R., and Roghmann, K. J. (1990). Does Limited Access to NICU Services Account for Higher Neonatal Mortality Rates among Blacks? *American Journal Perinatology, 7,* 227–231.

Lillie-Blanton, M., Martinez, R. M., Taylor, A. K., and Robinson, B. G. (1999). Latina and African American Women: Continuing Disparities in Health. In K. Charmaz and D. A. Paterniti (Eds.), *Health, Illness, and Healing* (pp. 395–414). Los Angeles: Roxbury Publishing.

Lin-Fu, J. S. (1993). Asian and Pacific Islander Americans: An Overview of Demographic Characteristics and Health Care Issues. *Asian American Pacific Islander Journal of Health, 1,* 20–36.

Marin, B. V. and Gomes, C. A. (1998, November). Latinos and HIV: Cultural Issues in AIDS Prevention. *The AIDS Knowledge Database.* San Francisco: University of California.

Martin, L. M., Callee, E. E., Wingo, P. A., and Heath, C. W. J. (1996). Comparison of Mammography and Pap Test Use from the 1987 and 1992 National Health Interview Surveys: Are We Closing the Gaps? *American Journal of Preventive Medicine, 12,* 82–90.

Mayberry, R. M., Mili, F., Isam, G. M., Samadi, A., Ofili, E., McNeal, M. S., Griffith, P. A., and LaBrie, G. (1999, October). *Racial and Ethnic Differences in Access to Medical Care: A Synthesis of the Literature.* Washington, DC: Kaiser Family Foundation.

McCord, C. and Freeman, H. (1990). Excess Mortality in Harlem. *New England Journal of Medicine, 322,* 173–177.

McLemore, S. D. and Romo, H. D. (1998). *Racial and Ethnic Relations in America,* 5th ed. Boston: Allyn & Bacon.

Meadows, M. (2000, August). More Research Needed on Breast Cancer in Black Women. *Closing the Gap.* Washington, DC: Office of Minority Health, U.S. Department of Health and Human Services.

Mettlin, C. J. and Murphy, G. P. (1994). The National Cancer Data Base Report on Prostate Cancer. *Cancer, 74,* 1640–1648.

Mettlin, C. J., Murphy, G. P., Cunningham, M. P., and Menck, H. R. (1997). The National Cancer Data Base Report on Race, Age, and Region Variations in Prostate Cancer Treatment. *Cancer, 80,* 1261–1266.

Mitchell, J. B. and McCormack, L. A. (1997). Time Trends in Late-Stage Diagnosis of Cervical Cancer. *Medical Care, 35,* 1220–1224.

Moore, R. D., Stanton, D., Gopalan, R., and Chaisson, R. E. (1994). Racial differences in the Use of Drug Therapy for HIV Disease in an Urban Community. *New England Journal of Medicine, 330,* 763–768.

National Academy on an Aging Society. (2000, July). Depression, No. 9. *Challenges for the 21st Century: Chronic and Disabling Conditions.* Washington, DC: National Academy on an Aging Society.

National Center for Health Statistics. (2001, June 26). *Mortality Declines for Several Leading Causes of Death in 1999.* Hyattsville, MD: U.S. Department of Health and Human Services.

National Center for Health Statistics. (2000). *Health United States, 2000.* Hyattsville, MD: U.S. Department of Health and Human Services.

Naumburg, E. H., Franks, P., Bell, B., Gold, M., and Engerman, J. (1993). Racial Differentials in the Identification of Hypercholesterolemia. *Journal of Family Practice, 36,* 425–430.

Navarro, V. (1990). Race or Class versus Race and Class: Mortality Differentials in the United States. *Lancet, 336,* 1238–1240.

Oddone, E. Z., Horner, R. D., Diers, T., et al. (1998). Understanding Racial Variation in the Use of Carotid Endarterectomy: The Role of Aversion to Surgery. *Journal of the National Medical Association, 90,* 25–33.

Oddone, E. Z., Horner, R. D., Monger, M. E., and Matchar, D. B. (1993). Racial Variations in the Rates of Carotid Angiography and Endarterectomy in Patients with Stroke and Transient Ischemic Attack. *Archives Internal Medicine, 153,* 2781–2786.

Optenberg, S. A., Thompson, I. M., Friedrichs, P., Wojcik, B., Stein, C. R., and Kramer, B. (1995). Race, Treatment, and Long-Term Survival from Prostate Cancer in an Equal-Access Medical Care Delivery System. *JAMA, 274,* 1599–1605.

Oropeza, L. (2001, Spring). Native Americans Strategize to Integrate HIV Prevention and Substance Abuse. *HIV Impact.* Washington, DC: Office of Minority Health, U.S. Department of Health and Human Services.

Oxendine, J. (2000, June–July). Diabetes Programs Have Local Style. *Closing the Gap.* Washington, DC: Office of Minority Health, U.S. Department of Health and Human Services.

Oxendine, J. (1999, February–March). Who Has Diabetes? *Closing the Gap.* Washington, DC: Office of Minority Health, U.S. Department of Health and Human Services.

Parham, G., Phillips, J. L., Hicks, M. L., Andrews, N., Jones, W. B., Shingleton, H. M., and Menck, H. R. (1997). The National Cancer Data Base Report on Malignant Epithelial Ovarian Carcinoma in African-American Women. *Cancer, 80,* 816–826.

Philibin, E. F. and Di Salvo, T. G. (1998). Influence of Race and Gender on Care Process, Resource Use, and Hosptial-Based Outcomes in Congestive Heart Failure. *American Journal of Cardiology, 82,* 76–81.

Pua'ala'okalani, A. (2000, June–July). Comparing Native Hawaiians' Health to the Nation. *Closing the Gap.* Washington, DC: Office of Minority Health, U.S. Department of Health and Human Services.

Regulus, T. A. (1995). Gang Violence. In R. L. Edwards (Ed.-in-Chief), *Encyclopedia of Social Work,* 19th ed. (Vol. 2, pp. 1045–1055). Washington, DC: National Association of Social Workers.

Rhoades, E. R., Mason, R. D., Eddy. P., Smith, E. M., and Burns, T. R. (1988, November–December). The Indian Health Service Approach to Alcoholism among American Indians and Alaska Natives. *Public Health Reports, 103,* 621–627.

Schoendorf, K. C., Hogue, C., Kleinman, J., and Rowley, D. (1992). Mortality among Infants of Black as Compared with White College-Educated Parents. *New England Journal of Medicine, 326,* 1522–1526.

Schulman, K. A., Berlin, J. A., Harless, W., Kerner, J. F., Sistrunk, S., Gersh, B. J., Dube, R., Taleghani, C. K., Burke, J. E., Williams, S., Eisenberg, J. M., Escarce, J. J., Ayers, W. (1999). The effect of race and sex on cardiac catheterization. *New England Journal of Medicine, 340,* 8, 618–626.

Shapiro, M. F., Morton, S. C., McCaffrey, D. F., Senterfitt, J. W., Fleishman, J. A., Perlman, J. F., et al. (1999). Variations in the Care of HIV-Infected Adults in the U.S.: Results from the HIV Cost and Services Utilization Study. *JAMA, 281,* 2305–2375.

Smith, G. D., Neaton, J. D., Wentworth, D., Stamler, R., and Stamler, J. for the MRFIT Research Group. (1998, March 28). *Lancet, 351,* 9107.

Snipp, C. M. (1986, October). American Indians and Natural Resource Development: Indigenous Peoples' Land, Now Sought After, Has Produced New Indian–White Problems. *American Journal of Economics and Sociology,* 457–473.

Sorlie, P. D., Backlund, E., Johnson, N. J., and Rogot, E. (1993). Mortality by Hispanics in the U.S. *JAMA, 270,* 2464–2468.

Svensson, C. K. (1989). Representation of American Blacks in Clinical Trials of New Drugs. *JAMA, 261,* 263–265.

Taylor, P. (1991, March 14). Gunshot Leading Killer of Teenage Boys. *Concord Monitor,* p. A10.

Therrien, M. and Ramirez, R. R. (2001). *The Hispanic Population in the U.S.: March 2000.* Current Population Reports, P20-535. Washington, DC: U.S. Census Bureau.

Tulchinsky, T. H. and Varavikova, E. A. (2000). *The New Public Health.* San Diego, CA: Academic Press.

U.S. Census Bureau. (2000). March Demographic Profile. *Current Population Surveys* (Online). Available at www.census.gov/population/socdemo.

U.S. Department of Health and Human Services. (1998). *Racial and Ethnic Disparities in Health, Response to President's Initiative on Race.* Washington, DC.

U.S. Department of Health and Human Services. (1986). *Report of the Secretary's Task Force on Black and Minority Health.* Volumes I–VIII. Washington, DC: U.S. Government Printing Office.

U.S. General Accounting Office. (2000a, March). *HIV/AIDS: Use of Ryan White CARE Act and Other Assistance Grant Funds* (HEHS-00-54). Washington, DC: U.S. Government Printing Office.

U.S. General Accounting Office. (2000b, May). *Women's Health: NIH Has Increased Its Efforts to Include Women in Research* (HEHS-00-96). Washington, DC: U.S. Government Printing Office.

U.S. General Accounting Office. (1993, April). *Indian Health Service—Basic Services Mostly Available; Substance Abuse Problems Need Attention.* (GAO/HRD-93-48). Washington, DC: U.S. Government Printing Office.

U.S. General Accounting Office. (1992, January). *Hispanic Access to Health Care—Significant Gaps Exist* (GAO/PEMD-92-6). Washington, DC: U.S. Government Printing Office.

Vega, W. A. and Amaro, H. (1994). Latino Outlook: Good Health, Uncertain Prognosis. *Annual Review of Public Health, 15,* 39–67.

Wang, F. and Javitt, J. C. (1996). Eye Care for Elderly Americans with Diabetes Mellitus: Failure to Meet Current Guidelines. *Opthamology, 103,* 1744–1750.

Wenneker, M. and Epstein, A. (1989). Racial Inequalities in the Use of Procedures for Patients with Ischemic Heart Disease in Massachusetts. *Journal of the American Medical Association, 261,* 253–257.

West, J. (1999, February–March). National Diabetes Education Program. *Closing the Gap.* Washington, DC: Office of Minority Health, U.S. Department of Health and Human Services.

Whittle, J., Conigliaro, J., Good, C. B., and Lofgren, R. P. (1993). Racial Differences in the Use of Invasive Cardiovascular Procedures in the Department of Veterans Affairs Medical System. *New England Journal of Medicine, 329,* 621–627.

7 Disparities in Health: Gender and Age-Based Differences

This chapter addresses gender and age-based differences in health risks in our society. Women face greater health risks than men as a result of their social status and discriminatory treatment. These risks extend to infants, children, and adolescents because women's health is inexorably linked to children's health through the childbearing role. Family planning services and prenatal care are critical to maternal, prenatal, and child health. Women are also particularly vulnerable to the risk of mortality and injury that stems from domestic and sexual violence.

Individuals also confront health risks at vulnerable stages during their lifespan. For example, infants and children are dependent on parents and guardians who must protect them from disease and illness. Adolescents experiment with tobacco, alcohol, and other substances as they seek approval from their peers and independence from their parents or guardians. Elderly adults confront chronic illness and impairments that limit their ability to function independently. In addition, these age-related risk factors are exacerbated by sociopolitical factors, including socioeconomic status and discrimination. In general, poor children, adolescents, and elderly adults are at greater risk for ill health.

This chapter, similar to Chapter 6, highlights some of the major health areas, including infant mortality, cardiovascular disease, HIV/AIDS, and infectious diseases that have been targeted by the U.S. Public Health Service. The primary focus of this chapter, however, is health risks specific to the experiences of women and age-based health disparities that stem from human growth and development and socioeconomic conditions. Unlike Chapter 6, this chapter provides information about federal policies, programs, and services that address these health issues and problems.

Women and Infants

The health status of women is inseparable from the social status of women in society, and women are still not equal to men in their access to power, prestige, or wealth. Although it is clear that women's stature has improved, women still experience discrimination in every aspect of social life. Disparities are found in occupational segregation, job discrimination, pay inequity, gender-specific education, sexual harassment, domestic violence, and representation in political structures (National Association of Social Workers, 2000e).

In the area of health, gender roles and behaviors have certainly had an impact on health outcomes. Traditional male behaviors and risk factors—including smoking, alcohol consumption, risk-taking behavior, occupational hazards, and violent sports—have contributed to lower rates of life expectancy for men. In 1996, average life expectancy for a woman was 79 years, while average life expectancy for a man was six years shorter, or 73 years (Agency for Health Care Policy and Research [AHCPR], 1999).

However, women still bear disproportionately the health consequences of living in poverty and lower socioeconomic status. Approximately two-thirds of poor people over age 18 are women. While women may have longer life expectancies than men, they are more likely to experience chronic illness during their lifetimes, and more likely to experience mental illness. They also make use of health care facilities and prescription drugs more frequently and, during old age, are more dependent on long-term care due to multiple chronic conditions (Agency for Health Care Policy and Research [AHCPR], 1999; Lambrew, 2001).

The government first recognized disparities in health for women when it enacted the Women's Health Equity Act of 1990, introduced by Representative (D) Patricia Schroeder, and established the Office of Women's Health in 1991. The broad purpose of the bill was to improve women's health care and to address the ongoing exclusion of women from medical research. Studies from the late 1980s conducted by the U.S. Public Health Service and the National Institutes of Health indicated that so little data were available on women's health that it was difficult to understand women's health care needs (Shumaker and Smith, 1999).

Cancer and Cardiovascular Disease

Heart disease and cancer are the primary causes of death for both women and men (Gottlieb, 1995). Heart disease is the leading cause of death for all women, and those over age 75 are at greatest risk (AHCPR, 1999). However, myths still seem to persist about heart disease being a mostly male health problem. For example, both female and male physicians are far less likely to refer women for cardiac catheterization, the most definitive test for heart disease (Schulman et al., 1999). Women are also less likely to be treated with therapy (clot busting) or to undergo surgery (coronary bypass) or surgical procedures (angiography or angioplasty) after hospital admissions, and thus are 20 percent more likely than men to die of a heart attack while still in the hospital (Iezzoni et al., 1997). They are also less likely than men to be treated for heart disease with lifesaving drugs (aspirin, beta blockers, etc.) (Canto et al., 2000).

Younger women, ages 35–44, are far more likely to die from cancer than heart disease, but here, too, myths about the dangers of different cancers seem to persist. Although breast cancer is the most common form of cancer women experience, since 1987, lung cancer has caused more deaths than breast cancer (*Healthy People 2000,* 1998b). However, low-income women are more likely to die from breast cancer than are other women because diagnosis tends to occur at a more advanced stage of the disease (AHCPR, 1999).

HIV/AIDS

Although the vast majority of adult AIDS cases are men (83 percent) and most of these cases are gay men (55 percent), the HIV virus and the disease of AIDS are of serious concern for women (U.S. Census Bureau, 1998). HIV/AIDS has been growing at a faster rate for heterosexual women than heterosexual men since the disease was first recognized in 1981. The number of cases has increased from 7 percent of women in 1985 to an alarming 20 percent in 1998 (AHCPR, 1999). Women are more susceptible because the virus is more easily transmitted from male to female. Poor women of color, as discussed earlier, are at especially high risk.

Young women ages 15–44 are especially vulnerable during their reproductive years because transmission of the virus occurs most often during this period. HIV/AIDS is the fourth leading cause of death among women ages 25–44 (AHCPR, 1999; *Healthy People 2000,* 1998b). On a more positive note, advances have been made in reducing the number of babies infected with AIDS by their mothers during pregnancy. This is the result of prenatal treatments with the drug AZT. Between 1992 and 1997, the number of babies with AIDS declined by two-thirds to a total of less than 300 babies (Coleman, 1999).

HIV/AIDS also generates other health-related problems that women face. For poor women, poverty is a compounding factor that makes dealing with this disease that much more difficult. For all women with HIV/AIDS, the need for psychological support has received less attention than it has for gay men, and few support groups exist. Many women are the primary caregivers in their households and continue to struggle with this role while caring for their own health. HIV/AIDS can also be traumatic for children who experience the loss of a parent to the disease (Hackl et al., 1997).

The Ryan White Comprehensive AIDS Resources Emergency (CARE) Act of 1990 (P.L. 101-381) was enacted to serve vulnerable, underserved populations with HIV/AIDS. The U.S. General Accounting Office (2000) reports that women and people of color "generally receive less appropriate care for their disease" (p. 11) and are assisted by the CARE Act at rates disproportionate to their representation in the AIDS population. The CARE Act provides funds to states, localities, schools, and organizations for prevention programs, medical treatment, and support services, including housing and case management.

Maternal and Infant Mortality

Maternal mortality, compared to other women's health issues, is not a serious risk; maternal mortality rates have declined steadily over the past fifty years (Agency for Healthcare Research and Quality [AHRQ], 2000). The maternal mortality rate declined from 8.2 deaths per 100,000 live births in 1990 to 7.5 deaths in 1997 (*Healthy People 2000,* 1999b). During the past decade, all women experienced increased access to prenatal care during the first trimester of pregnancy, which is of vital importance to the health of pregnant women and their babies (Healthy People 2000, 1998b). Women who lack prenatal care are more likely to have low-birth-weight babies, who in turn are at significant risk for neurological, congenital, and respiratory problems and disabilities (Balsanek, 1997). Low birth weight is responsible for almost 70 percent of infant mortality (AHRQ, 2000).

Infant mortality also declined during the past decade, but, compared to other industrialized countries, the United States ranks only twenty-fifth in low infant mortality rates (*Healthy People 2000,* 1999b). In addition, low-income women are at greater risk for poor birth outcomes. Inadequate prenatal care during the first trimester of pregnancy (*Healthy People 2000,* 1997), poor nutrition, and inadequate psychosocial supports are contributing factors (Homan and Korenbrot, 1998). "Mothers are less likely to obtain adequate...prenatal care if they are young, poor, unmarried, relatively uneducated, uninsured, or living in inner cities or rural areas" (Balsanek, 1997). Another concern is tobacco smoking. Overall, the use of tobacco during pregnancy decreased during the past decade (*Healthy People 2000,* 1999b), but pregnant low-income women are at greater risk for the stress-related use of drugs, alcohol, and cigarettes (Zambrana and Scrimshaw, 1997).

Maternal, Prenatal, and Child Health Services

A number of federal policies impact the availability and delivery of maternal, prenatal, and child health services. Title V of the Social Security Act of 1935 enacted the Maternal and Child Health Services (MCHS) program, as well as Crippled Children's Services (CCS) and Child Welfare Services (CWS). Title V has undergone many legislative changes, however. Funding to the states for maternal and child health services for low-income children is now administered through the Maternal and Child Health Block Grant established in 1981. The Maternal and Child Health Bureau in the U.S. Public Health Service provides leadership for the development of maternal and child health services and administers the program. Two of the primary goals of the block grant are to reduce infant mortality and increase women's access to prenatal care. *Healthy Start* is a special initiative that began in 1991 and focuses on at-risk or underserved areas with high infant mortality rates (Jaros and Evans, 1995).

The 1972 Special Supplemental Food program for Women, Infants, and Children (WIC) (P.L. 92-433) helps low-income women and their children attain adequate nutrition. In 1998, WIC provided food assistance to 1.7 million women, 1.8 million infants, and 3.6 million children. However, the Children's Defense Fund has encouraged expansion of the program because its funding ceiling does not allow it to reach everyone who is eligible (Edelman, 1999).

Community health centers, which were established by the Health Centers Consolidation Act of 1966 (P.L. 104-299), play a significant role in the provision of services to vulnerable and underserved women of childbearing age. The centers were originally created to increase access to health care for low-income people. Today, approximately 600 nonprofit community-based health centers provide services to about 10 million poor and low-income people in rural and urban areas that are medically underserved. In some areas, the centers are the only source of primary care for this population. Most are young women and children, many of whom are eligible for Medicaid or are uninsured. The centers play a vital role in the provision of prenatal, maternal, and infant care (U.S. General Accounting Office, 2000).

Family Planning Services

Family planning services and safe, legal abortions are essential services in the delivery of women's health care. Family planning prevents unwanted pregnancies and, in doing so, helps to reduce the incidence of abortion. Women who use family planning services are more likely to have prenatal care. Thus, they are also more likely to have healthy babies and less likely to give birth to low-birth-weight babies or to lose their children in childbirth. Family planning also improves maternal health for women and decreases maternal mortality. However, access to family planning is still a problem in the United States. About half of all pregnancies are unintended, and approximately one-fourth of these are aborted (*Healthy People 2000*, 1999a).

One of the primary concerns with family planning is the lack of coverage by private health insurers for contraceptive services. Medicaid provides the greatest support for reproductive services, but as discussed in Chapter 3, many people are ineligible for Medicaid (*Healthy People 2000*, 1999a). Title X, Family Planning and Population Research, of the Public Health Service Act (1970), does provide services for millions of women (and men) through a network of approximately 4,600 clinics across the country. Eighty-five percent of clinic users have low incomes, and about a third are adolescents (*Healthy People 2000*, 1999a).

However, Congress has not taken action to reauthorize Title X since 1985 due to political pressures from the influential, right-wing anti-choice movement, even though it does not represent the majority in the United States who support a woman's right to reproductive choice (National Association of Social Workers, 2000c). Congress has continued to appropriate funds, but between 1980 and 1990, federal funding for Title X has declined significantly, particularly when adjusted for inflation.

The primary method for the prevention of unwanted pregnancy is contraception, but contraceptives are not fail proof. In these cases, women need access to safe, legal abortions. However, the right to an abortion for low-income women on Medicaid has been threatened since 1976 when the Hyde amendment was enacted to prevent the use of federal funds for abortions. In addition, access to physicians and clinics that perform abortions has been jeopardized by the sometimes-violent actions, including bombings, arsons, assaults, and murders, organized by segments of the pro-life movement to prevent women from entering these facilities.

In 1994, Congress passed the Freedom of Access to Clinic Entrances Act (P.L. 103-259) to protect women, physicians, and other medical staff from these acts of violence, but the number of physicians and clinics that perform abortions has declined steadily. In 1999, only 4 percent of the counties in the United States had a health care provider who performed abortions (National Association of Social Workers, 2000c). The U.S. Food and Drug Administration approved the controversial French abortion drug RU-486 (September 28, 2000) under President Clinton, but this method has come under the scrutiny of the Bush administration. RU-486 provides an alternative to surgical abortions for women in the early stage of pregnancy, though it is not a substitute for most women and is unlikely to be covered by Medicaid. The right to safe and legal abortions, first granted by the U.S. Supreme Court decision *Roe v. Wade* in 1973, still needs enormous support and protection.

Violence against Women

In the United States, men and women are both subject to societal violence. However, women are more likely to be victims of sex crimes (rape, incest), whereas men are more likely to experience physical violence (warfare, assault, homicide, suicide, injury, disability) (Gilligan, 1996). These differences are rooted in "the cultural construction of masculinity and femininity" (p. 229) and the gender roles into which men and women are socialized. For example, in *Real Boys' Voices*, Pollack (2000) describes our tolerance for "dangerous bullying" among boys as a "national disgrace," and the increasing fear among boys of "being victimized by the rage and violence of other boys" (p. 199).

Gender-based socialization, coupled with women's traditional economic dependence on men, provides a social context for understanding domestic violence, which generally refers to violence between intimate partners. Legal definitions of domestic abuse typically refer to acts or threats of physical abuse, including rape or sexual assault, whereas clinical definitions are likely to include patterns of psychological or economic coercion, as well (Fantuzzo and Mohr, 1999).

Although men and women can experience domestic violence, men have historically inflicted physical abuse against women and women have had little recourse against it. Wife beating was actually sanctioned by English common law, was not prohibited in the United States until 1883, and was not even taken seriously as deviant or criminal behavior until the 1970s. Before the 1970s, domestic violence was viewed as a private, family matter, not a legal issue, and police departments, until the 1980s, discouraged arrests in cases of domestic violence.

Today, with the changes in social roles that have occurred, even if men and women are more likely to engage equally in physical abuse toward their partners or spouses (Brush, 1990), women are still more likely to suffer physical injury because men are usually physically stronger than women. In fact, studies (Browne, 1987; Schwartz, 1987) show that the vast majority (95 percent) of abuse victims are women. Women are also still more likely to remain in abusive relationships because of their economic dependence on men, and poor and low-income women are at even greater risk for spousal abuse (Dibble and Straus, 1990; Gelles and Cornell, 1990).

From a health perspective, violence against women is a major concern. Each year, approximately 4 million women suffer physical abuse from their partners (AHCPR, 1999; Bell et al., 1996). Violence in the form of rape increased from 1986 to 1994, though there has been a more positive downward trend since then (*Healthy People 2000*, 1998b). In 1997, the incidence of rape and attempted rape was 156 per 100,000 for all females (over age 12) and 349 per 100,000 for females aged 12–34 (*Healthy People 2000*, 1999c). The FBI reports that one-third to one-half of all homicides are women who die from partner abuse (National Association of Social Workers, 2000e). Emergency rooms report that one out of every four women treated has been injured due to domestic violence (AHCPR, 1999). Domestic violence also puts women at greater risk for mental health problems, including depression and suicide (AHCPR, 1999; Bell et al., 1996). Women that have experienced sexual or physical assault often experience posttraumatic stress disorder (Browne, 1993).

For many years, the widespread problem of violence against women in the United States received little attention, but in the past thirty years, a number of legal and social reforms have occurred. In the early to mid-1970s, grassroots efforts by women's groups to help "battered" women led to the development of shelters or safe houses across the country. Divorce laws also changed during this period, making it easier for women to leave their husbands. The NIMH sponsored research on sexual assault during the 1970s, and between 1979 and 1981, the federal government established and administered the Office of Domestic Violence.

In 1984, the first federal effort to address domestic violence, the Family Violence Prevention and Services Act, was enacted to give states funds to raise awareness about domestic violence and to establish temporary shelters for abused women. It also provided funds for training and family violence services. In 1984, the Victims of Crime Act was also enacted to give women compensation for crime-related costs.

With growing awareness and concern for victims of domestic violence, Congress enacted the Violence Against Women Act (VAWA) of 1994 (as part of the Violent Crime Control and Law Enforcement Act, P.L. 103-3222). This bill placed more emphasis on prevention and expanded federal funding for state-supported domestic violence prevention and training programs. It also classified sex crimes as hate crimes, increased penalties against offenders, and improved legal protections for victims of abuse, including the protection of battered immigrant women from deportation (Mathews, 1999). Battered immigrant women who depend on the legal citizenship or permanent resident status of their spouses for their own immigration status have been afraid to leave their spouses.

By 1999, over 2,000 agencies existed across the country providing services to battered women and their children, including emergency hot lines, crisis counseling, support groups for women and men, vocational counseling, and assistance with housing, legal services, and health and mental health care. These agencies also offer training and education programs to improve public awareness and understanding of the problem and improve collaboration among law enforcement agencies, child protective services, and health care services (Saathoff and Stoffel, 1999).

Depression

According to *Mental Health: A Report of the Surgeon General* (U.S. Dept. of Health and Human Services, 1999b),

> socioeconomic factors affect individuals' vulnerability to mental illness and mental health problems. Certain demographic and economic groups are more likely than others to experience mental health problems and some disorders. Vulnerability alone may not be sufficient to cause a mental disorder; rather, the causes of most mental disorders lie in some combination of genetic and environmental factors, which may be biological or psychosocial (p. xiv).

The social roles of women in the United States have changed considerably since the 1960s, and patterns of gender-based inequity are improving. However, women today still experience adverse socioeconomic conditions, including occupational segregation, disparities in earnings, and disproportionate rates of poverty, as well as harmful psychosocial risks, such as sexual harassment at work or school, or domestic violence. Women at all socioeconomic levels often bear the double burden and stress of caring for children and working outside the home. Older women are more likely to experience the stress of a spouse's death, since women have a longer life expectancy than men.

Men and women have about the same rates of mental illness, but women are at greater risk for depression, while men are at greater risk for alcohol and drug abuse (Glied and Kofman, 1995; Kessler, Abelson, and Zhao, 1998). National studies from the 1980s (the National Institute of Mental Health, Epidemiologic Catchment Area studies) and 1990s (the National Comorbidity Survey) show that women are at greater risk than men for affective disorders (Glied and Kofman, 1995; Proctor and Stiffman, 1998). In fact, women are twice as likely as men to be diagnosed with depression, and younger women ages 25–44 are particularly vulnerable (National Academy on an Aging Society, 2000). Women are also treated for depression more often than men (Wetzel, 1994).

The reasons for these differences between women and men are as yet unclear. Certainly, the socioeconomic and psychosocial factors that affect women's lives play a role in their mental health, but why are women at particular risk for depression? It may be that because men tend to see depression as a weakness, they are more likely to exhibit depressive symptoms through alcohol and substance abuse.

Women in Medical Research

A different, but related kind of disparity for women is found in the nation's health research agenda. In the 1980s, the National Institutes of Health (NIH) agreed that women were excluded from research studies (many included only men), and few studies were designed to research women's health issues. The NIH is the federal agency with primary responsibility for medical research. It has a multibillion-dollar budget to conduct research through twenty-five institutes and centers, each of which focuses on a major disease or health concern, such as cancer. In 1990, NIH established the Office of Research on Women's Health and started a Women's Health Initiative in 1991 to study (1) the prevention of cardiovascular disease, breast cancer, and osteoporosis through hormone replacement therapy and other preventive measures; (2) the relationship between lifestyle and specific disease outcomes; and (3) the role of community prevention efforts to promote healthy lifestyles, particularly among women of color. The results of these studies will provide new information about (1) health conditions unique to women or more prevalent among women, (2) differences between women and men in medical risks, and (3) health conditions with insufficient clinical data based on research using women as subjects (U.S. General Accounting Office, 2000).

Children and Adolescents

The federal government recognizes that children have special health needs. In 1999, the U.S. Agency for Health Care Policy and Research was reauthorized by Congress and renamed the U.S. Agency for Healthcare Research and Quality (AHRQ) under P.L. 106-129. AHRQ, which is responsible for research efforts to improve health care services and their access, identified children as one of its priorities and recognized children's health needs as different from those of adults (AHRQ, 2000).

   According to AHRQ (2000), children (under age 19) have the lowest mortality rates, but the highest rates of *acute* illness and, therefore, the need for frequent medical care. The rates of *chronic* illness for children and adults are about the same, but children experience different chronic illnesses, including asthma and attention deficit disorder. As children grow and change developmentally from infancy to adolescence, they are constantly vulnerable to new and changing environmental hazards, such as infectious diseases, as well as behavioral risks, such as alcohol and drug abuse, teenage pregnancy, and suicide. Finally, and most importantly, children are dependent on adults for their health and well-being.

   Over twenty-five years ago, medical researchers at Harvard (Newberger, Newberger, and Richmond, 1976) raised serious questions and concerns about the inability of the U.S. health care system to "reach and treat the children most in need of them" and the impact of "environmental forces" (p. 249) on child health, particularly among poor and "nonwhite" children. They were concerned with the impact of accidents, lead poisoning, physical abuse and other "causal" environmental factors that are readily viewed as risks to child health. However, they also raised broader concerns about the "relationship between adult dysfunction and childhood illness" (p. 271) and the wider context of child health. Children are clearly dependent on adult care, and parents who are unable to provide fully for their children, because of their own socioeconomic needs, place their children at risk for ill health, no matter how unintentional this may be. In other words, poverty "appears to cause—directly or indirectly—a great amount of morbidity and mortality in children" (p. 272).

Today, the "state of America's children" (Edelman, 1999) and its potential impact on child health has not improved; surprisingly, it has worsened. In 1975, the child poverty rate was 16 percent (U.S. Census Bureau, 1976); in 1999, the poverty rate among children was 16.9 percent. This is particularly alarming because the overall poverty rate in 1999 (11.8 percent) was at its lowest in twenty-one years (U.S. Census Bureau, 2000).

Poor children are at greater risk for ill health. For example, poor children are more vulnerable to iron deficiency, which causes anemia and can affect children's attention, concentration, and motor coordination. Poor children are more likely to live in cold, damp, moldy housing that exacerbates asthma and other respiratory diseases. Cockroach infestations are found in damp housing conditions that stem from lack of heat, uneven heat, or leaky pipes, and cause allergies and asthma for poor children. Poor children are more likely to be exposed to rats and mice, which can lead to respiratory problems; lead paint, which causes poisoning; and overcrowding, which contributes to stress, infection, injuries, and accidents. Homeless children are at greater risk for exposure to infectious diseases in shelters and have higher rates of asthma and inadequate immunizations (Sherman, 1994). Poor children are more likely to be exposed to secondhand smoke (twenty or more cigarettes per day) which puts them at greater risk for asthma and chronic bronchitis (Gergen et al., 1998; Williams, 1990).

Infectious Diseases

To address the need for all children to be immunized from infectious diseases, Congress supported President Clinton's initiative for a federal vaccine program in 1993. Prior to this legislation, children's access to vaccination was dependent on their access to providers and health insurance coverage. Children enrolled in the Medicaid program were particularly vulnerable, because physicians found it costly to purchase the vaccines and then wait for reimbursement from Medicaid. Instead physicians made referrals to public health clinics, and in the process, poor children often became infected before they had a chance to be immunized.

Under the Vaccines for Children Act, the federal government purchases the vaccines and distributes them at no cost to physicians to administer. The program has made an enormous difference in the rates of vaccination against diptheria, tetanus, pertussis, measles, mumps, rubella, and polio. For example, from 1992 to 1997, the number of two-year-olds fully immunized against these contagious diseases increased by 33 percent (Edelman, 1999). Public health clinics continue to play an important role in immunization, particularly in rural areas, where access to medical care is more limited (Slifkin et al., 1997).

Risky Behaviors: Substance Abuse

Substance abuse refers to the use of alcohol, tobacco, illicit drugs (marijuana, cocaine, heroin, hallucinogens), nonprescription and prescription drugs (depressants, such as sleeping pills or valium; stimulants, such as amphetamines), and common household products often used as inhalants (glues, solvents, butane, gasoline, and aerosols) in a way that results in "health consequences or impairment in social, psychological, and occupational functioning" (National Association of Social Workers, 2000a). The profession of social work is increasingly concerned with the prevalence of substance use in our society and its widespread impact on social work practice (Gray, 1995), and more social workers are needed in substance abuse treatment (Magura, 1994).

Millions of people in the United States use drugs everyday. Some do so responsibly without incident; others are at risk for habitual, chronic use that results in personal, familial, or legal problems. Substance abuse is difficult to assess because it not only is linked with other physical, psychological, and social problems, but also is influenced by cultural norms. Substance abuse can be the *cause* of physical or psychological problems, or it can be the *result* of individual efforts to cope with other preexisting conditions or diseases.

Substance abuse is associated with a wide range of physical illnesses including cancer, heart disease, liver and pancreatic disease and respiratory arrest; mental illness, including psychosis, depression, and anxiety disorders; and drug-related deaths and injuries that result from accidents or violence. The use of shared "dirty" needles among intravenous drug users is a risk factor for HIV/ AIDS, and other infectious diseases. Substance abuse among adolescents is of particular concern because experimental or social drug use could lead to abuse and eventually to dependence or addiction in adulthood.

Youth Smoking.   In 1995, the Maternal and Child Health Bureau established a new Office of Adolescent Health (OAH) in an effort to make the health of adolescents a national priority. OAH is concerned with several disturbing health trends among youth in the United States. One area of concern is teenage smoking, which, according to studies funded by the National Institute of Drug Abuse (Johnson et al., 2000) reached a peak in 1976. From 1977 to 1992, smoking among teens declined, but since 1992, there has been a sharp increase in teenage smoking (Gruber and Zinman, 2000). In 1997, the teenage smoking rate was 20 percent (*Healthy People 2000,* 1998a) (about twice the rate for adults). Gruber and Zinman (2000) raise concerns about the relationship between teenage smoking and adult smoking, and estimate that 25 percent to 50 percent of adolescent smokers continue this habit as adults.

Smoking is widespread and not confined to poor and low-income youth. In fact, white or suburban youth smoke even more than do African American or urban youth. Gruber and Zinman (2000) estimate that 25 percent of the reason for this increase in smoking is the decline in cigarette prices that occurred in the early 1990s (until 1998) and the advertising efforts of cigarette companies to target youth. Studies show that boys and girls choose to smoke for similar reasons, including the need to relieve stress, because others around them smoke, to experiment, and to have "fun." Girls of color are less likely to smoke than are boys across all racial lines, and Hispanic boys are more likely to smoke than are white, African American, or Asian American boys. Abused boys and girls are at greater risk for smoking as a means of relieving stress (Schoen et al., 1998).

Youth Drinking.   Although much attention has been paid to the use of illegal drugs by youth, alcohol is the most widely used and abused drug by teenagers. For some youth, the consumption of alcohol becomes a major problem in itself, especially if it involves "binge" drinking, whereas for others, alcohol abuse is but one of many high-risk behaviors that reflect other psychosocial difficulties. The National Household Survey on Drug Abuse and the National Survey of High School Seniors conducted by the Substance Abuse and Mental Health Services Administration (SAMHSA) define heavy, episodic, or "binge" drinking as five or more successive drinks per occasion on five or more days a month.

Although the legal minimum drinking age in the United States is 21, many teenagers consume alcohol, and teenagers are at high risk to start drinking at a young age, often between ages 13 and 15 (Johnson et al., 1995). In 1988, more than half of all adolescents (ages 12–17) had consumed alcohol during their lifetime (U.S. Department of Health and Human Services, 1998). In 1999, 24 percent of eighth graders, 40 percent of tenth graders, and 51 percent of twelfth graders consumed alcohol (during the month prior to being surveyed) (Johnson et al., 2000).

Alcohol use among all teens (during the month prior to being surveyed) *declined* between 1988 and 1997, dropping from 33 percent to 21 percent (U.S. Department of Health and Human Services, 1998). However, drinking among teens remains a major concern given its potentially devastating health consequences. The leading causes of death among youth are vehicular accidents, homicides, and suicides (*Healthy People 2000,* 1998a). Alcohol is the primary cause of fatal automobile and motorcycle accidents that involve adolescent drivers (Long, Brendtro, and Johnson, 1993) and is also associated with homicide and suicide (Holinger et al., 1994). Studies of suicide and drinking do not clearly show a causal relationship between these two factors, but they do show a correlation (Felts et al., 1992; Garrison et al., 1993; Kinkel et al., 1989).

In addition to fatalities, alcohol abuse is linked to risky sexual behavior, as well as to mental illness among youth. For example, one study of teenagers in Massachusetts found that adolescents who had consumed alcohol were more likely to engage in sexual intercourse and less likely to use contraceptives (condoms) (Strunin and Hingson, 1992). Studies (Kushner and Shor, 1993) of college students show that youth with anxiety disorders or depression are more likely to abuse or depend on alcohol. However, it is unclear whether mental illness leads to alcohol abuse or alcohol abuse leads to mental illness. Some studies do show that depression is more likely to precede alcohol abuse (Deykin et al., 1987; Deykin et al., 1992).

Youth Drug Abuse.   Adolescents are at risk for drug use for many of the same reasons that they abuse alcohol. In addition to psychiatric disorders and other troubling childhood behaviors, such as impulsiveness or aggressiveness, adolescents confront many psychosocial risk factors, including the attitudes and behaviors of parents and peer pressure. The role of parental attitudes and behaviors on adolescent substance abuse is unclear. Some studies, as reported by de Anda (1995), show that the attitude and behavior of parents toward drugs have both "direct and indirect effects," while others show "no significant relationship." The role of peers seems to be far more significant, however. Studies show that peer pressure to use substances may be the greatest risk factor for use and abuse of drugs by adolescents (de Anda, 1995).

Like alcohol abuse, the problem of substance abuse among teenagers is widespread. *Monitoring the Future,* an annual survey of thousands of adolescents and college students conducted by the University of Michigan's Institute for Social Research (since 1975) with funding from the National Institute on Drug Abuse, is one of the best sources of data on substance abuse. According to the survey, between 1975 and 2000, "young Americans achieved extraordinary levels of illicit drug use, either by historical comparisons in this country or by international comparisons with other countries" (Johnson et al., 2000).

In 1975, more than half (55 percent) of all adolescents had experimented with illegal drugs by the time they graduated from high school; the percentage increased to 66 percent by 1981. The survey shows a general decline in the use of illegal drugs from 1981 to 1992, a steady increase from 1992 to 1996 (a recent peak year), and a slow decline in the last few years. In 1999, the percentage of adolescents who had tried drugs before finishing high school had come full circle in the survey's history to 55 percent. The illegal drug used and abused more than any other is marijuana (Johnson et al., 2000).

Child Abuse and Neglect

Some childhood illnesses "represent symptoms of severe distress in…families" (Newberger, Newberger, and Richmond, 1976, p. 277). Although child abuse receives more attention, the neglect of children is far more widespread and, therefore, a more damaging risk to children. Child abuse refers to an act of intent to harm, or the "recurrent infliction of physical or emotional injury on a dependent minor, through intentional beatings, uncontrolled corporal punishment, persistent ridicule and degradation, or sexual abuse" (National Association of Social Workers, 1999, p. 70). Child neglect refers to an act of omission due to limited resources or abilities, or "the failure of those responsible for the care of a minor to provide the resources needed for healthy physical, emotional, and social development. Examples include inadequate nutrition, improper supervision, or [insufficient]… provisions for educational or health care requirements" (p. 72).

In 1997, there were approximately 984,000 cases of child abuse and neglect. More than half were cases of neglect, approximately one-quarter were physical abuse cases, and the remaining quarter were cases of sexual abuse, psychological abuse, medical neglect, or other forms of maltreatment. The age group at greatest risk was infants, and children under age 4 were by far at greatest risk for fatality. Three-fourths of the perpetrators were parents (U.S. Department of Health and Human Services, 1999a).

State-level child abuse and neglect reporting laws to protect children from harm have been in place since the early 1960s. Federal child abuse and neglect prevention efforts began in the mid-1970s with the enactment of the 1974 Child

Abuse Prevention and Treatment Act (CAPTA) (P.L. 93-247). CAPTA established the National Clearinghouse on Child Abuse and Neglect (NCCAN), which developed model reporting requirements and procedures and required the states to establish protective legislation. However, each state relies on its own definition of child abuse and neglect.

The 1980 Adoption Assistance and Child Welfare Act (P.L. 96-272) was a response to the increasing problem of ineffective foster care services for abused and neglected children. Hundreds of thousands of children—particularly those from vulnerable populations, including children of color, older children, children with disabilities, children with AIDS/HIV, and medically needy children—were languishing in foster homes for years. This legislation emphasized permanency planning and reunification with families. The states must make reasonable efforts to keep families together.

In 1988, CAPTA was amended (P.L. 100-294) to create the U.S. Advisory Board on Child Abuse and Neglect to allow for an evaluation of CAPTA's efforts and impact. In 1990, the Advisory Board found that child abuse and neglect was a "national emergency"; in 1995, it reported that abuse and neglect was a leading cause of death for very young children (under age 4) (National Association of Social Workers, 2000). In 1993, Congress enacted the Family Preservation and Family Support Services Act (P.L. 103-66) to continue emphasizing family unification, but to give states resources to shift their attention toward prevention and crisis intervention. The "family preservation" model encouraged by the policy relies on intensive, short-term community-based case management services for high-risk families to help them avoid and cope with crises.

By 1997, Congress was concerned that neither bill had had significant impact on the problems of foster care. The Adoption and Safe Families Act of 1997 (P.L. 105-89) was passed to place renewed emphasis on permanency in planning for children's care, and to deal once again with the thousands of children placed far too long in "temporary" foster care. The new policy required quicker action on the child's first permanency hearing (within twelve months rather than eighteen months), encouraged termination of parental rights for children in foster care for more than a year, and amended the Family Preservation and Family Support Services Act, renaming it the Safe and Stable Families Program, to encourage permanency planning efforts as soon as children entered the system. The policy recognized the psychological and emotional trauma of being left in limbo for long periods of time that was being imposed on children.

Exposure to Violence

The impact of violence in the lives of children in the United States is especially troubling. Homicide rates among young men are about twenty times greater than the rates found in most industrialized countries (Powell, 1999). Homicide is the second leading cause of death among young people in the United States 15 to 24 years of age (*Healthy People 2000*, 1998). Children of color who live in poor inner-city communities are particularly vulnerable to neighborhood violence. They witness shootings and beatings, often drug and/or gang related, and far too often fall victim to these behaviors (Powell, 1999). This kind of frequent exposure to guns and other weapons, drugs, and neighborhood violence is sometimes referred to as chronic community violence (Osofsky, 1999). In 1985, Surgeon General C. Everett Koop held a Conference on Violence as a Health Problem to recommend a public health solution to the problem of violence. Rather than reacting to harmful environmental influences, Koop's public health approach suggested the need for changes in the environments of children through education and public information campaigns (Prothrow-Stith and Quaday, 1995).

Studies show that poverty exacerbates individual and family problems and increases the risk of domestic violence and violence among peers. Violent influences in the home or in the community lead children and adolescents to resolve conflicts with violence, particularly if there are no mediating positive forces in their lives (Powell, 1999; Prothrow-Stith and Quaday, 1995). However, communities and schools from all socioeconomic sectors of the country are concerned with violent behavior and the problem of children carrying weapons to school. All children are exposed to violence—in their communities, in their own families, or through the media. According to the American Psychiatric Association (APA), by age 18, the typical child in the United States has seen 16,000 simulated murders and 200,000 acts of violence through television, movies, video games, and the Internet (American Psychiatric Association, 1998).

The public health approach to the prevention of violence involves *primary* efforts to "create alternative problem-solving strategies, reward non-violent problem-solving" through "mass media messages, classroom education, peer leadership and mediation, and community-based training programs" (Prothrow-Stith and Quaday, 1995). Starting in the mid-1980s, communities across the country began to establish violence prevention programs with private and public funds. For example, one model program, the Boston Violence Prevention Program, taught anger management and conflict resolution to youth and used mass media to create a different attitude toward violent behavior.

The public health approach to the prevention of violence also involves *secondary* efforts to reach children and adolescents who are at greater risk of violence or who have already been exposed to or engaged in acts of violence. These are efforts to stop harmful behaviors through "mentoring/nurturing programs, individual and group counseling, 'in-school' suspension, first-offender programs, and special efforts for hospitalized children who were shot or stabbed" (Prothrow-Stith and Quaday, 1995). Programs for children exposed to domestic violence have received attention only recently.

Although domestic violence has been accepted as a serious threat to women's health, less attention has been paid to the impact of exposure to domestic violence on children. The number of empirical studies conducted in the past ten to fifteen years to examine the impact of exposure to violence is limited, but there are indications from these studies that children exposed to domestic violence are at risk for a wide range of emotional, cognitive, behavioral, and social problems. The data available about the number of children exposed to domestic violence are also limited. Estimates from current research range from 3.3 million to 10 million children (Carter et al., 1999).

Studies show that children who witness violence have difficulty knowing whom to trust. They develop defensive behaviors against their fears, regressive behaviors and anxieties in response to trauma, and feelings of guilt for the violence around them. Children who witness a single act of abuse or violence often feel helpless or out of control, whereas children exposed to repeated abuse or violence often engage in denial of their experiences. These emotional and behavioral responses can be detrimental to a child's growth and development and can impact his or her personal relationships through adolescence and adulthood. Extreme inner-city conditions of recurrent violence can cause symptoms similar to post-traumatic stress disorder, including nightmares, excessive clinging to parents, and dulled affect. Studies of resilience in children exposed to violence point to similar contributing factors—caring parent(s) (protection, support), community supports (schools, churches and synagogues, community centers), and individual resources (intelligence, interpersonal skills, self-esteem, contact with positive role models, opportunities to access community resources, socioeconomic status) (Prothrow-Stith and Quaday, 1995).

Elderly

Elderly people in the United States also experience discrimination and disparities in social status, and like women, their health is often associated with their social status. In the 1960s, one out of three elderly people in the United States lived in poverty and the vast majority depended on Social Security as their only source of income. Congress enacted the Older Americans Act (OAA, P.L. 89-73) in 1965 and established the Administration on Aging as part of President Johnson's War on Poverty, in an effort to ensure the health and well-being of elderly people. With the passage of Medicare in 1965, and the introduction of cost of living adjustments to Social Security pensions in 1972, the rate of poverty among seniors has fallen dramatically (11 percent in 1998) (Federal Interagency Forum on Aging-Related Statistics, 2000). However, older people are still at greater risk for poverty than other adults.

Within the elderly population, women, people of color, and older seniors are at even greater risk for poverty. Although there has been a significant increase in the financial assets and net worth of seniors since the 1980s, elderly people of color have not fared as well (Ozawa and Tseng, 2000). This population has a history of lower employment earnings, fewer financial assets, and smaller retirement pensions. Indeed, the poverty rate among elderly African Americans (26.4 percent in 1998) and Latinos/as (21.0 percent in 1998) is substantially higher than it is for elderly whites (8.2 in 1998) (Federal Interagency Forum on Aging-Related Statistics, 2000).

Older seniors over age 85 also experience higher rates of poverty, primarily because most are women. Women make up about 70 percent of older seniors over age 85. These women are more likely to live alone and less likely to be currently married than are older male seniors. These conditions compound an already weak financial position that older women face because of their limited lifetime employment earnings. For example, older men are about twice as likely as older women to be college graduates (Federal Interagency Forum on Aging-Related Statistics, 2000). Ozawa and associates (1999) found that the net worth of individuals with at least some college is significantly higher than the net worth of those who did not attend college.

To protect older workers from the economic impact of employment discrimination, Congress passed the Age Discrimination and Employment Act in 1978. This law prevents employers from age-based discrimination in hiring, firing, promotion, and other discriminatory treatments. However, employers have found ways to get around this law by using demotions, changes in work schedules, or additional work without additional pay, to force older employees out of the workforce. Such actions exacerbate the problems of older workers who often find it difficult to obtain comparable employment. With the "aging" or "graying" of society, assumptions about age norms have certainly changed, but in the area of employment, the demand for productivity still places older people at risk for discrimination.

In the area of health, life expectancy has increased dramatically and people in the United States are living longer than ever. However, old age increases the risk for disease and functional disability and many older people suffer from serious chronic health conditions, such as high blood pressure and arthritis. The oldest old (over age 85) experience multiple chronic conditions, debilitating disabilities, and frailty (Federal Interagency Forum on Aging-Related Statistics, 2000).

Healthy People 2010, the government's renewed public health initiative to eliminate disparities in health, identifies chronic disease, long-term care, and cancer and cardiovascular disease as major health risks and concerns for older people (Office of Minority Health, 2000). Since 1980, death rates from heart disease for people over age 65 have declined substantially, but cardiovascular disease is still the leading cause of death. On the other hand, death rates from cancer, the second leading cause of death, increased slightly during this period. Chronic health problems also play a major role in mortality. Of the six leading causes of death, four are chronic conditions: stroke (heart disease), chronic obstructive pulmonary disease, pneumonia and influenza, and diabetes (Federal Interagency Forum on Aging-Related Statistics, 2000).

People over age 65 are also vulnerable to mental and physical disabilities, including Alzheimer's disease and other brain disorders, which limit their ability to function independently during old age. Approximately 16 million people, or one-third of all people with disabilities living in the community, are over age 65 (*Healthy People 2000,* 1997). "The typical recipient [of caregiving] is a 77-year-old woman who lives alone and has a chronic illness" (Oxendine, 2000, p. 4). A smaller population of disabled seniors (approximately 2 million) receives care in nursing homes, mental hospitals, and other institutional settings (*Healthy People 2000,* 1997). With the aging of the population, it is estimated that the need for long-term care among the elderly will double by 2030 (Congressional Budget Office, 1999).

Long-Term Care

Long-term care is a "marked departure from the traditional acute care model of health services and insurance." Traditional medicine focuses on the treatment and cure of disease; the purpose of long-term care is to "minimize, rehabilitate, or compensate for chronic illness or functional limitations" (National Association of Social Workers, 2000, p. 209). Long-term care refers to the delivery of services to persons with functional disabilities over a prolonged period of time. These individuals need assistance with everyday activities of daily living (ADL), such as eating and dressing, and instrumental activities of daily living (IADL), such as preparing meals and shopping. Skilled and therapeutic care for individuals with chronic conditions is also provided (Feder, Komisar, and Niefeld, 2000).

The highly fragmented public/private health insurance system in the United States offers little protection against the high cost of long-term care. Private health insurance plans and long-term-care insurance, which is fairly new to the industry, is a very small market and finances only about 7 percent of the nation's long-term care expenditures for nursing facility and home care (Feder, Komisar, and Niefeld, 2000). More people are purchasing long-term-care insurance, but it is very expensive and unaffordable for most middle-aged and senior adults. It is also difficult for people with chronic illnesses, disabilities, or serious preexisting conditions to buy long-term-care insurance.

Medicare does not cover long-term care unless it is a medical necessity. As a result, it finances only about 20 percent of the nation's long-term care costs (Feder, Komisar, and Niefeld, 2000). To receive home health care, recipients must need intermittent skilled nursing care, such as intravenous feeding or physical therapy, and be confined to their residence. Medicare provides twenty-one days of daily care and intermittent care thereafter with no limits on the number of days of service. To receive nursing facility care, recipients must be hospitalized for at least three consecutive days and need daily rehabilitative skilled nursing care. Medicare provides up to one hundred days of care and requires a significant copayment after the first twenty days.

Individuals bear a significant portion of the nation's cost of long-term care. They are responsible for up to eighty days of Medicare co-insurance payments for skilled nursing care and pay "out-of-pocket" for home and nursing facility services not covered by insurance. As a result, elderly adults finance about 25 percent of the nation's cost of long-term care (Feder, Komisar, and Niefeld, 2000). However, given the high cost of long-term care, most elderly people rely on informal (unpaid) care. One estimate, using 1994 data, found that it would cost $94 billion per year to replace informal (unpaid) care with formal (paid) care (Oxendine, 2000).

The 1996 National Alliance for Caregiving and AARP survey of caregivers found that more than 7 million informal (unpaid) caregivers provide an average of twenty hours of care per week. Most of these caregivers are spouses, and most spouses in the caregiving role are women. "The typical caregiver is a 46-year-old woman who is employed and also spends around eighteen hours per week caring for her mother who lives nearby" (Oxendine, 2000, p. 4). The study also shows that people of color are more likely than whites to take on the caregiver role, to live with the recipient of care, and to provide care for more than one person.

The physical and emotional stress that often accompanies caregiving, the demands of juggling work and caregiving, the changing role of women, and the complex changes in the structure of families, have all played a role in the need to address caregiving as a problem in itself. They have also increased the need to find ways to support formal caregiving. When Congress reauthorized the Older Americans Act in 2000, it legislated President Clinton's initiative for a National Family Caregiver Support Program. This program provides funds for respite care, adult day care, training, counseling, and support for caregivers, and other caregiver support services.

Medicaid, which supports two-thirds of all nursing facility residents, is the most important insurer of long-term care (Krauss and Altman, 1998). Medicaid provides coverage for long-term-care services for poor individuals or those who become impoverished as a result of "spending down" their personal incomes and assets to state eligibility levels. Medicaid finances about 40 percent of the nation's cost of long-term care; most of these dollars are spent on nursing facilities (Feder, Komisar, and Niefeld, 2000). In most states, even with efforts to reduce nursing facility care and increase home health care, Medicaid continues to emphasize institutional care. This is due primarily to fears that home health care will become an added expense, rather than a substitute for institutional care. Long-term-care services for an individual in a nursing facility cost about $46,000 *annually* and Medicaid is a publicly financed program.

Medicaid long-term-care benefits also vary widely from state to state. Home health services must be provided, but states are not required to offer personal care. States control the number of nursing facility beds available and set the rates for reimbursement to nursing facilities for Medicaid residents. Optional services, including "case management, psychosocial rehabilitation, clinical services entailing outpatient therapy, partial hospitalization, and home-based personal care by non-physician providers" vary from state to state (National Association of Social Workers, 2000).

Overall, the inadequacy of insurance for the potentially catastrophic cost of long-term care raises serious concerns for the future. Seniors who need care often go without it because services are either too expensive, unavailable, or too difficult to find. Elderly people often need to impoverish themselves before services can be made available, which, as Feder and colleagues (2000) indicate, "seems excessively harsh." The number of people over age 65 who need long-term care is expected to double, and nursing facility expenditures are projected to increase almost fivefold by 2030 (Shactman and Altman, 2000). Reform efforts to expand long-term-care coverage failed with the demise of the Health Security Act of 1993, and today, long-term-care policy lags far behind current and projected needs.

Elder Abuse

State and national efforts to address child abuse during the 1960s and family violence during the 1970s, led to growing awareness of the problem of elder abuse and laid the basis for legislation to protect elderly adults. In 1981, Congress passed the Prevention, Identification, and Treatment of Elder Abuse Act, which was modeled after federal child abuse prevention legislation. The House Select Committee on Aging investigated elder abuse and published a major report on the "hidden problem" of elder abuse (Tatara, 1995a).

However, concerns were raised about the appropriateness of the child abuse model for adult protection. Mandatory reporting laws, similar to the child abuse reporting system, would stereotype elderly adults as dependents, would ignore the problem of elderly spouse abuse, and could potentially violate civil rights. Therefore, in 1987, Congress authorized a federal elder abuse prevention program as part of the Older Americans Act (OAA) and authorized funds for the program in 1990. For the first time, federal funds were made available to the states for prevention and treatment programs. The Administration on Aging established two national resource centers on elder abuse: the National Center on Elder Abuse (1988), and the National Eldercare Institute on Elder Abuse and State Long-Term Care Ombudsman Services (1991). In virtually all states, Adult Protective Services agencies serve as the primary vehicle for reporting and investigating suspected elder abuse. These agencies were initially established during the mid-1970s as a result of amendments to the Social Security Act amendments that established state-mandated reporting systems for *all adults* over age 18 (Wolf, 2000; Tatara, 1995a).

The term *elder abuse* refers to physical, sexual, emotional or psychological abuse, neglect, financial or material exploitation, and self-abuse and neglect. Acts of elder abuse and neglect are similar to child abuse only in that they include intentional acts of abuse, as well as acts of omission, or neglect. A primary difference, however, is the variation in the types of abusers and the complexity of these adult relationships. Abusers include family members (spouses, siblings, adult children, adult grandchildren, other relatives), informal (unpaid) or formal (paid) caregivers, staff of residential or institutional settings, other service providers, neighbors, friends, and other adults. The OAA specifically includes deprivation by a caretaker of essential goods or services in its definition of abuse.

Exploitation and *self-abuse/neglect* are types of mistreatment that are specific to elderly adults. The OAA defines exploitation as the illegal or improper use of an older person's resources for monetary or personal gain. Self-abuse or neglect is defined as the failure to provide for one's own essential needs, particularly if it threatens his or her life or safety. In doing so, it recognizes the need to protect elders whose disabilities or limitations may prevent them from taking proper care of themselves.

Studies of elder abuse in the United States (Pillemer and Finkelhor, 1988; Tatara, 1995b; Tatara et al., 1997; National Center on Elderly Abuse, 1998) show that between 4 percent and 6 percent of the elderly population reports experiences of abuse or neglect. However, researchers and service providers believe this rate of abuse is grossly underestimated. Elder abuse is more difficult to identify than is child abuse or domestic violence. Many seniors live alone. They also have limited contact with members of the community; often, their only contact is with family members. Adult Protective Services agencies are more likely to receive reports about the most obvious and visible incidents of abuse, but much less likely to receive reports of neglect or less obvious forms of abuse. In addition, no incidence data on elder abuse in nursing facilities are available, but various reports and surveys of personnel indicate that a significant problem exists. A 2001 congressional review of state inspection records showed that elder abuse occurred in almost one of every three nursing homes between January 1999 and January 2001; these facilities were cited for 9,000 abuse violations (McQueen, 2001).

The National Center on Elderly Abuse (1998) incidence study commissioned by Congress provides the best data on the prevalence of elder abuse, and represents the first attempt to estimate the incidence of *unidentified* and *unreported* cases. This study found that, in 1996, unidentified and unreported incidents of elder abuse were at least five times greater than the number of cases reported to APS agencies. The study also found a 150 percent increase in the number of reported cases from 1986 to 1996, even though the size of the elderly population over age 60 increased only 10 percent during this same period. Ninety percent of the abusers were family members, primarily adult children. Most of the victims were women and the oldest old (defined as over age 80), and women were especially vulnerable to financial and psychological abuse. African American elders were more likely to be self-neglectors. The study raises important questions for further study, and it highlights the important role of health and mental health practitioners and financial institutions (banks) in the identification of abuse and neglect.

Highlights

■ Women experience disparities in health for a variety of reasons, many of which are linked to their social status and discriminatory treatment. Congress recognized these disparities by enacting the Women's Health Equity Act of 1990 and establishing the Office of Women's Health.

■ Differences between women and men in medical risks exist, yet little research has been done to understand them better. Before 1990, heart disease and cancer, the leading causes of death for women, were treated as "male" diseases and few clinical studies included women as subjects. Even worse, some studies show that women today are still less likely to be treated for heart disease than are men.

■ Women experience health conditions that are unique to women or more prevalent among women than men.

More research is needed to prevent and treat breast cancer and osteoporosis.

Maternal, prenatal, and child health services are essential to the health of both women and children. Poor women are especially vulnerable to inadequate nutrition and medical care during pregnancy.

AIDS/HIV has been growing at a faster rate for heterosexual women, especially poor women from inner cities or rural areas, than for heterosexual men, and has increased to alarming rates.

Sexual and domestic violence against women is a serious mortality and health risk for women.

■ Age-based disparities also exist, some of which stem from greater vulnerability at various stages of human growth, such as infancy or old age; other disparities are caused by socioeconomic inequity and discrimination. Elder abuse is a good example of the latter.

■ Children have the highest rates of chronic illness and, as they proceed from infancy to adolescence, are constantly vulnerable to new and changing health risks. Children are dependent on adults for their health and well-being, and are at risk for child abuse and neglect, and exposure to domestic violence. Poor children are particularly vulnerable.

■ Adults over age 65 are more vulnerable to life-threatening diseases (heart disease and cancer) and physical and mental disabilities. Elderly adults, like children, are at greater risk for poverty, which exacerbates the health problems and conditions of old age, particularly the need for long-term care.

Websites to Obtain Updated and Additional Information

www.commonwealthfund.org
The Commonwealth Fund

www.urban.org
Urban Institute
Assessing the New Federalism

www.mchpolicy.org
Maternal and Child Health Policy Research Center

www.childrensdefense.org
Children's Defense Fund

www.aahsa.org
American Association of Homes and Services for the Aging

www.ahrq.gov
Agency for Healthcare Research and Quality
U.S. Department of Health and Human Services

REFERENCES

Agency for Health Care Policy and Research (AHCPR). (1999, April). *AHCPR Women's Health Highlights,* Fact Sheet, AHCPR Pub. No. 99-PO17 (Online). Available at www.ahrq.gov/research/womenh1.htm.

Agency for Healthcare Research and Quality (AHRQ). (2000). *Performance Plans for FY 2000 and 2001 and Performance Report for FY 1999* (Online). Available at www.ahrq.gov/about/gpra2001/gpra01a.htm.

American Psychiatric Association. (1998). *Psychiatric Effects of Media Violence*, APA Fact Sheet Series (Online). Available at www.psych.org/public_info/media_violence.html.

Balsanek, J. (1997). Addressing At-Risk Pregnant Women's Issues through Community, Individual, and Corporate Grassroots Efforts. *Health and Social Work, 22*, 1, 63–69.

Bell, R. et al. (1996). *Violence Against Women in the U.S.: A Comprehensive Background Paper.* New York: Commonwealth Fund Commission on Women's Health.

Browne, A. (1993). Violence against Women by Male Partners: Prevalence, Outcomes, and Policy Implications. *American Psychologist, 48*, 10, 1077–1087.

Browne, A. (1987). *When Battered Women Kill.* New York: Free Press.

Brush, L. D. (1990). Violent Acts and Injurious Outcomes in Married Couples: Methodological Issues in the National Survey of Families and Households. *Gender and Society, 4*, 1, 56.

Canto, J. G., Allison, J. J., Kiefe, C. I., et al. (2000, April). Relationship of Race and Sex to the Use of Reperfusion Therapy in Medicare Beneficiaries with Acute Myocardial Infarction. *New England Journal of Medicine, 15*, 1094–1100.

Carter, L. S., Weithorn, L. A., and Behrman, R. E. (1999). Domestic Violence and Children: Analysis and Recommendations. In R. E. Behrman (Ed.), *The Future of Children, 9*, 3, (pp. 4–20). Los Altos, CA: David and Lucile Packard Foundation.

Coleman, B. C. (1999, August 11). New Therapy Decreases Number of AIDS Babies. *Concord Monitor*, p. 3.

Congressional Budget Office. (1999, March). *Projections of Expenditures for Long-Term Care Services for the Elderly.* Washington, DC: CBO.

de Anda, D. (1995). Adolescence Overview. In R. L. Edwards (Ed.-in-Chief), *Encyclopedia of Social Work,* 19th ed., (pp. 16–133). Washington, DC: National Association of Social Workers.

Deykin, E. Y. et al. (1992). Depressive Illness among Chemically Dependent Adolescents. *American Journal of Psychiatry, 149*, 10, 1341–1347.

Deykin, E. Y. et al. (1987). Adolescent Depression, Alcohol and Drug Abuse. *American Journal of Public Health, 77*, 2, 178–182.

Dibble, V. and Straus, M. E. (1990). Some Structure Determinants of Inconsistency between Attitudes and Behaviors: The Case of Family Violence. In M. A. Straus and R. J. Gelles (Eds.), *Physical Violence in American Families.* (pp. 167–180). New Brunswick, NJ: Transaction.

Edelman, M. W. (1999). *The State of America's Children.* Boston: Beacon Press.

Fantuzzo, J. W. and Mohr, W. K. (1999). Prevalence and Effects of Child Exposure to Domestic Violence. *The Future of Children, 9*, 3, (pp. 21–32). Los Altos, CA: David and Lucile Packard Foundation.

Feder, J., Komisar, H. L., and Niefeld, M. (2000). Long-Term Care in the U.S.: An Overview. *Health Affairs, 19*, 1, 40–56.

Federal Interagency Forum on Aging-Related Statistics. (2000). *Older Americans 2000: Key Indicators of Well-Being* (Online). Available at www.agingstats.gov/chartbook2000.html.

Felts, W. M. et al. (1992). Drug Use and Suicide Ideation and Behavior among North Carolina Public School Students. *American Journal of Public Health, 82*, 6, 870–872.

Garrison, C. Z. et al. (1993). Aggression, Substance Abuse, and Suicidal Behaviors in High School Students. *American Journal of Public Health, 83*, 2, 179–184.

Gelles, R. J. and Cornell, C. P. (1990). *Intimate Violence in Families,* 2nd ed. Newbury Park, CA: Sage.

Gergen, P. J., Fowler, J. A., and Mauter, K. R. (1998, February). The Burden of Environmental Tobacco Smoke Exposure on the Respiratory Health of Children 2 Months through 5 Years of Age in the U.S.: Third National Health and Nutrition Examination Survey, 1988–1994. *Pediatric Electronic Pages, 101,* 2 (Online). Available at www.pediatrics.org.

Gilligan, J. (1996). *Violence—Our Deadly Epidemic and Its Causes.* New York: G. P. Putnam's Sons.

Glied, S. and Kofman, S. (1995). *Women and Mental Health: Issues for Health Reform.* New York: Commonwealth Fund.

Gottlieb, N. (1995). Women Overview. In R. L. Edwards (Ed.-in-Chief), *Encyclopedia of Social Work,* 19th ed. (pp. 2518–2529). Washington, DC: National Association of Social Workers.

Gray, M. C. (1995). Drug Abuse. In R. L. Edwards (Ed.-in-Chief), *Encyclopedia of Social Work,* 19th ed. (pp. 795–803). Washington, DC: National Association of Social Workers.

Gruber, J. and Zinman, J. (2000). *Youth Smoking in the U.S.: Evidence and Implications* (Working Paper No. 7780). Cambridge, MA: National Bureau of Economic Research.

Hackl, K. I., Somlai, A. M., Kelly, J. A., and Kalichman, S. C. (1997). Women Living with AIDS: The Dual Challenge of Being a Patient and Caregiver. *Health and Social Work, 22,* 1, 53–62.

Healthy People 2000. (1999a, March 3). *Progress Review. Family Planning.* Washington, DC: U.S. Department of Health and Human Services.

Healthy People 2000. (1999b, May 5). *Progress Review. Maternal and Infant Health.* Washington, DC: U.S. Department of Health and Human Services.

Healthy People 2000. (1999c, October 6). *Progress Review. Violent and Abusive Behavior.* Washington, DC: U.S. Department of Health and Human Services.

Healthy People 2000. (1998a, July 9). *Progress Review. Adolescents and Young Adults.* Washington, DC: U.S. Department of Health and Human Services.

Healthy People 2000. (1998b, May 20). *Progress Review. Women's Health. Washington, DC: U.S. Department of Health and Human Services.*

Healthy People 2000. (1997, October 30). *Progress Review. People with Low Income.* Washington, DC: U.S. Department of Health and Human Services.

Holinger, P. C., Offer, D., Barter, J. T., and Bell, C. C. (1994). *Suicide and Homicide among Adolescents.* New York: Guilford Press.

Homan, R. K. and Korenbrot, C. C. (1998). Explaining Variation in Birth Outcomes of Medicaid Eligible Women with Variation in the Adequacy of Prenatal Support. *Medical Care, 36,* 2, 190–201.

Iezzoni, L. I., Ash, A. S., Schwartz, M., and Mackierman, Y. D. (1997, February). Differences in Procedure Use, In-Hospital Mortality, and Illness Severity by Gender for Acute Myocardial Infarction Patients: Are Answers Affected by Data Source and Severity? *Med Care, 35,* 2, 158–171.

Jaros, K. J. and Evans, J. C. (1995). Maternal and Child Health. In R. L. Edwards (Ed.-in-Chief), *Encyclopedia of Social Work,* 19th ed., (pp. 1683–1689) Washington, DC: National Association of Social Workers.

Johnson, L. D., O'Malley, P. M., and Bachman, J. G. (2000). *Monitoring the Future National Results on Alcohol Drug Abuse, Overview of the Findings, 1999.* Bethesda, MD: National Institute on Drug Abuse.

Johnson, L. D., O'Malley, P. M., and Bachman, J. G. (1995). *National Survey Results on Drug Use from the Monitoring the Future Study, 1975–1998:* Volume I, *Secondary School Students.* (NIH Pub. No. 99-4660). Bethesda, MD: National Institute on Drug Abuse.

Kessler, R. C., Abelson, J. M., and Zhao, S. (1998). The Epidemiology of Mental Disorders. In J. B. W. Williams and K. Ell (Eds.), *Mental Health Research* (pp. 3–24). Washington, DC: National Association of Social Workers.

Kinkel, R. J. et al. (1989). Correlates of Adolescent Suicide Attempts: Alienation, Drugs, and Social Background. *Journal of Alcohol and Drug Education, 34,* 3, 85–96.

Krauss, N. A. and Altman, B. M. (1998, December). *Characteristics of Nursing Home Residents—1996,* MEPS Research Finding No. 5. Rockville, MD: Agency for Health Care Policy and Research.

Kushner, M. G. and Sher, K. J. (1993). Comorbidity of Alcohol and Anxiety Disorders among College Students: Effects of Gender and Family History of Alcoholism. *Addictive Behaviors, 18,* 543–552.

Lambrew, J. M. (2001, August). *Diagnosing Disparities in Health Insurance for Women: A Prescription for Change.* New York: Commonwealth Fund.

Long, N., Brendtro, L., and Johnson, J. (1993). Alcohol and Kids: Facing Our Problem. *Journal of Emotional and Behavioral Problems, 2,* 2–4.

Magura, S. (1994). Social Workers Should Be More Involved in Substance Abuse Treatment. *Health and Social Work, 19,* 1, 3–5.

Mathews, M. A. (1999). The Impact of Federal and State Laws on Children Exposed to Domestic Violence. In R. E. Behrman (Ed.), *The Future of Children* (pp. 50–66). Los Altos, CA: David and Lucile Packard Foundation.

McQueen, A. (2001, July 29). Abuse in Nursing Homes Widespread. *Concord Monitor,* p. A1.

National Academy on an Aging Society. (2000, July). *Challenges for the 21st Century: Chronic and Disabling Conditions, No. 9 Depression.* Washington, DC: National Academy on an Aging Society.

National Association of Social Workers. (2000a). Alcohol, Tobacco, and Other Substance Abuse. *Social Work Speaks,* 5th ed. Washington, DC: National Association of Social Workers.

National Association of Social Workers. (2000b). Child Abuse and Neglect. *Social Work Speaks,* 5th ed. Washington, DC: National Association of Social Workers.

National Association of Social Workers. (2000c). Family Planning and Reproductive Choice. *Social Work Speaks,* 5th ed. Washington, DC: National Association of Social Workers.

National Association of Social Workers. (2000d). Long-Term Care. *Social Work Speaks,* 5th ed. Washington, DC: National Association of Social Workers.

National Association of Social Workers. (2000e). Women's Issues. *Social Work Speaks,* 5th ed. Washington, DC: National Association of Social Workers.

National Association of Social Workers. (1999). *The Social Work Dictionary.* Washington, DC: National Association of Social Workers.

National Center on Elder Abuse. (1998, September). *National Elder Abuse Incidence Study, Final Report* (Online). Available at www.aoa.gov/abuse/report.html.

Newberger, E. H., Newberger, C. M., and Richmond, J. B. (1976). Child Health in America: Toward a Rational Public Policy. *Milbank Memorial Fund Quarterly/Health and Society, 54,* 3, 249–298.

Office of Minority Health. (2000, May). *Healthy People 2010: Objectives for Older Adults.* Washington, DC: U.S. Department of Health and Human Services.

Osofsky, J. D. (1999). The Impact of Violence on Children. In R. E. Behrman (Ed.), *The Future of Children* (pp. 33–49). Los Altos, CA: David and Lucile Packard Foundation.

Oxendine, J. (2000, May). Who Is Helping the Caregivers? *Closing the Gap.* Washington, DC: Office of Minority Health, U.S. Department of Health and Human Services.

Ozawa, M. N., Lum, Y. S., and Tseng, H. Y. (1999). Net Worth at Retirement and 10 Years Later. In S. S. Nager (Ed.), *The Substance of Public Policy* (pp. 245–275). New York: Nova Science.

Ozawa, M. N. and Tseng, H. Y. (2000). Differences in Net Worth between Elderly Black People and Elderly White People. In S. Keigher, A. Fortune, and S. Witkin (Eds.), *Aging and Social Work* (pp. 67–82). Washington, DC: National Association of Social Workers.

Pillemer, K. A. and Finkelhor, D. (1988). The Prevalence of Elder Abuse: A Random Sample. *The Gerontologist, 28,* 1, 51–57.

Pollack, W. S. (2000). *Real Boys' Voices.* New York: Random House.

Powell, K. B. (1999). Correlates of Violent and Nonviolent Behavior among Vulnerable Inner-City Youth. In J. G. Sebastian and A. Bushy (Eds.), *Special Populations in the Community.* Gaithersburg, MD: Aspen Publishers.

Proctor, E. K. and Stiffman, A. R. (1998). Background of Services and Treatment Research. In J. B. W. Williams and K. Ell (Eds.), *Mental Health Research* (pp. 259–286). Washington, DC: National Association of Social Workers.

Prothrow-Stith, D. and Quaday, S. (1995). *Hidden Casualties: The Relationship Between Violence and Learning.* Washington, DC: National Health and Education Consortium.

Saathoff, A. J. and Stoffel, E. A. (1999). Community-Based Domestic Violence Services. In R. E. Behrman (Ed.), *The Future of Children* (pp. 97–110). Los Altos, CA: David and Lucile Packard Foundation.

Schoen, C., Davis, K., DesRoches, C., and Shekhdar, A. (1998, June). *The Health of Adolescent Boys: Commonwealth Fund Survey Findings.* New York: Commonwealth Fund.

Schulman, D., Berlin, J., William, H., Kerner, J., and Ayers, W. (1999). The effects of race and sex on physicians' recommendations for cardiac catheterization. *New England Journal of Medicine, 340,* 618–627.

Schwartz, M. D. (1987). Gender and Injury in Spousal Assault. *Sociological Focus, 20,* 61–75.

Shactman, D. and Altman, S. H. (2000). Conference Report: The U.S. Confronts the Policy Dilemmas of an Aging Society. *Health Affairs, 19,* 3, 252–258.

Sherman, A. (1994). *Wasting America's Future, Children's Defense Fund Report on the Costs of Child Poverty.* Boston, MA: Beacon Press.

Shumaker, S. A. and Smith, T. R. (1999). The Politics of Women's Health. In K. Charmaz and D. A. Paterniti (Eds.), *Health, Illness, and Healing.* Los Angeles: Roxbury Publishing.

Slifkin, R. T., Clark, S. J., Strandhoy, S. E., and Konrad, T. R. (1997, Fall). Public Sector Immunization Coverage in 11 States: The Status of Rural Areas. *Journal of Rural Health, 13,* 4, 334–341.

Strunin, L. and Hingson, R. (1992). Alcohol, Drugs, and Adolescent Sexual Behavior. *International Journal of the Addictions, 27,* 2, 129–146.

Tatara, T. (1995a). *An Analysis of State Laws Addressing Elder Abuse, Neglect, and Exploitation.* Washington, DC: National Center on Elder Abuse.

Tatara, T. (1995b). Elder Abuse. In R. L. Edwards (Ed.-in-Chief), *Encyclopedia of Social Work,* 19th ed., (pp. 834–842). Washington, DC: National Association of Social Workers.

Tatara, T., Kuzmeskas, L., and Duckhorn, E. (1997). *Elder Abuse in Domestic Settings. Informational Series.* Washington, DC: National Center on Elder Abuse, American Public Welfare Association.

U.S. Census Bureau. (2000). Current Population Report (Online). Available at www.census. population.html.

U.S. Census Bureau. (1998). HIV/AIDS Trends. *Statistical Abstract of the United States, 1998.* Washington, DC: U.S. Government Printing Office.

U.S. Census Bureau. (1976). Current Population Report (Online). Available at www.census. population.html.

U.S. Department of Health and Human Services, (1999a). *Child Maltreatment 1997: Reports from the States to the National Child Abuse and Neglect Data System.* Washington, DC: Administration on Children, Youth, and Families.

U.S. Department of Health and Human Services. (1999b, December). *Mental Health: A Report of the Surgeon General.* Rockville, MD: U.S. Department of Health and Human

Services Substance Abuse and Mental Health Services Administration, Center for Mental Health Services, National Institute of Mental Health.

U.S. Department of Health and Human Services. (1998). *National Household Survey on Drug Abuse.* Washington, DC: Substance Abuse and Mental Health Service Administration.

U.S. General Accounting Office. (2000, March). *Community Health Centers: Adapting to Changing Health Care Environment Key to Continued Success* (HEHS-00-39). Washington, DC: U.S. General Accounting Office.

Wetzel, J. W. (1994). Depression: Women-at-Risk. In M. M. Olson (Ed.), *Women's Health and Social Work: Feminist Perspectives* (pp. 85–108).

Williams, D. R. (1990). Socioeconomic Differentials in Health: A Review and Redirection. *Social Psychology Quarterly, 53,* 2, 81–99.

Wolf, R. S. (2000, Fall). The Nature and Scope of Elder Abuse. *Journal of the American Society on Aging, 24,* 2.

Zambrana, R. E. and Scrimshaw, S. C. (1997, May–June). Maternal Psychosocial Factors Associated with Substance Use in Mexican-American Origin and African American Low-Income Pregnant Women. *Pediatric Nursing, 23,* 3, 253–259, 274.

8 New Directions for Health and Health Care Policy

The final chapter of this book considers the future of health, health *care* policy, and *health* policy and draws implications for social work. Previous chapters have examined the history and status of the health care delivery system in the United States. This chapter shifts our focus from the delivery of health care services to a broader framework for understanding health and health policy; this new framework focuses on the *social determinants* of morbidity and mortality. As Evans, Barer, and Marmor (1994) have asked: *Why Are Some People Healthy and Others Not?*

Going beyond Health Care

Before addressing the determinants of health, we must ask, what is health? Although the answer to this question may seem obvious, or something we know intuitively, defining health is a complex task. For many years, health was understood as the absence of illness or disease. One was either sick or not, in good health or poor health. This definition is misleading, however. First, it is too static and abstract. Health is not an either/or phenomenon but a relative, or quantitative, one (Rose, 1993). It is difficult to define precisely where health ends and illness begins. Rather, health seems much more a matter of degree. Second, the definition is too narrow. It focuses our attention on individuals, not the broader context in which they live and flourish. Today, however, we know that health is as much a social process as an individual or biological one (Berkman and Kawachi, 2000).

In 1946, the World Health Organization (WHO) advanced a broader definition of health. Challenging the static, either/or approach, WHO defined health as "a state of complete physical, mental and social well-being and not simply the absence of disease or infirmity" (WHO, 1958, as cited in Sagan, 1987, p. 8). Under this definition, individuals could be well physically, yet have serious psychological, social, or other problems. The WHO definition also grasped health as a goal, or moving target, an unfolding process, which one does not necessarily achieve.

Yet, the WHO definition is somewhat abstract. If health encompasses every aspect of "physical, mental, and social" well-being, then anything and everything, including *all* social policy, is health related (Evans and Stoddart, 1994). Although this may be true in a broad sense, it leaves us with the question of how, or even whether, to consider specific *health* policies and issues. If everything is health related, then health reform can take place only through fundamental social transformation. Although this may make sense from a theoretical perspective, it does little to address the practical problems of our society, such as infant mortality, lack of health care coverage, and the cost of health care. If the earlier definition was too narrow, the WHO definition seems too broad.

Determinants of Health: A Biopsychosocial Perspective

Social work has developed a more concrete approach to health, known as the *biopsychosocial* perspective (Berkman and Volland, 1997). The biopsychosocial perspective considers the impact on health and well-being of **biological** (genetics and the human aging process), **psychological** (perception, cognition, emotion), and **social** (lifestyle, culture, politics, race and ethnicity, class, gender) factors. Although these factors, or determinants, are distinct, they are also interrelated. In fact, the interaction among these factors has become the focus of recent frameworks of health (Evans and Stoddart, 1994).

Let us first briefly consider the role of biological, psychological, and social factors as distinct entities, or determinants. This will lay the foundation for analyzing the interactions among these influences and a discussion of the biopsychosocial framework.

Biological Factors.   Longres (1990) identifies four basic ways in which biology underlies "individual functioning." First, humans' genetic structure, anatomy, and physiology impose fundamental limits on the species' behavior, growth, and development. Second, biological and genetic factors play a role in psychological well-being. For example, researchers have linked schizophrenia with the "lateral and third ventricles" and the temporal lobes of the brain (Farmer and Pandurangi, 1997, p. 110). Bipolar disorder seems largely genetic, showing "a nearly 100 percent rate of concordance among identical twins" (Ratey and Johnson, 1998, p. 120). Third, "illness, injury, or disability" can change an individual's cognition, emotions, and behavior. Finally, "physical growth," from fertilization to old age, provides impetus for "personal change and development" (Longres, 1990, p. 24).

Psychological Factors.   Longres (1990) also discusses three essential "subsystems" of the "psychological domain"—cognition, affect, and behavior. Cognition consists of "perception, sensation, memory, imagination, judgment, and language, as well as intelligence and other aspects of intellectual functioning such as knowledge, beliefs, and opinions" (Longres, 1990, p. 24). Cognitive processes enable the individual to interpret and grasp the external world. Affect involves feeling and emotion and an individual's "sense of well-being or ill-being" (Longres, 1990, p. 25). Behavior refers to "the ways individuals express themselves in action" and includes "mannerisms, habits, and…communication skills" (Longres, 1990, p. 25). Although humans express cognition and affect through behavior, the latter, unlike the former, directly involves what "people say and do" (Longres, 1990, p. 25).

Finally, as Longres points out, cognition, affect, and behavior "form increasingly larger and more complex systems within the individual" (p. 26). A good example of this is the development of attitudes, which includes a cognitive level (what an individual believes), an affective level (what an individual feels), and a behavioral level (a predisposition to behave in a certain way).

Social Factors.   Individuals are also social beings who exist within physical and social environments. From a sociological perspective, both culture and social structure are essential to human behavior. Culture refers to the beliefs, values, language, traditions, and material objects shared by a people. Social structure refers to the social organization of society. Most sociologists identify increasingly complex levels of social organization, beginning with statuses and roles, and including dyads, families, groups, organizations, communities, and complex social institutions. Belief systems and traditions shape human behavior. Social structures provide social norms (informal and formal social rules of conduct) and include social statuses (social ranking based on race, class, gender, and/or age) that play a significant role in shaping human behavior. Social institutions, including the health care system, include policies, programs, and services that exact enormous influence on individuals.

Biopsychosocial Dynamics.   The Council on Social Work Education (CSWE) (1995) requires that social work programs "provide content about theories and knowledge of human bio-psycho-social development" (pp. 102, 140). This biopsychosocial approach is rooted in early holistic approaches to understanding human behavior. Theoretical foundations include Richmond's (1917) social diagnosis, Gordon's (1969) general systems approach, Bartlett's (1970) common base of practice, Germain's ecological perspective (1973), and Germain and Gitterman's (1980) life model of social work practice.

The National Association of Social Workers (NASW) funded the development of PIE, Person-in-Environment classification system, in an effort to establish "uniform descriptions of a client's interpersonal, environmental, mental, and physical health problems" (Karls and Wandrei, 1995, p. 1818). The PIE approach to assessment and intervention focuses on the interaction between people and their environments (Karls and Wandrei, 1995). PIE conceptualizes practice in terms of processes, what Weick (1986) calls "fields of interaction between people and their multiple environments," rather than "static, linear relationships" (p. 552). From this perspective, the client is less the individual than the individual within a system. The system consists of interacting biological, psychological, and social factors. The generalist practitioner plans intervention based on the clients' physical, emotional, social, and economic needs. This requires intervention on multiple levels to help change individual, familial, group, and organizational or community behavior. The biopsychosocial perspective captures these multiple levels, or dimensions, of human existence and activity.

Unfortunately, most discussions of the biopsychosocial perspective focus on the interaction that occurs among these dimensions. Yet, to understand and appreciate the biopsychosocial perspective fully, one must also acknowledge the *relative,* or partial, identity of these factors. By this, we mean that, in addition to being separate, each factor also contains within it something of the others. This is not as complicated as it sounds.

Consider, for example, the age-old debate over nature and nurture. Is human behavior determined by biology or by the social environment? From a biopsychosocial perspective, the question itself is misleading. Nature and nurture are not only separate and distinct but also interrelated. From a biopsychosocial perspective, human behavior is "100 percent hereditary" *and* "100 percent environmental" (Ferris, 1996, p. 26). How can this be?

Take the human brain. In recent years, our understanding of the growth and development of this organ has undergone dramatic change. At the 1997 White House Conference on Early Childhood Development and Learning, Hillary Rodham Clinton summarized the state of knowledge:

> Fifteen years ago, we thought...a baby's brain structure was virtually complete at birth. Now, we understand that it is a work in progress, and that everything we do with a child has...potential physical influence on that rapidly-forming brain. A child's earliest experiences, their relationships with parents and care-givers, the sights and sounds and smells and feelings they encounter, the challenges they meet determine how their brains are wired. And that brain shapes itself through repeated experiences.... The brain is the last organ to become fully mature anatomically. Neurological circuitry for many emotions isn't completed until a child reaches 15 (Clinton, H., 1997, pp. 1–2).

In short, the brain is not "hard-wired," or fixed, at birth but is in a continual state of change and development. This plasticity may even continue into adulthood. Researchers at UCLA have found that cognitive and behavioral modification can actually alter the brain and "'genetic disposition'" of individuals with obsessive-compulsive disorder (Schwartz, 1996).

Social factors have a profound impact on the development of the brain (Kotulak, 1997). According to Siegel, social experience "'selectively shapes genetic neuronal potential and thus directly influences the structure and function of the brain'" (cited in Mate', 1999, p. 77). Emotional deprivation can "warp" an infant's "developing neural circuits" and irreversibly alter "the way an organism behaves and responds to the world around it" (Hotz, 1997). Depriving a child of hugging, caressing, and other forms of caring touch can change the brain's biochemistry (Hotz, 1997). Emotional support—the ability to respond actively and positively to a child's needs—plays a central role in the development of intelligence as well (Greenspan, 1997).

Not surprisingly, violence can have a particularly adverse impact on the chemistry of the brain and individual development. Children living in violent neighborhoods are at risk of developing a form of posttraumatic stress disorder that limits one's capacity to learn and develop interpersonal relationships

(Prothrow-Stith and Quaday, 1995). Many abused children grow up to become "antisocial" adults, as "violence begets violence" (Ferris, 1996, p. 23). Gilligan (1992), a former director of mental health in Massachusetts' prisons, found that, in many cases, adult violence was linked with feelings of shame originating in early abuse and neglect.

In short, the human brain is not only a *biological* phenomenon but also a *social* (and *psychological*) one. As Levins (1998) puts it:

> As mammals, we are born partly formed. Our development depends on regularly occurring environmental factors that have become incorporated into our developmental biology. The development of vision requires light. The development of muscles and bone require exercise. Brain development requires stimulation. Intellectual development needs challenge. Emotional and social development require touch, attention and loving care (p. 12).

From this perspective, the biological, psychological, and social dimensions of life are separate and interrelated. Although this may seem contradictory, it is a contradiction of real life, not theory. This is the true insight of the biopsychosocial perspective.

A Biopsychosocial Approach to Health

In the mid-1980s, Weick (1986) developed a "health model" based on a biopsychosocial approach to health. She contrasted her perspective with the medical model, which focuses largely on the individual. According to Weick (1986), the medical model reduces the study of human health to the study and treatment of disease and seeks to uncover "specific, identifiable causes and antidotes for particular disease conditions" (p. 553). The traditional roles of doctor and patient are deeply rooted in this model. The physician is the trained expert and authority who diagnoses and treats the patient; the patient relies on the judgment of the doctor and cooperates with the prescribed treatment. The medical model has promoted research into the causes of disease and the development of new means of treatment. Few of the dollars spent on health care have been spent on health promotion or prevention (Weick, 1986).

In contrast with the medical model, the health model goes beyond linear explanations for health and disease and focuses on the multiple influences that shape individual health. The complexity of interactions among these influences creates conditions that may have an even greater effect on individual health.

The health model also views treatment from this perspective. Weick (1986) argues that a central assumption of the health model is "the capacity of humans to heal themselves" (p. 556). "The human body contains innate, self-correcting mechanisms that respond to a continuously changing environment" (p. 556). Thus, treatment requires an active role on the part of patients in achieving health. In the health model the goal is to empower individuals to use their capacities to heal themselves. However, Weick recognizes that ultimately individuals can be well only if society takes responsibility for the promotion of good health and access to resources.

Finally, Weick (1986) discusses the consistency between the health model and social work, both of which emphasize strengths, self-determination, and social context.

> At any given moment, an individual's state of health reflects the capacity of the individual and the capacity of the social-physical environments, both past and present, to provide the necessary raw materials and resources for healing to take place…rather than confining ourselves to questions about how growth and development fail to occur…, a health perspective asks how we can create environments in which people have the best chance for maximum healing-health-wholeness …we ask how people can be helped to develop their strengths more fully (p. 558).

Weick (1986) makes an important contribution to our understanding of health from a biopsychosocial perspective. She stresses that environment determines the health of individuals. In the years since Weick's article, scholars have come closer to understanding *which* environmental factors are most important.

What Determines Good Health?

During the past twenty-five years, scholars from Western Europe and North America have increasingly focused on the role of *social* factors in shaping the health of populations (Evans, Barer, and Marmor, 1994). This growing body of literature reinforces the biopsychosocial perspective and therefore has important implications for social work.

In a sense, the social determinants of health approach is not a new one. Speculation about the relationship between health and society has gone on for years. During the 1830s and 1840s, Villerme in France and Virchow in Germany argued that "social conditions," such as inadequate housing, malnutrition, and poor sanitation, contributed to high rates of disease and mortality among working and poor people (Amick III et al., 1995). In 1842, Edwin Chadwick issued a *Report on an Enquiry into the Sanitary Conditions of the Labouring Population of Great Britain* (Amick III et al., 1995). "Chadwick called for organized public health, and he defined its mission as one of sanitary cleanup" (Garrett, 2000, p. 284).

There were similar developments in the United States. In 1850, Lemuel Shattuck issued a *Report of the Sanitary Commission of Massachusetts*, which led to the creation of the first state board of health in the nation and became a "blueprint" for public health in this country (Moroney, 1995). During the late 1880s, in response to developments in Europe, particularly the emergence of Pasteur's theory linking disease to germs, officials in New York City established "the nation's first public health laboratory" (Garrett, 2000, p. 293). By the turn of the century, public health leaders, armed with newly developed vaccines,

> routinely deployed police officers and zealous nurses or physicians to the homes of those suspected of carrying disease…. In some cases, police officers pinned the arm

of those who refused while a city nurse jabbed it with a vaccination needle (Garrett, 2000, p. 299).

The U.S. Public Health Service was created in 1902, and public health programs were established at major universities during the 1920s (Moroney, 1995; Amick III et al., 1995).

As noted earlier, during the 1950s, the World Health Organization (WHO) (1958) challenged the static notion of health as the absence of disease. One factor behind this shift was increased life expectancy. In the 1800s, only three out of ten newborn infants lived beyond the age of 25 years (McKeown, 1994). Infant mortality was high and life expectancy short, and childhood diseases were often fatal. By 1992, in the United States, the infant mortality rate (per 1,000 live births) had risen to 8.52 and life expectancy to 72 years. Today, in the United States, few infants are victims of infectious disease, and infant death is most often associated with low birth weight and poverty (Turnock, 1997).

Social scientists have studied the declines in mortality for decades. Early studies emphasized the role of medicine and health care in improving health status. During the 1950s and 1960s, however, researchers began to call this view into question (McKinlay and McKinlay, 1994). In a seminal work, McKeown (1979) showed that medical care played a relatively limited role in reducing mortality in the West. Thus, in England and Canada, death rates from tuberculosis began to decline before the discovery of streptomycin. Extending this work to the United States, McKinlay and McKinlay (1994) contended that "medical measures" could account for "at most 3.5 percent of the decline in mortality" between 1900 and 1973 (p. 21).

If health care does not explain the reduction in mortality, what does? McKeown (1994) argued that increased income, improved nutrition, and public health efforts played a far more important role than medical care in improving life expectancy. Building on this work, Reves (1985) suggested that family planning and smaller families were also central factors by improving conditions for women and children. Sagan (1987) developed this further, arguing that an "increased sense of psychological well-being," stimulated by economic growth, may have increased resistance to infection and reduced rates of mortality (p. 126). Fogel (1994) emphasized the role of improved nutrition in reducing mortality.

Inequality and Health

As researchers delved more deeply into the health of populations, they discovered that countries with the greatest wealth, as measured by per capita gross national product and median income, did not necessarily have the healthiest populations (Wilkinson, 1996). Although the United States is the wealthiest nation in the world and spends more per capita on health care than any other country, we have "poorer health than 20 developed countries, including all European Union (EU) nations" (Wilkinson, 2001, p. 30). Indeed, during the 1980s, males living in Bangladesh, one of the poorest nations in the world, had a greater chance of living to age 65 than did males living in Harlem (McCord and Freeman, 1994).

This does not mean that economic growth has played no role in population health. For much of human history, material deprivation, or *absolute* poverty, limited the lives of most of the world's people. During the past few centuries, however, due to what Wilkinson (1997) and others have called the epidemiological transition, a dramatic change has taken place.

The epidemiological transition refers to changes in patterns of morbidity and mortality. Until around 1800, infectious diseases, such as smallpox, diphtheria, and measles, were the major cause of death (Tarlov, 1996). Since then, the death rate from these diseases has rapidly declined and "life expectancy nearly doubled" (Tarlov, 1996). Much of this change is attributable to economic growth and resulting improvements in material standards of living (Wilkinson, 1996). At the same time, mortality from chronic diseases, such as heart disease, cancer, and diabetes, have increased, and these diseases "now account" for three out of four deaths in the United States (Tarlov, 1996). This raises two important questions. First, why has economic growth failed to reduce the incidence of all disease (i.e., infectious as well as chronic)? Second, what explains the increasing importance of chronic disease?

The answer to the first question seems to be that the relationship between economic growth and population health, while real, is also limited (Duleep, 1995). Wilkinson (1996) estimated that as a country's per capita income approaches $5,000, the returns to health of economic growth begin to diminish. At this point, the distribution of income becomes a more important determinant of health than the level of economic growth. As the distribution of income grows increasingly important, so too does the role of *relative* poverty, or inequality. Inequality helps explain why economic growth has a limited impact on mortality and chronic disease has replaced infectious disease as a major cause of death (Wilkinson, 1997).

Absolute versus Relative Poverty.   What is relative poverty? Why does it matter? Absolute poverty is a state of material deprivation. It implies a minimal standard of need, below which survival becomes difficult or impossible. Relative poverty, on the other hand, is not a state or condition, but a social relationship. One can be unequal only in a relative sense, that is, in contrast, or relation, to others (DeLone, 1979). Relative poverty suggests a gap between an individual's social position and his or her potential (Calman, 1997). Individuals with incomes above an absolute level of poverty can, and generally do, fall into relative poverty. Relative and absolute poverty can overlap. In the United States, homelessness and hunger are forms of both material deprivation and extreme inequality.

Inequality and Mortality.   Numerous researchers have found a relationship between inequality and mortality (Flegg, 1982; Le Grand, 1987). After examining income distribution and infant mortality in seventy nations, Waldmann (1999) concluded:

> Comparing two countries in which the poor have equal real incomes, the one in which the rich are wealthier is likely to have a higher infant mortality rate (p. 14).

Wennemo (1993) also discovered a relation between inequality and infant mortality in wealthy nations. In a study of income distribution and life expectancy in several countries, Wilkinson (1999c) found a "strong relation" between a country's distribution of income and its "average life expectancy" (p. 32). He also noted that if Britain had a distribution of income similar to that in the "most egalitarian European countries," it would add "about two years…to the population's life expectancy" (Wilkinson, 1999c, p. 33).

In the United States, Kaplan and associates (1999) reported that, between 1980 and 1990, states with the widest income gaps (in 1980) had "smaller declines in mortality" than other states (p. 55). They also found a relationship between age-adjusted death rates and income (Kaplan et al., 1999). In another state-by-state study, Kennedy and associates (1999) found a correlation between income inequality and rates of mortality, infant mortality, heart disease, cancer, and murder. In an analysis of 273 metropolitan areas, Shi and Starfield (2001) also found a significant relation between income inequality and mortality among blacks and whites.

The Whitehall studies of British civil servants provide particularly detailed information on the relationship between inequality and health (Marmot, 1994). The first series of studies (Whitehall I), which included only males, found that the mortality rate for lower-level workers (clerical and manual workers) was three times higher than the rate for workers at the highest level (senior administrators). Obvious risk factors, such as blood pressure, cholesterol, and smoking, explained less than half this difference. Absolute poverty, or material deprivation, also had little to do with the difference in mortality. All the participants in the study belonged to the middle or upper class, worked in white-collar settings, and had job security (Marmot, 1994).

Inequality did seem to play a role, however. Remarkably, at every level, individuals in higher job grades had lower rates of mortality and morbidity than individuals directly beneath them had (Marmot, 1994). Someone with a home and two automobiles enjoyed better health than someone who rented and owned one automobile; individuals in the "highest income group" had better health "than *those* only slightly less well-off" (Wilkinson, 1994, p. 70).

The researchers even found these gradations in health status among smokers. After controlling for "pack-years…tar content," and other factors, administrators who smoked twenty cigarettes a day were less likely to die from lung cancer than were clerical and manual workers who smoked twenty a day (Marmot, 1994, p. 206). The Whitehall studies suggest that merely living in a hierarchical, or stratified, society is a threat to one's health (Wilkinson, 2000). Researchers call this relationship the socioeconomic, or *health,* gradient (Daniels, Kennedy, and Kawachi, 2000; Marmot, 2000; Marmot and Wilkinson, 2001).

Now it is important to note that not everyone accepts the existence of a relationship between inequality and health (Kawachi, Wilkinson, and Kennedy, 1999; Wolfson et al., 1999). Critics argue that this research is subject to what sociologists call "the ecological fallacy," that is, assuming that what holds at a macro, or population, level necessarily holds at a micro, or individual, level (Macintyre and Ellaway, 2000). In this case, critics assert, researchers have not taken into account the well-known fact that people in poverty are usually in poorer health than other people (Kawachi, Wilkinson, and Kennedy, 1999). Thus, "the apparent impact of inequality on health" may reflect "the larger number of poor people in the areas being studied" (Kawachi and Kennedy, 2001, p. 20).

Although disagreement over this and other issues remains unresolved, it is difficult to see how inequality does not play a critical role in the health of populations (Kawachi and Kennedy, 2001; Kaplan and Lynch, 2001). After all, there seems little doubt that, at a certain point, economic growth has a diminishing impact on health status (Fuchs, 1994; Duleep, 1995). At the same time, as noted above, the wealthiest nations, such as the United States, do not necessarily have the healthiest populations (Wilkinson, 1996; Sen, 1993). If material wealth (or lack of it) does not explain health differences *between* countries, it is difficult to see how it explains differences *within* them (Wilkinson, 1999a). In addition, the often-noted relationship between individual poverty and poor health may reflect, at least in part, a relationship between relative poverty and health (Wilkinson, 1999b). Inequality might also be a "crude proxy" for hierarchical and "authoritarian" relationships, which may also have an adverse impact on health status (R. Wilkinson, personal communication).

The Impact of Inequality on Health

For many years, researchers and policy makers had assumed that socioeconomic factors primarily influenced the health of people in poverty (Adler, 2001). The discovery of a far wider-reaching relation between *inequality* and health undermined this view. It now appears that, at least in developed countries, *relative poverty* poses a greater threat to health than does absolute poverty. This section examines four factors that researchers believe may explain this relation: psychosocial variables, social cohesion, childhood development, and material conditions (Smith and Egger, 1996).

Psychosocial Variables.   Wilkinson (1996) and others have argued that psychosocial variables associated with living in a stratified society are a central cause of the relation between inequality and health. Although these theorists do not deny the role of material factors, such as inadequate diet, poor housing, and pollution, they stress the importance of "variables such as control, anxiety, insecurity, depression," and "social affiliations" (Marmot and Wilkinson, 2001, p. 1233). Brunner (1997) also links psychosocial factors with "social position." He includes among these factors "perceived financial strain, job insecurity, low control and monotony at work, stressful life events and poor social networks," and "fatalism" (Brunner, 1997, p. 1473).

Psychosocial variables have both direct and indirect effects on health (Wilkinson, 1997). The direct effects are the "physiological" consequences "of chronic mental and emotional stress" (Wilkinson, 1997, p. 592). Chronic stress can increase one's chances of developing potentially deadly conditions (e.g., hypertension and heart disease), weaken immunity, and accelerate aging (Brunner, 1997; Meaney, 1997). The indirect, or mediated, effects are the behavioral risks, such as smoking, overeating, and alcohol and drug abuse, which individuals engage in to manage or deaden stress (Wilkinson, 1997).

It would be surprising if psychosocial factors did *not* play a central role in the health gradient. If, as the gradient suggests, inequality is an important determinant of health, psychosocial factors must be involved in some way. After all, as noted above, relative poverty is fundamentally a social relationship. One is poor or deprived, not in the abstract but in relation, or comparison, to others. These evaluations affect how people think and feel about themselves (Beck, 1991; Burns, 1980; Ellis, 1996). Individuals who cannot live up to society's standards often develop a sense of shame or self-hatred (Gilligan, 1996).

Shame is also a function of power and control. To shame people is to expose them, to catch them with their "pants down" (Erikson, 1963). When we reveal someone's secrets or inner being, we also render that person powerless. Powerlessness, in turn, has well-documented effects on health (Wilkinson, 1996; Brunner, 1997; Meaney, 1997). Researchers have "repeatedly" found that "health and well-being" depend on an individual's ability to influence the "forces" impacting his or her "life" (Syme, 1996, p. 85).

Whitehall II, a follow-up study of British civil servants, which, unlike Whitehall I, included women, revealed the importance of psychosocial factors (Marmot et al., 1994; Marmot and Wilkinson, 2001). Again, researchers found that workers in lower occupational categories were less healthy than workers in higher categories were (Marmot et al., 1994). Lower-level workers also had less control over their jobs and fewer sources of social support (Marmot, Bobak, and Smith, 1995). This suggests that lack of control, or powerlessness, contributes to the development of the health gradient (Syme, 1994; Marmot and Wilkinson, 2001). Studies from Sweden, the United States, and Germany substantiate the findings of Whitehall II (Wilkinson, 1996).

Kawachi and associates (1994) have also addressed the issue of control. According to them, "frustrated aspirations," or "gaps between aspirations and rewards," can be "detrimental to health" (Kawachi et al., 1994, p. 11). They note that even if the income of the entire population rises, individuals will feel deprived if their own incomes do not increase as quickly as they had expected or as quickly as the incomes of others increase. Because people "evaluate their...well-being in relative terms," their frustration may increase even during periods of rapid economic growth (Kawachi et al., 1994, p. 11). An individual's failure to live up to community expectations can result in frustration and a wide range of mental and physical disorders.

Finally, animal studies have contributed to our understanding of the influence of social rank on health. In extensive observations of wild baboons in Kenya, Sapolsky (1994) found that dominant animals were much healthier than subordinate ones. This does not necessarily prove that high social rank leads to better health. Indeed, it could be the other way around; that is, healthier individuals may rise in the social hierarchy. In a study of captive monkeys, Shively and Clarkson (1994) discovered that manipulating an individual's status (i.e., making a dominant monkey subordinate, and a subordinate one dominant) adversely affected the health of both animals. However, change in status had a far greater impact on previously dominant animals than on previously subordinate ones (Shively and Clarkson, 1994). This seems to indicate that social rank influences health status, rather than the other way around (Sapolsky, 1994).

Sapolsky also found a link between personality type and physiological health. Independent of social status, baboons that were best able to cope with stressful situations, and thus had some measure of control over their environment, were healthier than their counterparts. However, social relationships played a critical role as well. The most psychologically adjusted baboons were those "most capable of developing friendships," or social supports (Sapolsky, 1994, p. 264).

Smith (1996), a contributor to the Whitehall studies, has raised questions about the role of psychosocial factors. He notes that although changes in inequality may explain mental and emotional "distress" and deaths from "accidents and violence," they seem to have minimal influence on "major causes of death," such as cardiovascular disease and cancer (Smith, 1996, p. 988). Lynch and colleagues (2000) also question the importance of psychosocial factors.

Social Cohesion.   Researchers have also linked the health gradient to social cohesion. By social cohesion, scholars mean the level of interaction and cooperation between and among members of a society (Kawachi and Berkman, 2000). A half century ago, Durkheim (1951), a French social theorist, found that rates of suicide varied according to the "degree" of cohesion, or "integration," within a community (p. 209). Catholic countries, where social ties were relatively strong, had lower suicide rates than did Protestant countries, where social ties were weaker. The importance of this work was that it examined suicide as a social phenomenon and not "purely in terms of individual psychology and circumstances" (Wilkinson, 1996, p. 15).

Bruhn and Wolf (1979) addressed the relationship between social cohesion and health in their study of the town of Roseto, Pennsylvania. The population of Roseto largely descended from individuals who had emigrated from Italy during the 1880s. Although they had lifestyles similar to those of residents of neighboring towns, the citizens of Roseto had significantly lower rates of mortality from heart disease (Wilkinson, 1996). A central factor in Roseto's success seemed to be the town's "egalitarian ethos." Although Roseto had class differences, social pressure kept them muted. According to Bruhn and Wolf:

> The local priest emphasised [sic] that when the preoccupation with earning money exceeded the unmarked boundary it became the basis for social rejection, irrespective of the standing of the person.... Despite the affluence of many, there was no atmosphere of 'keeping up with the Joneses'" (cited in Wilkinson, 1996, p. 117).

During the 1960s, Roseto began to change. As the town grew more prosperous, and the population more educated, social and class differences became more obvious. With increasing stratification, and social division, Roseto lost its "health advantage" (Wilkinson, 1996). By "the 1980s, Roseto's new generation of adults had a heart attack rate above that of their neighbors in a nearby and demographically similar town" (Putnam, 2000, p. 329). These findings have been corroborated by other researchers as (Lasker et al., 1994, Egolf et al., 1992).

Researchers have also explored the links among income equality, social cohesion, and health outcomes (Wilkinson, 1997). The inspiration for much of this work has come from Robert Putnam, a Harvard political scientist. In 1993, Putnam and two colleagues published a study of regional governments in Italy. They discovered that the "hallmarks of a successful region" were a tradition of citizen involvement through civil and "community organizations" and other "horizontal" networks (Putnam, 2000, p. 345). Putnam characterized these forms of association as "social capital" (cited in Kawachi and Kennedy, 1997). As specific examples of social capital, Putnam (2000) mentions extended families, bridge and Rotary clubs, "ethnic fraternal groups," civic organizations, parent–teacher organizations, and "the network of professional acquaintances recorded in your address book" (pp. 20–22).

Social capital also includes people's feelings and attitudes about the nature and character of their fellow citizens and society. Individuals who belong to civic organizations and engage in community activity are likely to have positive feelings about their fellow citizens and society. Communities with a high degree of citizen participation and trust are thus rich in social capital. In Italy, the regions with the most social capital also had the least income inequality (Wilkinson, 1996). Although Putnam and his colleagues did not specifically address health-related issues, they did find an inverse correlation between the degree of civic engagement in a community and its rate of infant mortality (cited in Wilkinson, 1996).

Building on this work, Kawachi and associates (1997) examined the relationship among social capital, income inequality, and mortality in thirty-nine states in the United States. To measure social capital, they relied on survey data from the National Opinion Research Center, which includes questions on "social trust and organizational membership" (Kawachi et al., 1997, p. 1491). The authors found an inverse relationship between inequality and levels of social trust and citizen involvement in organized activity. At the same time, low levels of trust and involvement correlated with high rates of mortality. The authors concluded that a low level of social capital may be "one of the pathways through which growing income inequality exerts its effects on population-level mortality" (Kawachi et al., 1997, p. 1495).

This suggests that social capital plays a mediating role, linking a society's distribution of income with its rate of morbidity and mortality. The distribution of income is also a force for cohesion or division. A relatively equitable distribution of income promotes social cohesion, whereas a relatively inequitable distribution undermines cohesion and promotes social division.

Childhood Development.   Childhood experiences also contribute to the relation between inequality and health (Bartley et al., 1997). As noted above, from infancy, environmental, and particularly socioeconomic, factors have a profound impact on the brain's growth and development (Hertzman, 1994). The brain, in turn, "influences" the development of "cardiovascular...immune," and other systems, as well as the "sensory, cognitive, and social skills necessary to guide the organism through life" (Cynader, 1994, pp. 155, 163).

Socioeconomic factors affect more than an infant's brain, however. Hertzman (1994, p. 169) notes that birth itself has a more adverse impact on "lower-class" children than on "upper-class children." Social rank even "buffers" upper-class children from the effects of "exposure to lead in the environment" (Hertzman, 1994, p. 170). Thus, the "quality" of early experiences can have a lasting impact on an "individual's social responsivity throughout life" (Cynader, 1994, p. 162).

In an effort to explain how childhood experiences influence health outcomes, researchers have developed two approaches. The "latency," or critical periods, model assumes that individuals go through critical biological and social periods (Hertzman, 1994). Thus, some researchers believe babies' brains are "open to experience of a particular kind only during narrow periods of opportunity" (Gopnik, Meltzoff, and Kuhl, 1999, p. 189). Distinct events, particularly in the early stages of life, can reverberate throughout the life cycle (Hertzman, 1994).

The "pathways model," on the other hand, focuses on the "cumulative effects of life events and the ongoing importance of the conditions of life" (Hertzman, 1994, p. 174). This approach relies on studies showing that an accumulation of events influences health status (Bartley, Blane, and Montgomery, 1997). The pathways model does not deny the importance of critical events. However, it stresses that "if appropriate stimulation is missed at a specific time in early childhood, the function can be developed through other forms of stimulation later in life" (Hertzman, 1994, p. 177).

Both perspectives acknowledge the importance of inequality. For example, Hertzman (1994) notes that early education may prevent "a decline in mental function in late life" (p. 171). If children do not learn to read at a young age, their brains may fail to develop in crucial ways that could protect them later against the ravages of dementia (Hertzman, 1994). Not surprisingly, the risk of dementia is lower among high school graduates than among individuals with less than a secondary education (Hertzman, 1994). Lack of education has clear links with poverty and inequality.

In terms of the pathways model, Hertzman (1994) has discussed how events related to socioeconomic status can lead to adverse outcomes throughout the life cycle. The disadvantages associated with being born into a poor or low-income family can trigger a chain of events that result in "failure in school" and "low levels of well-being in early adulthood" (Hertzman, 1994, p. 174). This, in turn, can push an individual into poorly paying jobs with "high" demands and "low levels of control" and lead to "disability and absenteeism" and eventually an early death (Hertzman, 1994, p. 174). Although it is possible to break this chain at any stage, it becomes harder and more unlikely as the life cycle unfolds. Smith (1996) argues that illnesses with lengthy gestation periods are likely rooted in long-term "cumulative factors, such as "wealth, family assets," and "lifetime earnings" (p. 987).

Material Conditions.   Material conditions also seem to play a role in the development of the health gradient. Lynch and colleagues (2000) have developed a "neo-material" interpretation, which stresses the "combination of negative exposures and lack of resources held by individuals, along with systematic underinvestment across a wide range of human, physical, health, and social infrastructure" (p. 1201). According to them, an inequitable distribution of income is part of a wider "cluster of neo-material conditions," including education, health care, food, housing, and jobs, which "affect population health" (Lynch et al., 2000, p. 1201).

To illustrate the impact of "neo-material conditions" on health, they cite, as a "metaphor," the difference between first- and economy-class air travel. Individuals traveling first class receive benefits, such as good food and comfortable seats, that enable them to "arrive fresh and rested," which economy-class passengers, who "arrive feeling a bit rough," do not receive (Lynch et al., 2000, p. 1201).

Conclusion.   Although the existence of the health gradient is widely accepted, the reasons for it remain in dispute (Tarlov, 1999). Although the social cohesion and psychosocial explanations are persuasive, they have not convinced everyone (Smith and Egger, 1996). Many studies suffer from methodological flaws and rely on inadequate data (Kawachi et al., 1994). Some scholars have noted the difficulty of defining and measuring social cohesion and social capital (Kaplan and Lynch, 1997; Kawachi et al., 1997). On other hand, some observers seem to deny the impact of social cohesion and psychosocial factors (Lynch et al., 2000). This view seems too extreme and does not fit the evidence (Marmot and Wilkinson, 2001). The relation between inequality and health seems best explained by a combination of psychosocial variables, social cohesion, childhood experience, and material conditions (R. Wilkinson, personal communication; I. Kawachi, personal communication).

Implications for Health Policy and Social Work

We started this chapter by asking if health policy could lead to good health. We end it by asserting that inequality is bad for health. For national health policy to play a significant role in promoting health, it must incorporate the research on social determinants of health summarized in this chapter. Accomplishing this complex task will require a new framework for health policy.

A New Framework for Health Policy

Evans and Stoddart (1994) developed a multidimensional, universal framework for health and health policy based on the social determinants of health, which may serve as a framework. This framework identifies five stages of development: (1) disease and health care, (2) escalating costs, (3) a new concept for health, (4) a new framework for health policy, and (5) the costs and benefits of health policy.

Stage One: Disease and Health Care.   According to Evans and Stoddart (1994), traditional approaches to health policy have been based on a narrowly conceived "thermostat" model that defines illness as a deviation from a normal state of health. Just as cold weather encourages us to turn up the thermostat in our homes, medicine responds to illness by turning up the level of treatment and services. Medicine's *traditional* response takes the following path:

Medicine's Traditional Path
DISEASE ⇒ Individual may/may not *seek* and may/may not have *access* to **MEDICAL CARE** ⇒ **NEED** for care and **RESPONSE** determined by **HEALTH CARE SYSTEM** ⇒ **LEVEL OF CARE** determined by **ACCESS** ⇒ **DISEASE** reduced through **CURE** and **CARE** (Evans and Stoddart, 1994)

In this model, the "level of health of a population is the negative or inverse of the burden of disease" and "professionally defined needs for care are themselves adjusted according to the capacity of the health care system and the pressures on it" (Evans and Stoddart, 1994, p. 21). More and more resources are expended for health care, rather than health. "As one need is met another is discovered" (Evans and Stoddart, 1994, p. 22).

Stage Two: Escalating Costs.   By the 1970s, with the exception of the United States, all of the world's developed countries had established universal, comprehensive systems of health care delivery. In all of these countries "ever-increasing needs" were in conflict with "increasingly restrained resources." In Evans and Stoddart's (1994) model, public concern is expressed as follows:

Medicine's Traditional Response to Needs
DISEASE ⇒ addressed by **HEALTH CARE SYSTEM** ⇒ **INCREASED RESPONSE** ⇒ has led to **GROWING HEALTH CARE COSTS** (Evans and Stoddart, 1994)

According to Evans and Stoddart (1994), there is little scientific evidence to support much of the health care that is provided. In fact, there is evidence that some of the health care provided leads to poor health outcomes. Consequently, there seems to be relatively little payoff to society for the ever-increasing resources expended on health care. In addition, variations in health care spending among countries do not lead to demonstrable differences in health.

Stage Three: A New Concept of Health.   To "shift the focus of health policy from an exclusive concern with health care" (Evans and Stoddart, 1994, p. 25) to health, Evans and Stoddart proposed three categories for determinants of health—lifestyles, environment, and human biology. From this perspective, the delivery of health care is viewed as only one of many ways that public policy can address health outcomes and raises larger questions for policy analysts and planners. What else can and should nations do? To what extent should government be involved? Are individuals responsible for their lifestyle behaviors? What are the obligations and responsibilities of government and the private corporate sector? To focus on health outcomes, Evans and Stoddart (1994) have offered a revision of the "thermostat model" of health:

> *Determinants of Health*
> <u>**LIFESTYLE**</u> ⇔ <u>**ENVIRONMENT**</u> ⇒ <u>**HUMAN BIOLOGY**</u>
>
> ⇓   ⇓   ⇓
>
> **DISEASE** ⇒ Individual may/may not *seek* and may/may not have *access* to
> **MEDICAL CARE** ⇒ **NEED** for care and **RESPONSE** determined by
> **HEALTH CARE SYSTEM** ⇒ **LEVEL OF CARE** determined by **ACCESS** ⇒
> **DISEASE** reduced through **CURE** and **CARE** (Evans and Stoddart, 1994)

Stage Four: A New Framework for Health Policy.   Evans and Stoddart (1994) incorporated the findings of McKeown, Marmot, and others concerning the role of social relationships, social class, and hierarchy in determining health outcomes to establish a new framework. They included the important findings that a health gradient exists and that relative poverty is a greater risk to health than is absolute poverty. Environmental factors, in the broadest sense of the term, are a health issue for *all* of us, not *some* of us.

Evans and Stoddart (1994) offered the following:

> *A New Framework for Health Policy*
> **DISEASE** ⇒ addressed by **HEALTH CARE SYSTEM**
>
> **HEALTH** and **FUNCTION** ⇒ experienced by **INDIVIDUALS**
>
> **ILLNESS** does not necessarily equal **DISEASE**
>
> **DISEASE, HEALTH CARE,** and **HEALTH** ⇒ affected by
> **SOCIAL ENVIRONMENT, PHYSICAL ENVIRONMENT,**
> and **GENETIC ENDOWMENT**
>
> **ULTIMATE GOAL OF HEALTH POLICY** ⇒ **INDIVIDUAL, SOCIAL,** and
> **ECONOMIC WELL-BEING** (Evans and Stoddart, 1994)

From this perspective, whether individuals become "sick" depends on the *interactions* of their genetic endowments with the physical and social environment. On a societal level, the "relationship between the health care system and the health of the population becomes even more complex" (Evans and Stoddart, 1994, p. 29).

Stage Five: The Costs and Benefits of Health Policy. A health *care* policy of "ever increasing needs" leads to escalating costs. In addition, the expansion of health care inevitably means that societal resources are reduced for other uses. Evans and Stoddart (1994) suggest that the "positive effects of health care on health may be outweighed by its negative effects through competition for resources with other health-enhancing activities" (p. 32). To shift from health *care* policy to a *health* policy requires an all-encompassing framework:

> *All-Encompassing Health Policy*
> **DISEASE** ⇒ addressed by **HEALTH CARE SYSTEM**
>
> **HEALTH** and **FUNCTION** ⇒ experienced by **INDIVIDUALS**
>
> **ILLNESS** does not necessarily equal **DISEASE**
>
> **DISEASE, HEALTH CARE** and **HEALTH** ⇒ affected by **SOCIAL ENVIRONMENT, PHYSICAL ENVIRONMENT,** and **GENETIC ENDOWMENT**
>
> **ULTIMATE GOAL OF HEALTH POLICY** ⇒ **INDIVIDUAL, SOCIAL,** and **ECONOMIC WELL-BEING**
>
> **PROSPERITY** ⇒ affects **DISEASE, HEALTH CARE, HEALTH,** and **WELL-BEING** (Evans and Stoddart, 1994)

Ultimately, "[A] society that spends so much on health care that it cannot or will not spend adequately on other health-enhancing activities may actually be *reducing* the health of its population through increased health spending" (Evans and Stoddart, 1994, p. 32).

International Policy Efforts

The social determinants perspective has had an impact on some government policies, primarily in Canada and the United Kingdom. In 1974, the Canadian government published *A New Perspective on the Health of Canadians* (1974), or the Lalonde Report. The Lalonde Report argued that genes, the environment, and individual behavior were more important than medical care in determining health status (Marmor, Barer, and Evans, 1994). Although the Lalonde Report proved highly influential and helped transform thinking about determinants of health, its primary focus was still on individual habits (Armstrong and Armstrong, 1996; Rachlis and Kushner, 1989).

In 1976, the British government appointed a commission, chaired by Sir Douglas Black, to investigate increasing mortality among people with low incomes (Wilkinson, 1996). The subsequent Black report, which the government of Margaret Thatcher attempted to suppress, offered "compelling evidence that poverty causes ill health" (Rachlis and Kushner, 1989, p. 179; Dean, 1994). This report ushered in a new era of research on the social causes of health and illness in the developed world, much of it under the leadership of Richard Wilkinson and Michael Marmot, two British researchers (Wilkinson, 1996, p. ix).

In 1997, in light of the research findings on social determinants of health, the government of Tony Blair appointed a commission chaired by Sir Donald Acheson to investigate inequality and health (Davey-Smith, Morris, and Shaw, 1998). The so-called Acheson report summarized data on trends in health inequality and the socioeconomic determinants of health and recommended steps to reduce inequalities (Independent Inquiry into Inequalities in Health Report, 1998).

Reaction to the report was mixed. In an editorial in the *British Medical Journal,* Davey-Smith, Morris, and Shaw (1998) welcomed the report but criticized it for being "too cautious and vague" in its recommendations (p. 1465). On the other hand, Alvin Tarlov (1999), a physician and leading health policy theorist in the United States, praised the report as a "major accomplishment" and called it a possible "beacon guide for many nations" (p. 1466).

Implications for Health and Health Care Policy in the United States

The social determinants perspective has profound implications for efforts for national health care in the United States. To begin with, as previously noted, health care seems to have played a relatively limited role in declines in mortality and growth of life expectancy. Evidence suggests that health care continues to play a relatively limited role in population health (I. Kawachi, personal communication). Some researchers believe that "acute care" may actually have an adverse impact (Bezruchka, 2001). In addition, in some countries with national health care, "health disparities" have not disappeared (Daniels, Kennedy, and Kawachi, 2000).

However, this does not mean that United States should not join the rest of the developed world in providing health care to all its citizens. Indeed, the opposite is true. Medicine and access to health care are vitally important to individuals who are sick or in poor health. As Shi and Starfield (2001) point out, the supply of primary care physicians in an area seems to have a significant influence on mortality, particularly among whites. Medicine's primary weakness is that its ability to promote health and wellness is relatively limited.

Universal coverage, or the lack of it, also seems to have an indirect impact on health status. A comparative study of the United States and Canada found a strong association between income inequality and mortality in the former but none in Canada, at either the provincial "or the metropolitan level" (Ross et al., 2000, p. 902). What explains this difference? It may be that Canada's universal system of health care not only narrows the gap between rich and poor but also serves as a form of social capital, and thus a force for cohesion, and helps reduce psychosocial stress. If this is true, enacting universal coverage in the United States could help reduce inequality and help improve the health status of the population.

Implications for Social Work

Social workers, and NASW in particular, have long been in the forefront of the struggle for universal coverage, and they should not rest until they achieve success. Social justice and advocacy have been an integral part of social work's mission as a profession, and it must continue to support legislative and community-based efforts to achieve universal access to health care. However, in light of the relationship between health and inequality, there is evidence that efforts to reduce inequality in the United States will contribute to the nation's health.

Social work should also take note of the links between the health gradient and its biopsychosocial approach. In fact, the health gradient is a biopsychosocial relation. It is biological because humans are fundamentally biological beings, and morbidity and mortality are rooted in interruptions of biological processes. It is social because it is linked with distribution of income and relative deprivation, which are fundamentally social relationships. Finally, the gradient is also a psychological phenomenon. The link, or pathway, between income inequality and the distribution of morbidity and mortality is, at least in part, the mental and emotional stress associated with relative deprivation. (Even Smith [1996], who questions the immediate importance of psychosocial factors, acknowledges their link with violence, accidents, and similar phenomena, and their role throughout the life span.)

The literature on social determinants of health shows that health is essentially a biopsychosocial phenomenon. The practice of social work is rooted in a biopsychosocial perspective. As the largest group of mental health providers and as professionals in a wide range of health settings, social workers have an important role to play in providing further insight into the psychosocial dimensions of health.

Highlights

■ Individual and population health is a biopsychosocial process that encompasses biological (genetics and human aging process), psychological (perception, cognition, and emotion), and social (lifestyle, culture, politics, race and ethnicity, class, and gender) factors, which are both distinct and interrelated.

■ Weick's (1986) health model, in contrast to the traditional medical model, focuses on multiple influences that shape health status. Ultimately, individuals and the population as a whole can be well only if society takes responsibility for health promotion.

■ A growing body of research indicates that social factors are indeed critical determinants of health and begins to explain this phenomenon by identifying specific causal factors. Research shows that medical care has played a limited role in reducing mortality in Western nations, whereas factors such as increased income, improved nutrition, and public health efforts have played a greater role in the extension of human life.

■ However, Wilkinson (1996) discovered that countries with the greatest wealth do not necessarily have the healthiest populations in terms of mortality and morbidity. Thus, material standards of living (income and wealth) have a limited impact on mortality and morbidity.

■ Inequality or the distribution of income in a population seems to play a more significant role in population health than absolute poverty. The wider the income gap within a nation, the higher the mortality and morbidity rate. In other words, after a certain point or threshold, economic growth has a diminished impact on population health.

■ Relative poverty poses a greater threat to health than absolute poverty. Researchers have found four factors that help explain this relationship between inequality and health: (1) psychosocial variables, (2) social cohesion, (3) childhood development, and (4) material conditions.

■ The discovery of a relationship between inequality and health has implications for national health care in the United States and for the profession of social work. Evans and Stoddart (1994) developed a framework to conceptualize the role of inequality and incorporate research on the social determinants of health. In the final stage of their framework, they argue that the expansion of health *care* may do little to improve *health*. Nations must allocate resources toward health-enhancing activities to achieve healthy populations.

■ Canada and Britain have taken steps to apply this framework to health policy, but their efforts have been very limited. In the United States, universal access to health care services is a basic need that has not yet been met. However, long-range efforts to go beyond *health care* and toward *health* will require much broader socioeconomic reforms.

■ Social work has a special role to perform in efforts to achieve a healthy population. The practice of social work is rooted in a biopsychosocial perspective. Social workers can provide further insight into the psychosocial dimensions of health and make significant contributions to the social determinants of health perspective through their practice and research.

■ The role of social work in advocacy efforts to achieve social justice and equity may have implications for the nation's health.

REFERENCES

Adler, N. E. (2001). A Consideration of Multiple Pathways from Socioeconomic Status to Health. In J. A. Auerbach and B. K. Krimgold (Eds.), *Income, Socioeconomic Status, and Health: Exploring the Relationships* (pp. 56–66). Washington, DC: National Policy Association.

Amick III, B. C., Levine, S., Tarlov, A. R., and Walsh, D. C. (1995). In B. C. Amick III, S. Levine, A. R. Tarlov, and D. C. Walsh (Eds.), *Society and Health* (pp. 3–17). New York: Oxford University Press.

Armstrong, P. and Armstrong, H. (1996). *Wasting Away: The Undermining of Canadian Health Care.* Toronto: Oxford University Press.

Bartlett, H. M. (1970). *The Common Base of Social Work Practice.* New York: National Association of Social Workers.

Bartley, M., Blane, D., and Montgomery, S. (1997, April 19). Socioeconomic Determinants of Health: Health and the Life Course: Why Safety Nets Matter. *British Medical Journal, 314,* 1194–1198.

Bartley, M., Power, C., Blane, D., and Davey Smith, G. (1994). Birthweight and Later Socioeconomic Disadvantage: Evidence from the 1958 Birth Cohort Study. *British Medical Journal, 309,* 1475–1478.

Beck, A. (1991). Cognitive Therapy: A 30-Year Retrospective. *American Psychologist, 46,* 382–389.

Berkman, L. F. and Glass, T. (2000). Social Integration, Social Networks, Social Support, and Health. In L. F. Berkman and I. Kawachi, (Eds.), *Social Epidemiology* (pp. 137–173). New York: Oxford University Press.

Berkman, L. F. and Kawachi, I. (Eds.). (2000). *Social Epidemiology.* Oxford: Oxford University Press.

Berkman, B. and Vollard, P. (1997). Health Care Practice: Overview. In R. L. Edwards (Ed.). *Encyclopedia of Social Work,* 19th ed., Supplement, (pp. 143–149). Washington, DC: National Association of Social Workers.

Bezruchka, S. (2001, June 12). Societal Hierarchy and the Health Olympics. *Canadian Medical Association Journal, 164,* 12, 1701–1704.

Bosma, H., Marmot, M. G., Hemingway, H., Nicholson, A., Brunner, E., and Stansfeld, S. (1997). Low Job Control and Risk of Coronary Disease in Whitehall II (Prospective Cohort) Study. *British Medical Journal, 314,* 558–566.

Bruhn, J. and Wolf, S. (1979). *The Roseto Story.* Norman, OK: University of Oklahoma Press.

Brunner, E. (1997). Socioeconomic Determinants of Health: Stress and the Biology of Inequality. *British Medical Journal, 314,* 1472–1478.

Burns, D. D. (1980). *Feeling Good—The New Mood Therapy.* New York: Signet.

Calman, K. C. (1997, April 19). What Is Health for All? *British Medical Journal, 314,* 1187–1192.

Clinton, H. (1997, April 17). Remarks by the First Lady at the White House Conference on Early Childhood Development. Available at www.clinton.nara.com

Council on Social Work Education. (1995). Curriculum Policy Statement for Baccalaureate/ Master's Degree Programs in Social Work Education. *Handbook of Accreditation Standards and Procedures.* Alexandria, VA: CSWE.

Cynader, M. S. (1994, Fall). Mechanisms of Brain Development and Their Role in Health and Well-Being. *Daedalus, 123,* 4, 155–166.

Daniels, N., Kennedy, B., and Kawachi, I. (2000, February–March). Justice is Good for Our Health. *Boston Review, 25,* 1, pp. 4–19.

Davey-Smith, G., Morris, J. N., and Shaw, M. (1998, November 28). The Independent Inquiry into Inequalities in Health [Editorial]. *British Medical Journal, 317,* 1465–1466.

Dean, M. (1994). Beveridge Revisited and Restructured. *Lancet, 344,* 1285.

DeLone, Richard. (1979). *Small Futures—Children, Inequality, and the Limits of Liberal Reform.* New York: Harcourt Brace Jovanovich.

Duleep, H. C. (1995, Summer). Mortality and Income Inequality Among Economically Developed Countries. *Social Security Bulletin, 58,* 2, 34–50.

Durkheim, E. (1951). *Suicide: A Study in Sociology.* New York: Free Press.

Egolf, B., Lasker, J., Wolf, S., and Potvin, L. (1992). The Roseto Effect: A 50-Year Comparison of Mortality Rates. *American Journal of Public Health, 82,* 1089–1092.

Ellis, A. (1996). *Better, Deeper, and More Enduring Brief Therapy—The Rational Emotive Behavior Therapy Approach.* New York: Brunner/Mazel.

Epstein, H. (1998, July 16). Life and Death on the Social Ladder. *New York Review,* pp. 26–31.

Erikson, E. H. (1963). *Childhood and Society,* 2nd ed. New York: W. W. Norton.

Evans, D., Beckett, L., Albert, M., Hebert, L., Scherr, P., Funkenstein, H., and Taylor, J. (1993). Level of Education and Change in Cognitive Function in a Community Population of Older Persons. *Annals of Epidemiology, 3,* 71–77.

Evans, R. G., Barer, M. L., and Marmor, T. R. (1994). *Why Are Some People Healthy and Others Not?* New York: Aldine de Gruyter.

Evans, R. G. and Stoddart, G. L. (1994). Producing Health, Consuming Health Care. In P. R. Lee and C. L. Estes, (Eds.), *The Nation's Health,* 4th ed. (pp. 14–33). Boston: Jones and Bartlett Publishers.

Farmer, R. L. and Pandurangi, A. K. (1997). Diversity in Schizophrenia: Toward a Richer Bi-opsychosocial Understanding for Social Work Practice. *Health and Social Work, 22,* 2, 109–116.

Ferris, C. F. (1996, March–April). The Rage of Innocents. *The Sciences,* 22–26.

Flegg, A. (1982). Inequality of Income, Illiteracy, and Medical Care as Determinants of Infant Mortality in Developing Countries. *Population Studies, 36,* 441–58.

Fogel, R. W. (1994, April). *Economic Growth, Population Theory, and Physiology: The Bearing of Long-Term Processes in the Making of Economic Theory.* Working Paper No. 4638. Cambridge: National Bureau of Economic Research.

Fonagy, P. (1996). Patterns of Attachment, Interpersonal Relationships, and Health. In D. Blane, E. Brunner, and R. Wilkinson (Eds.), *Health and Social Organization, Towards a Health Policy for the Twenty-First Century* (pp. 21–31). London and New York: Routledge.

Fuchs, V. R. (1994). A Tale of Two States. In P. Conrad and R. Kern (Eds.), *The Sociology of Health and Illness,* 4th ed., (pp. 55–61). New York: St. Martin's Press.

Garrett, L. (2000). *Betrayal of Trust: The Collapse of Global Public Health.* New York: Hyperion.

Germain, C. B. (1973). An Ecological Perspective in Casework Practice. *Social Casework, 54,* 323–330.

Germain, C. B. and Gitterman, A. (1980). *The Life Model of Social Work Practice.* New York: Columbia University Press.

Gilligan, J. (1996). *Violence, Our Deadly Epidemic and Its Causes.* New York: Grosset/Putnam.

Gopnik, A., Meltzoff, A., and Kuhl, P. K. (1999). *The Scientist in the Crib: Minds, Brains, and How Children Learn.* New York: William Morrow.

Gordon, W. E. (1969). Basic Constructs for an Integrative and Generative Conception of Social Work. In G. Hearn (Ed.), *The General Systems Approach: Contributions Toward an Holistic Conception of Social Work* (pp. 5–12). New York: Council on Social Work Education.

Greenspan, S. I. with Benderly, B. L. (1997). *The Growth of the Mind and the Endangered Origins of Intelligence.* Reading, MA: Addison-Wesley.

Hertzman, C. (1994, Fall). The Lifelong Impact of Childhood Experiences: A Population Health Perspective. *Daedalus, 123,* 4, 167–180.

Hill, H. (1961). Racism Within Organized Labor: A Report of Five Years of the AFL-CIO. New York: NAACP Labor Department.

Hotz, R. L. (1997, October 28). Lack of Maternal Love Can Affect Brain Chemistry. *Concord Monitor,* p. A2.

House, J. S., Landis, K. R., and Umberson, D. (1994). Social Relationships and Health. In P. Conrad and R. Kern (Eds.), *The Sociology of Health and Illness,* 4th ed. (pp. 83–92). New York: St. Martin's Press.

Independent Inquiry into Inequalities in Health Report. (1998, November 26). The Stationary Office (Online). Available at www.official-documents.co.uk/document/doh/ih/ih.htm.

Kaplan, G. A. and Lynch, J. W. (2001, March). Is Economic Policy Health Policy? *American Journal of Public Health, 91,* 3, 351–354.

Kaplan, G. A. and Lynch, J. W. (1997). Whither Studies on the Socioeconomic Foundations of Population Health? [Editorial]. *American Journal of Public Health, 87,* 9, 1409–1413.

Kaplan, G. A., Pamuk, E., Lynch, J. W., Cohen, R. D., and Balfour, J. L. (1999). Income Inequality and Mortality in the United States. In I. Kawachi, B. P. Kennedy, and R. G. Wilkinson (Eds.), *The Society and Population Health Reader.* Volume I, *Income Inequality and Health* (pp. 50–59), New York: New Press.

Karls, J. M. and Wandrei, K. E. (1995). Person-in-Environment. In R. L. Edwards (Ed.-in-Chief), *Encyclopedia of Social Work,* 19th ed. (pp. 1818–1827). Washington, DC: National Association of Social Workers.

Kawachi, I. and Berkman, L. (2000). Social Cohesion, Social Capital, and Health. In L. F. Berkman and I. Kawachi (Eds.), *Social Epidemiology* (pp. 174–190). New York: Oxford University Press.

Kawachi, I. and Kennedy, B. P. (2001). How Income Inequality Affects Health: Evidence from Research in the United States. In J. A. Auerbach and B. K. Krimgold (Eds.), *Income, Socioeconomic Status, and Health: Exploring the Relationships* (pp. 16–28). Washington, DC: National Policy Association.

Kawachi, I. and Kennedy, B. P. (1997, April 5). Health and Social Cohesion: Why Care about Income Inequality. *British Medical Journal, 314,* 1037–1040.

Kawachi, I., Kennedy, B., Lochner, K., and Prothrow-Stith, D. (1997). Social Capital, Income Inequality, and Mortality. *American Journal of Public Health, 87,* 9, 1491–1498.

Kawachi, I., Levine S., Miller, M., Lasch, K., and Amick III, B. (1994). *Income Inequality and Life Expectancy—Theory, Research and Policy.* Society and Health Working Group Paper Series No. 94-2. Boston, MA: Harvard School of Public Health.

Kawachi, I., Wilkinson, R. G., and Kennedy, B. P. (1999). Introduction. In I. Kawachi, B. P. Kennedy, and R. G. Wilkinson (Eds.), *The Society and Population Health Reader.* Volume I, *Income Inequality and Health* (pp. xi–xxxiv). New York: New Press.

Kennedy, B. P., Kawachi, I., and Prothrow-Stith, D. (1999). Income Distribution and Mortality: Cross Sectional Ecological Study of the Robin Hood Index in the United States. In I. Kawachi, B. P. Kennedy, and R. G. Wilkinson (Eds.), *The Society and Population Health Reader.* Volume I, *Income Inequality and Health* (pp. 60–68) New York: New Press.

Kotulak, R. (1997). *Inside the Brain: Revolutionary Discoveries of How the Mind Works.* Kansas City: Andrews McMeel Publishing.

Lasker, J., Egolf, B. P., and Wolf, S. (1994). Community Social Change and Mortality. *Social Science Medicine, 39,* 53–62.

Le Grand, J. (1987). Inequalities in Health: Some International Comparisons. *European Economic Review, 31,* 182–191.

Levins, R. (1998). *Looking at the Whole: Toward a Social Ecology of Health.* Robert H. Ebert Lecture. (Available from the Department of Population and International Health, Harvard School of Public Health, Cambridge, MA.)

Longres, J. F. (1990). *Human Behavior and the Social Environment.* Itasca, IL: Peacock Publishers.

Lynch, J. W., Davey Smith, G., Kaplan, G. A., and House, J. S. (2000, April 29). Income Inequality and Mortality: Importance to Health of Individual Income, Psychosocial Environment, or Material Conditions. *British Medical Journal, 320,* 1200–1204.

Macintyre, S. and Ellaway, A. (2000). Ecological Approaches: Rediscovering the Role of the Physical and Social Environment. In L. F. Berkman and I. Kawachi (Eds.), *Social Epidemiology* (pp. 332–348). New York: Oxford University Press.

Marmor, T. R., Barer, M. L., and Evans, R. G. (1994). The Determinants of a Population's Health: What Can Be Done to Improve a Democratic Nation's Health Status? In R. G. Evans, M. L. Barer, and T. R. Marmor (Eds.), *Why Are Some People Healthy and Others Not?* (pp. 217–230). New York: Aldine de Gruyter.

Marmot, M. (2000). Multilevel Approaches to Understanding Social Determinants. In L. F. Berkman and I. Kawachi. *Social Epidemiology* (Eds.), (pp. 349–367) New York: Oxford University Press.

Marmot, M. G. (1994, Fall). Social Differentials in Health Within and Between Populations. *Daedalus, 123,* 4, 197–216.

Marmot, M. G. (1986). Social Inequalities in Mortality: The Social Environment. In R. G. Wilkinson (Ed.), *Class and Health: Research and Longitudinal Data.* London: Tavistock.

Marmot, M. G., Bobak, M., and Smith, G. D. (1995). Explanations for Social Inequalities in Health. In B. C. Amick III, S. Levine, A. R. Tarlov, and D. C. Walsh (Eds.), *Society and Health* (pp. 172–210). New York: Oxford University Press.

Marmot, M. G., Smith, G. D., Stansfeld, S., Patel, C., North, F., Head, J., Brunner, E., and Feeney, A. (1991). Health Inequalities and Social Class. In P. R. Lee and C. L. Estes (Eds.), *The Nation's Health*, 4th ed. Boston: Jones and Bartlett Publishers.

Marmot, M. and Wilkinson, R. G. (2001, May 19). Psychosocial and Material Pathways in the Relation between Income and Health: A Response to Lynch et al. *British Medical Journal, 322,* 1233–1236.

Mate' G. (1999). *Scattered: How Attention Deficit Disorder Originates and What You Can Do About It.* New York: Dutton.

McCord, C. and Freeman, H. P. (1994). Excess Mortality in Harlem. In P. Conrad and R. Kern (Eds.), *The Sociology of Health and Illness: Critical Perspectives* (pp. 35–42). New York: St. Martin's Press.

McKeown, T. (1994). Determinants of Health. In P. R. Lee and C. L. Estes (Eds.), *The Nation's Health,* 4th ed. (pp. 6–13). Boston: Jones and Bartlett Publishers.

McKeown, T. (1979). *The Role of Medicine: Dream, Mirage, or Nemesis?* Oxford: Basil Blackwell.

McKeown, T. (1976). *The Modern Rise of Populations.* New York: Academic Press.

McKinlay, J. and McKinlay S. (1994). Medical Measures and the Decline of Mortality. In P. Conrad and R. Kern (Eds.), *The Sociology of Health and Illness: Critical Perspective* (pp. 10–23). New York: St. Martin's Press.

Meaney, M. M. (1997, Fall). *Stress and Disease, A Seminar for Health Professionals.* (Available from Institute for CorText Research and Development.)

Moore, R. D. and Webb, G. D. (1986). *The K Factor, Reversing and Preventing High Blood Pressure Without Drugs.* New York: Pocket Books, Simon & Schuster.

Moroney, R. (1995). Public Health Services. In R. L. Edwards (Ed.-in-Chief), *Encyclopedia of Social Work,* 19th ed. (pp. 1967–1973). Washington, DC: National Association of Social Workers.

Newman, D. M. (1987). *Sociology, Exploring the Architecture of Everyday Life.* Thousand Oaks, CA: Pine Forge Press.

Power, C., Bartley, M., Davey Smith, G., and Blane, D. (1996). Transmission of Social and Biological Risk across the Life Course. In D. Blane, E. Brunner, and R. Wilkinson (Eds.), *Health and Social Organization—Toward a Health Policy for the Twenty-First Century.* New York: Routledge.

Prothrow-Stith, D. and Quaday, S. (1995). *Hidden Casualties: The Relationship Between Violence and Learning.* (Available from National Health and Education Consortium, c/o Institute for Educational Leadership, 1001 Connecticut Ave., NW, Suite 310, Washington, DC 20036.)

Putnam, R. D. (2000). *Bowling Alone: The Collapse and Revival of American Community.* New York: Simon & Schuster.

Putnam, R. D. (1993, Spring). The Prosperous Community: Social Capital and Economic Growth. *American Prospect,* 35–42.

Rachlis, M. and Kushner, C. (1989). *Second Opinion: What's Wrong with Canada's Health Care System and How to Fix It.* Toronto: HarperCollins.

Ratey, J. J. and Johnson, C. J. (1998). *Shadow Syndromes, the Mild Forms of Major Mental Disorders That Sabotage Us.* New York: Bantam Books.

Reves, R. (1985). Declining fertility in England and Wales as a Major Cause of the 20th Century Decline in Mortality. *American Journal of Epidemiology, 122,* 112–126.

Reynolds, A. J., Mann, E., Miedel, W., and Smikowski, P. (1997, Summer–Fall). *Focus, 19,* 1, 5–11. Madison, WI: University of Wisconsin-Madison, Institute for Research on Poverty.

Richmond, M. E. (1917). *Social Diagnosis.* New York: Russell Sage Foundation.

Rodgers, G. B. (1979). Income and Inequality as Determinants of Mortality: An International Cross-Section Analysis. *Population Studies, 33,* 343–351.

Rose, G. (1993). *The Strategy of Preventive Medicine.* Oxford: Oxford University Press.

Ross, N. A., Wolfson, M. C., Dunn, J. R., Berthelot, J., Kaplan, G. A., and Lynch, J. W. (2000, April 1). Relation between Income Inequality and Mortality in Canada and in the United States: Cross Sectional Assessment Using Census Data and Vital Statistics. *British Medical Journal, 320,* 898–902.

Sagan, L. A. (1987). *The Health of Nations—True Causes of Sickness and Well-Being.* New York: Basic Books.

Sapolsky, R. M. (1994). *Why Zebras Don't Get Ulcers, a Guide to Stress, Stress-Related Diseases, and Coping.* New York: W. H. Freeman.

Schwartz, J. M. (1996). *Brain Lock—Free Yourself from Obsessive-Compulsive Behavior.* New York: HarperCollins.

Schwartz, L. L. (1994, April). *The Medicalization of Social Problems: America's Special Health Care Dilemma—Special Report.* Washington, DC: American Health System Institute.

Sen, A. (1993, May). The Economics of Life and Death. *Scientific American,* 40–47.

Shi, L. and Starfield, B. (2001, August). The Effect of Primary Care Physician Supply and Income Equality on Mortality Among Blacks and Whites in U.S. Metropolitan Areas. *American Journal of Public Health, 91,* 8, 1246–1251.

Shively, C. A. and Clarkson, T. B. (1994). Social Status and Coronary Artery Atherosclerosis in Female Monkeys. *Arteriosclerosis and Thrombosis, 14,* 5, 721–726.

Smith, G. D. (1996, April 20). Income Inequality and Mortality: Why Are They Related? [Editorial]. *British Medical Journal, 312,* 987–988.

Smith, G. D. and Egger, M. (1996). Unequal in Death, Commentary: Understanding It All—Health, Meta-Theories, and Mortality Trends. *British Medical Journal, 313,* 1584–1585.

Strole, L., Langer, T., Michael, S., Opler, M., and Rennie, T. (1961). *Mental Health in the Metropolis,* Vol. 1. New York: McGraw-Hill.

Syme, S. L. (1996). To Prevent Disease: The Need for a New Approach. In D. Blane, E. Brunner, and R. Wilkinson (Eds.), *Health and Social Organization, Towards a Health Policy for the Twenty-First Century* (pp. 21–31). London and New York: Routledge.

Tarlov, A. R. (1999, March 3). Response to George D. Smith, et al., The Independent Inquiry into Inequalities in Health [Letter]. *British Medical Journal, 317,* 1465–1466.

Tarlov, A. R. (1996). Social Determinants of Health, the Sociobiological Translation. In D. Blane, E. Brunner, and R. Wilkenson, *Health and Social Organization.* New York: Routledge.

Turnock, B. J. (1997). *Public Health—What It Is and How It Works.* Gaithersburg, MD: Aspen Publishers.

Waldmann, R. J. (1999). Income Distribution and Infant Mortality. In I. Kawachi, B. P. Kennedy, and R. G. Wilkinson (Eds.), *The Society and Population Health Reader.* Volume I, *Income Inequality and Health* (pp. 14–27). New York: New Press.

Weick, A. (1986). The Philosophical Context of a Health Model of Social Work. *Social Casework, 67,* 9, 551–559.

Wennemo, I. (1993). Infant Mortality, Public Policy and Inequality—A Comparison of 18 Industrialized Countries 1950–1985. *Sociology of Health and Illness, 15,* 429–446.

Wilkinson, R. G. (2001). Why Is Inequality Bad for Health? In J. A. Auerbach and B. K. Krimgold (Eds.). *Income, Socioeconomic Status, and Health: Exploring the Relationships* (pp. 29–43). Washington, DC: National Policy Association.

Wilkinson, R. G. (2000). *Mind the Gap: Hierarchies, Health and Human Evolution.* London: Weidenfeld & Nicolson.

Wilkinson, R. G. (1999a). Health Inequalities: Relative or Absolute Material Standards? In I. Kawachi, B. P. Kennedy, and R. G. Wilkinson (Eds.), *The Society and Population Health Reader.* Volume I, *Income Inequality and Health* (pp. 148–160). New York: New Press.

Wilkinson, R. G. (1999b). Two Pathways, but How Much Do They Diverge? *British Medical Journal, 319,* 953–957.

Wilkinson, R. G. (1999c). Income Distribution and Life Expectancy. In I. Kawachi, B. P. Kennedy, and R. G. Wilkinson (Eds.), *The Society and Population Health Reader.* Volume I, *Income Inequality and Health* (pp. 28–35). New York: New Press.

Wilkinson, R. G. (1997). Income, Inequality, and Social Cohesion [Comment]. *American Journal of Public Health, 87,* 9, 1504–1506.

Wilkinson, R. G. (1996). *Unhealthy Societies, the Affliction of Inequality.* London and New York: Routledge.

Wilkinson, R. G. (1994). The Epidemiological Transition: From Material Scarcity to Social Disadvantage? *Daedalus, 123,* 4, 61–79.

Wolfson, M., Kaplan, G., Lynch, J., Ross, N., and Backlund, E. (1999, October 9). Relation between Income Inequality and Mortality: Empirical Demonstration. *British Medical Journal, 319,* 953–957.

World Health Organization. (1958). *The First Ten Years of the World Health Organization.* Geneva: World Health Organization.

GLOSSARY OF TERMS

Access An individual's ability to obtain health care services. Barriers to access are often financial (insufficient resources), geographic (distance to services), organizational (insufficient providers and services), and social (cultural, lingual, discrimination)

Activities of daily living (ADL) Self-care, including bathing, dressing, eating, and moving from one place to another. An index or scale is used to measure an individual's level of independence in these activities.

Acute care Medical care for short-term or episodic illness or health problems.

Behavioral health managed care Various strategies used to control mental health and substance abuse costs while maintaining quality and appropriate levels of care.

Beneficiary An individual eligible for and enrolled in a health insurance plan.

Capitation A prospective method of payment for health care services. Providers are typically paid a fixed amount for each enrolled member of a health care plan to provide a predetermined package of benefits and services over a specified period of time.

Carve-out plans A managed care organization that specializes in the management or provision of mental health or substance abuse benefits.

Catastrophic health insurance Health insurance that protects against high cost of treating severe or long-term illness or disability; usually these policies cover expenses beyond those covered by another insurance policy, up to a maximum limit.

Catchment area A geographically defined area served by a health program, institution, or plan; the area is determined on the basis of factors such as population distribution, natural geographic boundaries, and access to transportation. Typically, all residents within the area are eligible for services.

Categorically needy Individuals eligible for Medicaid based on family, age, or disability status (see Chapter 5 for full discussion of distinct population groups).

Charity care Medical services provided to individuals who cannot afford to pay for services, especially those who are uninsured and underinsured.

Chronic care Medical care for long-term illness or disability; often, these conditions are permanent, leave residual disability, are nonreversible, require patient training for rehabilitation, or require lengthy periods of supervision, observation, or care.

Coinsurance The beneficiary's share of a medical bill required by a health care plan after the deductible is paid. Typically, the health care plan pays 80 percent of the cost and the beneficiary pays 20 percent.

Community-based care Medical and social services provided in an individual or family's community residence to promote health and minimize the effects of illness and disability.

Community health center An outpatient or ambulatory health center that usually serves residents of a catchment area with scarce services or special needs; community or neighborhood health centers were established by the federal government during the 1960s to serve low-income families in medically underserved areas.

Today, these centers primarily provide services to uninsured and Medicaid populations who are in worse health than the general population.

Community mental health center   A center that provides ambulatory mental health services to residents within a catchment area; these centers were also established by the federal government during the 1960s. Today, these centers continue to provide services primarily to the most vulnerable populations who are poor or low income.

Copayment   A fixed amount paid by a beneficiary when covered services are received. Beneficiaries typically pay copayments ranging from $5 to $15 each time they receive medical benefits or services.

Cost sharing   The portion of the medical expenses of a health insurance policy or plan that individual enrollees are required to pay; typically, these expenses are paid through deductibles, copayments, and coinsurance.

Cost shifting   This occurs when providers are not reimbursed or fully reimbursed for their services. Providers charge the balance or a portion of the balance of their costs to those who do pay.

Covered services   Medical services eligible for payment by a health care plan.

Current Population Survey (CPS)   An annual national survey conducted by the U.S. Department of Commerce, Census Bureau, to gather annual statistics about the U.S. population. The CPS provides data on health status and insurance coverage.

Deductible   The fixed annual amount paid by a beneficiary for medical services before the health care plan covers expenses.

Deinstitutionalization   A policy to reduce treatment in hospital and institutional settings and provide community-based care; this occurred in mental health in the 1960s and 1970s.

Developmental disability   A chronic, severe mental and/or physical disability that manifests before adulthood (by age 21), usually continues indefinitely, and creates functional limitations in daily living. The need for special care is typically lifelong or extended.

Diagnostic-related groups (DRGs)   The classification system established by Medicare to pay hospitals a predetermined fee for patient care for specific diagnoses; each case is reimbursed at the same rate, regardless of the actual cost of patient care.

Disability   Any individual limitation of physical, mental, or social activity as compared to individuals of similar age, sex, and occupation; usually refers to vocational limitations, but includes functional and learning disabilities. Disabilities vary in degree and duration.

Disenrollment   The procedures required to cancel membership in a health care plan.

Dually eligible   Individuals entitled to Medicare who are also eligible for Medicaid because of their income status.

Durable medical equipment   Prescribed medical equipment that can be used for long periods of time, such as wheelchairs.

Enrolled population/enrollees   Individuals covered by a particular health plan.

Epidemiology   The study of the causes and patterns of illness and/or disease in human populations. Epidemiologists' aim is to apply their findings to disease prevention and health promotion.

Exclusions   Health care plans do not cover all health services, such as cosmetic surgery, or all services under all circumstances, such as nonemergency care in an emergency room.

Federal poverty level (FPL)   The U.S. Census Bureau has established an absolute measure or definition of poverty that is based on a minimal standard of living and income threshold. The poverty index is updated annually to account for inflation and is proportional to family size and composition.

Fee-for-service   A traditional payment method that pays providers for each service provided. Beneficiaries with traditional fee-for-service indemnity insurance would be reimbursed for all or part of the paid fee.

Group practice   A formal association of three or more providers; income is pooled and redistributed to the members according to a prearranged agreement.

Health insurance   Financial protection against medical costs that are related to disease, illness, or disability; it usually covers all or some of the costs and can be obtained on an individual or group basis.

Health maintenance organization (HMO)   A health care plan that provides a comprehensive set of health care services to a group of beneficiaries, usually in a geographic area, for a predetermined, prepaid fixed fee per enrollee. The payment is fixed without regard to actual services provided (costs incurred). Beneficiaries are often restricted to care provided by the HMO's network of providers and hospitals.

Health plan   An organization that provides a defined set of benefits, usually structured like an HMO.

Health promotion   Education and related interventions designed to improve or protect individual or population health.

Health status   The state of health of an individual, group, or population measured by subjective assessments, indicators of population mortality or morbidity, or incidence or prevalence of disease/illness.

Home health care   Services provided in the home to elderly, disabled, ill, or convalescent individuals rather than an institutional setting by visiting nurses, private duty nurses, home health agency, public health department, hospital, or other group. Nursing care, occupational and physical therapy, homemaker services, and social services are typically provided.

Hospice   Palliative and supportive care for terminally ill individuals and their families; hospice workers' care and support for family members often extends through their mourning period.

Hospital   A medical institution that provides inpatient diagnostic and therapeutic services, both surgical and nonsurgical; it also typically provides outpatient and emergency services. Hospitals can be classified as short- or long-term stay, teaching (affiliated with a university medical school) or nonteaching, specialized (such as psychiatric), or for-profit or nonprofit.

Incidence   In epidemiology, the number of cases of disease, infection, or other health condition or event, such as morbidity, that occurs within a prescribed period of time.

Indemnity plan   A fee-for-service health insurance plan.

Independent practice association (IPA)   A group practice that provides services on a prepaid, capitated, or fee-for-service basis. The providers remain in their own office settings, but contract with health plans to provide services.

Indigent care   Health care services provided to poor individuals or those unable to pay. Typically, these individuals are ineligible for Medicaid.

Inpatient   An individual admitted at least overnight to a hospital or health facility.

Intermediate care facility (ICF)   An institution licensed by a state to provide care and services to individuals who do not require hospital or skilled nursing care.

Katie Beckett children   Children with disabilities under age 18 who qualify for home health care coverage through a special Medicaid provision; Katie Beckett was a ventilator-dependent child who remained institutionalized in order to maintain her Medicaid eligibility.

License or licensure   Permission granted to individuals or organizations by public authorities to engage in a practice or occupation. The licensing process typically requires completion of an appropriate education, examination, and achievement of other performance measures, such as continuing education or practice supervision.

Lifetime limit   The maximum dollar amount paid by a health care plan for a beneficiary over his or her lifetime. A single catastrophic illness can cause a beneficiary to reach the lifetime limit.

Long-term care   Long-term personal care and social services provided to individuals who cannot function independently, regardless of age; services can be provided in an institution or at home, but traditionally have been provided in nursing care facilities.

Managed care   A variety of clinical, financial, and organizational methods used to reduce health care costs and achieve cost efficiency.

Medicaid (Title XIX of the Social Security Act)   A federal–state public insurance system that provides access to health care for certain low-income individuals who meet eligibility criteria. States determine benefits, eligibility, provider payment rates, and program administration (see Chapter 5).

Medically necessary   An insurance industry term used to define appropriate care and care provided according to general standards of practice. A proposed treatment plan may be reviewed to determine if it is medically necessary.

Medically needy   Individuals categorically eligible for Medicaid whose income, less accumulated medical expenses, is lower than state income eligibility limits. This determination of eligibility is referred to as "spending down."

Medically underserved population   A geographically or socially defined population that has a shortage of health services, such as Native Americans. The term is used to assess priority for federal assistance from certain programs.

Medicare (Title XVIII of the Social Security Act)   A federal social insurance system that provides access to health care for retired workers over age 65, disabled workers eligible for Social Security disability benefits, and certain individuals who need kidney transplants or dialysis (see Chapter 5).

Medigap policy   A private health insurance policy, strictly regulated by the federal government, offered to Medicare beneficiaries to cover expenses not covered by Medicare.

Morbidity   In epidemiology, the extent (incidence or prevalence) of illness, injury, or disability in a defined population.

Mortality   In epidemiology, the rate of death in a defined population in a prescribed period of time. *Crude death rates* are the total number of deaths in relation to total population during a year; *specified death rates* are the total number of deaths for specific diseases during a given year and can be further specified by age, race, gender, or other attribute.

Network   The health care providers, medical centers, clinics, and hospitals that have a contractual agreement with a health plan to provide services to its beneficiaries.

Open enrollment   A specific period each year when health plans must accept all who apply; this reduces the opportunity for insurance plans to exclude individuals who are considered poor health risks.

Out-of-network   The use of providers who are not part of the plan's provider network. HMO beneficiaries are typically prohibited from using out-of-network services except in an emergency. Members of preferred provider organizations and HMOs with point-of-service options can seek care out-of-network but are required to pay additional costs.

Out-of-pocket limit   The maximum dollar amount a health care plan requires a beneficiary to pay for deductibles, copayments, and coinsurance annually (excluding premiums).

Outpatient   An individual who receives ambulatory services without being admitted to the hospital.

Point-of-service (POS)   A health insurance benefits plan that gives beneficiaries the option to choose among different delivery systems (HMO, PPO, fee-for-service), rather than selecting one option during open enrollment. Typically, this is a more expensive option for enrollees.

Practice guidelines   A set of guidelines developed by health care professionals to determine the most effective treatments.

Preexisting condition   A diagnosed condition or problem that existed prior to enrollment in a health plan or insurance policy. Under the Health Insurance Portability and Accountability Act of 1997, insurers can no longer deny coverage for preexisting conditions until beneficiaries meet waiting period requirements.

Preferred provider organization (PPO)   A formal organization that typically includes hospitals and providers who receive discounted rates in exchange for a market share of beneficiaries, and expedited payments. Enrollees can receive services from PPO or non-PPO providers, but their cost sharing is lower if they stay within the PPO.

Primary care   Routine health care services provided by a physician trained in family medicine, internal medicine, or pediatrics, or a nurse practitioner or physician's assistant. Primary care physicians are considered the ideal point of entry into the medical system and should be responsible for overall coordination of patient care.

Privatization   The trend to shift functions traditionally performed by public entities to the private sector.

Prospective payment   Amounts or rates of payment determined in advance for a defined period; providers accept these amounts regardless of actual costs incurred.

Prospective payment system   The system established by Medicare to pay hospitals on a prospective basis using diagnostic-related groups (DRGs).

Provider   Hospital, facility, or licensed professional that provides health care services.

Public health   Organized health promotion activities, programs, and policies. Typical public health activities include immunizations, sanitation, health education, disease control, occupational health and safety programs, and air, food, and water quality.

Quality of care   Extent to which health care services meet professional standards and consumer satisfaction; providers, procedures, and outcomes can be measured.

Risk   An unpredictable level of need and associated costs for health care services; the potential difference between projected and actual costs.

Risk bearing entity   An organization that assumes financial responsibility for the provision of a set of benefits by accepting prepayment for *some* (partial risk) or *all* (full risk) of the cost of care.

Risk sharing   An arrangement among parties to share the financial responsibility for the provision of services.

Section 1115 Medicaid waiver   Establishes authority to waive certain Medicaid regulations to encourage demonstration or experimental projects; states allowed to change Medicaid provisions.

Section 1915(b) Medicaid waiver   Allows states to establish mandatory enrollment in managed care plans in an effort to reduce costs; often referred to as "freedom-of-choice waiver."

Seriously mentally ill   Individuals defined by the Community Mental Health Services Block grant as adults over age 18 who have been diagnosed with a mental illness that results in functional impairment and substantially limits activities of daily living.

Skilled nursing facility (SNF)   Nursing care facilities that meet specified regulations for services, staffing, and safety to participate in the Medicare and Medicaid programs.

Underinsured   Individuals with private or public insurance that does not cover all necessary health care services, resulting in out-of-pocket expenses that exceed ability to pay or represent a significant portion of income.

Uninsured   Individuals who lack private or public health insurance.

Utilization review   Evaluation of the use of health care services, procedures, and facilities, including necessity, appropriateness, and efficiency, conducted by a peer review group or a public agency. This process has been used to reduce unnecessary hospital admissions and reduce the length of hospital stays.

Index